CAMBRIDGE STUDIES IN PHILOSOPHY

The moral psychology of the virtues

CAMBRIDGE STUDIES IN PHILOSOPHY

General Editor SYDNEY SHOEMAKER

Advisory editors J. E. J. ALTHAM, SIMON BLACKBURN,
GILBERT HARMAN, MARTIN HOLLIS, FRANK JACKSON,
JONATHAN LEAR, JOHN PERRY, T. J. SMILEY,
BARRY STROUD

JAMES CARGILE *Paradoxes: a study in form and predication*
PAUL M. CHURCHLAND *Scientific Realism and the plasticity of mind*
N. M. L. NATHAN *Evidence and assurance*
WILLIAM LYONS *Emotion*
PETER SMITH *Realism and the progress of science*
BRIAN LOAR *Mind and meaning*
J. F. ROSS *Portraying analogy*
DAVID HEYD *Supererogation*
PAUL HORWICH *Probability and evidence*
ELLERY EELLS *Rational decision and causality*
HOWARD ROBINSON *Matter and sense*
E. J. BOND *Reason and value*
D. M. ARMSTRONG *What is a law of nature?*
H. E. KYBURG Jr. *Theory and measurement*
M. ROBINS *Promising, intending and moral autonomy*

The moral psychology
of the virtues

N.J.H. Dent

Lecturer in Philosophy
University of Birmingham

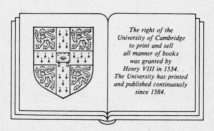

*The right of the
University of Cambridge
to print and sell
all manner of books
was granted by
Henry VIII in 1534.
The University has printed
and published continuously
since 1584.*

Cambridge University Press

Cambridge
London   New York   New Rochelle
Melbourne   Sydney

Published by the Press Syndicate of the University of Cambridge
The Pitt Building, Trumpington Street, Cambridge CB2 1RP
32 East 57th Street, New York, NY 10022, USA
296 Beaconsfield Parade, Middle Park, Melbourne 3206, Australia

First published 1984

Printed in Great Britain
at the University Press, Cambridge

Library of Congress catalogue card number: 83-26208

British Library Cataloguing in Publication Data
Dent, N. J. H.
The moral psychology of the virtues—
(Cambridge studies in philosophy)
1. Virtues
I. Title
179'.9   BV4630
ISBN 0 521 25726 3

For
Thomas and Anna

It is the concrete being that reasons; pass a number of years, and I find my mind in a new place; how? the whole man moves; paper logic is but the record of it.

John Henry Newman
Apologia Pro Vita Sua

Contents

Preface

Some of the material of this discussion develops and extends (and sometimes modifies) views I have suggested in previously published papers. But in no case is the argument of those papers simply reproduced, nor is acquaintance with them supposed; I have tried to make this work self-sufficient.

References in the text and footnotes to Aristotle's *Nicomachean Ethics* are given by the abbreviation E.N., followed by the Bekker numbering.

I should like to express my thanks to my former colleagues Dr R.S. Woolhouse and Professor R.F. Atkinson for reading and commenting on an earlier draft of this work. Professor Leon Pompa made numerous comments on the final draft, and gave me generous and sustained encouragement. I am very grateful to him. I also thank Mrs Shirley Shakespeare and Mrs Katherine Spencer for their help with typing.

N.J.H.D.

Introduction

In her paper 'Modern Moral Philosophy', G.E.M. Anscombe writes: '. . . it is not profitable for us at present to do moral philosophy; that should be laid aside at any rate until we have an adequate philosophy of psychology, in which we are conspicuously lacking.' A few pages further on, she continues: 'In present-day philosophy an explanation is required how an unjust man is a bad man, or an unjust action a bad one; to give such an explanation belongs to ethics; but it cannot even be begun until we are equipped with a sound philosophy of psychology. For the proof that an unjust man is a bad man would require a positive account of justice as a "virtue". This part of the subject-matter of ethics is, however, completely closed to us until we have an account of what *type of characteristic* a virtue is – a problem, not of ethics, but of conceptual analysis – and how it relates to the actions in which it is instanced . . .' (The sentence concludes, rather dauntingly, as follows: 'a matter which I think Aristotle did not succeed in really making clear'.)

This book is intended to make a contribution to achieving an account of what 'type of characteristic' a virtue is. It is, thus, basically an essay in philosophical psychology, at least in that part of the subject which treats of those concepts which have a crucial relation to ethics: concepts such as 'action', 'intention', 'pleasure', 'wanting' (these are Anscombe's suggestions); and also 'choice', 'deliberation', 'practical reason' and many others. This part of the philosophy of psychology I refer to as 'moral psychology'; and, therefore, this book is offered as a contribution to moral psychology.

In the second passage cited above, Anscombe emphasised that the proof that an unjust man is a bad man (or, come to that, cowardly, mean, licentious men are bad men) must wait upon an account of what type of characteristic a virtue, or a vice, is. I have here concentrated almost wholly upon this precondition for giving such a proof, and have not tried to move beyond that to 'ethics'. I have, that is, not tried to explain

1

here the value of virtues and the disvalue of vices, although it will be pretty clear from what I say in what direction I think we must look for such an explanation. This restriction of scope will be quite apparent, for example, in my discussion of the nature and workings of practical reason in chapter 4. There I have confined myself to trying to present and account for the distinctive characteristics of this capacity of mind as it contributes to the ordering and direction of desire and action; and I have not tried to present and defend any substantive norms or principles which would mark what 'right' practical reasoning is. I am quite aware of this omission; however, as I have just indicated, it is made in consonance with the overall intent and compass of the discussion.

This work falls roughly into two parts, after the opening chapter. In chapter 1, which is primarily intended to set the scene for the subsequent treatment, I identify the concerns which inform my discussion and say a little more generally about the place of inquiry into the nature of virtue in relation to the preoccupations of recent moral philosophy. The next three chapters (2–4 inclusive) are concerned with characterising three 'active powers' of men which are, as I judge, central in the determination of conduct, and out of the relations and connections of which are formed that type of characteristic which a virtue is. In these chapters I have been much influenced by the moral psychologies of Plato and Aristotle. But I have not often entered into detailed exegesis and discussion of their views; rather I have tried to argue afresh for the conceptions of the desiring elements in the human soul which are, as I believe, to be found in their writings. I think that their insights have too often been lost in subsequent philosophy of mind and morals, particularly that influenced by Humean notions of the nature, rôle and relations of reason and desire. And I have been concerned to try to recover these insights and to show their importance. Most centrally, I have tried to argue that some desires are based on or are answerable to practical reason for their existence, strength and direction, and thus that our purposes and concerns are open to rationally reflective assessment and modification. The idea that we are blessed (or cursed) with a set of desires by nature which, being simply parts of the fabric of our nature, neither take their rise from nor are modifiable by reflective understanding seems to me a deeply mistaken one, albeit that it has some proper application.

The three following chapters (5–7 inclusive) are concerned with discussing the nature and effects of relations and interdependencies between these active powers. I argue that it is in the existence of certain complex structures obtaining between them that we find that type of characteristic which a virtue is; and I try to describe the nature of these structures. I insist that not all virtues possess the same overall structure (even if they did, such a structure would, of course, be 'fleshed out' differently in the case of different virtues); and I try to explain why these structures are different, as a result of the differences in the characters of the active powers which, by interacting, go to form them. I also consider some ways in which there may be unsatisfactory or faulty inter-relations between these powers, particularly in chapter 7.

The discussion thus moves from a consideration of (sense-) desire, passion and practical rationality, as more or less independent, discrete, powers of mind to a consideration of them as they interact and are co-ordinated. This is, however, a framework of the account, and should not be taken as an historical account of how human behaviour and desire develops in complexity of structure and expression. Most of the interests and behaviour of adult humans exhibit, 'in one go' so to say, very many features in very complex relationships. Isolating these features, presenting them as the expression of different active powers and then reintegrating them through the account of forms of interdependency of these powers, is a method whereby one hopes to bring a perspicuous order into a confusing and complicated field, and should not be taken to have any strong ontological implications. The expression of the human soul in wish, desire, intent, action etc. is extraordinarily complex and, in the effort to master this complexity, one may present (parts of) that expression as the outcome of the interweaving of different powers. But this is a device by which one hopes to secure understanding, not a claim that such powers exist as self-contained psychological units in the soul each separately putting out effects which, by intermingling, produce the final result. The *basic* unit still remains the active life of a man.

I conclude with some general comments on the subject-matter and approach of this discussion. I have said that my concern will be with what type of characteristic a virtue is, with the elements and structure of such characteristics, rather than with the question of why possession and exercise of these characteristics may be desirable, admirable or whatever. But there still may be grave doubts about the whole enterprise. Is not the term 'virtue' hopelessly archaic; does it not sound merely stilted in present-day discussion (and even more so the term 'vice')? Also, is not discussion of these matters apt to be sanctimonious? I dare say that my remarks will, from time to time, sound both stilted and sanctimonious. But these are my faults, not flaws inherent in the subject. For, first, although the term 'virtue' may sound awkwardly in ordinary talk, people still do discuss a person's honesty, generosity, kindness, selfishness, greed, malice etc.; and in so talking they are talking of his virtues and vices even though these specific words are not used. On a more abstract level, too, there is a central place for trying to understand the significance of virtues and vices when trying to come to an overall understanding of the basis of the moral value of character and action, even though, once again, these words 'virtue' and 'vice' may be eschewed. (I argue this in chapter 1, sections iv and v.)

Secondly, although I shall be considering at some length the restraint of desire for pleasure (such as is involved in 'temperance' – another awkward word), the moderation of anger (such as is involved in having an equable temper) and so on, it is no part of my purpose to recommend, sanctimoniously or otherwise, such restraint and moderation (or to condemn it). I am only concerned to show how restraint and moderation may be possible given the character of the constituent phenomena involved; to show what the elements and structure of the relevant 'ordered' state might be; to show how such a state is displayed in actions and reactions; and so on. My attempt is to articulate the composition and organisation of complex characteristics of human beings, without comment upon whether or not in the end these characteristics are good to possess or good to be without.

It is true enough that I would hardly be so interested in, nor would I expect anyone else to be interested in, trying to elucidate the nature of these characteristics unless I thought they were *significant* human characteristics, ones worth remark. But this falls far short of having any wish to moralise about them. Furthermore, a good part of the interest there is in determining the elements and structure of virtues comes from the fact that, by doing this, a better understanding may be gained of certain issues in philosophical psychology – as I indicated earlier. This fact provides no occasion for moralising.

4

On the other hand, it will emerge that incorporated into virtues is an endeavour, on their possessor's part, to moderate feelings, desires, actions etc. by true judgement on the real importance of certain goods. Now, if this is true, then it would follow that to possess virtues is to possess attributes worth having just in so far as it is worth incorporating what is rightly believed to be good into the order and direction of one's desires and actions. But it is one thing to see that this consequence follows, and quite another to use it as a ground for extolling the desirability of becoming or being virtuous.

Any unease which protracted discussion of 'virtue' could engender might have different sources from those mentioned. It might be felt that the 'picture' of the human psyche implied by the notion of virtue, the categorisation of its components, of their respective natures etc., comprises a framework of understanding, a body of concepts and principles, which is outmoded, contains suppositions and implications which are inapplicable or is at least a framework less perspicuous than other frameworks of understanding might be. Perhaps the body of concepts and principles attendant upon employing the idea of virtue has just lost its use – in some degree – for us. (Thus Leavis writes of *Women in Love*, in a passage typical of many: 'I will revert to those aspects of Lawrence's astonishingly original art which, in the rendering of the manifestations of life in the actors, are *not* concerned with "character". The ways in which Lawrence brings into the drama the forces of the psyche of which the actors' wills have no cognizance, and which, consequently, do not seem to belong to their selves, are very various.')

This suggestion obviously raises very difficult questions with very extensive implications, and I cannot consider it here in any detail. I have to say, however, that I do not think that the notion of virtue, with its attendant notions of 'character', 'will', 'consciousness' etc., has lost its power to illuminate, has been shown to have no effective hold on the stuff of active life. I hope my overall discussion will substantiate this claim. But I do accept that the framework it imposes is not beyond question. I think the right attitude to take is to say that it offers us a way of making sense of (some parts of) ourselves, of which we can and do make use. And that it is in its way valuable to try to grasp more completely and consciously what this way of doing things amounts to, comprises. The 'external' question, of whether or not to continue to do things this way, is not one I engage with here. I take the body of concepts and principles

5

more or less as a 'given' and try to delineate it. I do not think that Hume, for example, was really trying to replace an inadequate framework with a more adequate one (in his view) in his discussions of the passions, desire etc. Rather, I think, he was misconstruing the nature of a particular framework. In this there is, perhaps, some contrast between Book 1 and Book 2 of the *Treatise*; Book 1 is, plausibly, more revisionary, Book 2 more descriptive – or misdescriptive (to invoke Strawson's well-known contrast). Nor do I think that Hume was describing (or revising) a different framework from our own, though this is a yet further question which may provoke disagreement.

There are other omissions from my discussion, though ones more to do with matters 'internal' to the body of notions I am considering. Thus I say very little about responsibility for character, feeling and action; or about such feelings as guilt, shame, remorse etc. which clearly form part of the 'psychology' of morals. I have not considered, except very informally, issues about 'stages' in moral development (after the fashion of Piaget and Kohlberg); neither have I looked much into questions about the deeper psychological roots of emotions and for the integration of the self. The reason, in each case, is that I have wanted to push forward along one main path of argument, and not to take up issues which, however interesting they are, did not clearly advance this movement. Although much has been omitted, I hope enough has still been included.

1

The virtues: themes and issues

i   THE SPIRIT IN ACTION

We generally think that we should not only try to do the right thing, but also aspire to do it in the right spirit. Our moral interest in ourselves and others does not stop at the question of what was done, but extends further to take in questions of motive, desire and intent as these were displayed in or revealed by what was done. One who saves a child from drowning solely to enjoy the acclaim and publicity his act would most likely bring, has done the right thing but not in the right spirit, has done a good thing but not done it well, with a good motive. This is not to say that if he cannot find it in him to act with any other end in view than this it would be better that he should do nothing at all, though in cases other than this that might be true. It is only to say that his act did not enact, was not the disply of, a concern for the life of the child as worth saving as such, a concern we take to be desirable.

It is an important question why acting 'in the right spirit' matters at all; and it is also important to consider how much acting in the right spirit matters relative to the need to perform some required act or to produce certain results, particularly when such performance or production would only be undertaken in a poor spirit or with a bad motive (on this question, see Dent 1975 and n.d.; Hume, *Treatise*, 477, 575; Irwin 1977: 162, 281; Strawson 1968: 75–6). This book is not, however, directly concerned with these questions. Rather, I shall discuss the question of what possession of the right spirit consists in, and of what it is for action to be undertaken in that spirit and to be expressive of it. In this chapter I shall explain, in a preliminary way, what treatment of these questions will involve; and show something of the bearing of these matters on more general issues in moral philosophy.

To be concerned with the spirit in which a man acts is to be concerned with the reasons he had for acting as he did, and upon which he acted; and with the desires, feelings, purposes and interests which found

7

expression in his conducting himself in the way he did at the time. It is to be concerned with the psychological background to a man's action and with the way in which his action gave a, perhaps only partial, expression to that background; gave to it, so to say, a certain degree of articulate utterance in his conduct.

Admittedly, when we ask in what spirit someone did something, for example, agreed to help with the washing-up, we are apt to be given an answer which speaks of the manner of his conduct, that he agreed reluctantly, resentfully, grudgingly or gladly, cheerfully and without hesitation. (For an account of virtue which lays emphasis on the 'manner' of action, see Peters (1962).) And this may seem to refer only to features of his outward behaviour. But even if we suppose that that is all that is spoken of when we speak of the spirit in which something is done, if we ask why one man's manner was grudging and another's glad we must surely appreciate that his manner in acting can, and usually does, indicate a good deal about what he likes and what he hates, what he thinks is worth doing and what is a waste of time. That is, we soon come to need to attend to the desires, feelings and reasons which bore upon and directed the person's behaviour in the case, and these are not all present as features of the manner of the outward behaviour undertaken at the time – they 'lie behind' it. Aristotle wrote: 'We must take as a sign of states of character the pleasure or pain that ensues on acts' (E.N. 1104b 4). The 'pleasure or pain' he has in mind is the gladness or delight we may feel at having done something, or the regret or annoyance we may likewise feel. And these retrospective reactions to what we have done are all of a piece with the prospective reactions of being glad to help or resenting having to help, which then also should be taken as a sign of states of character. Of course, they are but *one* sign, and states of character incorporate much more than this – a man's motives, feelings and ends as well. We are often happy to substitute for 'acting in the right spirit' the phrase 'acting from a good motive', as I indicated at the start. And our freedom to make this substitution clearly indicates that we recognise there is more to the spirit in which an act is done than the manner in which it is done, if we narrowly conceive this as comprehending only certain features of the exterior performance. For there is little even initial plausibility in supposing that in speaking of motives we refer only to such features.

We may say, then, that the inquiry is into what states of character comprise, and how action may embody a trait of character. Not, as I have said, into what makes one such state desirable and another deplorable, but into what the possession of either a desirable or a deplorable state of character comprehends, in terms of the elements and structure of a man's 'soul'. Of course, we *explain* nothing by equating acting in a certain spirit with acting from a certain state of character; anything obscure about the first notion is likely to be equally obscure about the second. However, making this connection enables us to move towards a more familiar area of discussion.

It would be possible to begin straightaway with a conceptual analysis of the notion of a 'state of character' (see, e.g., Brandt 1970). But I shall, instead, begin by discussing the nature of simpler psychological phenomena than the possession of a state of character, and by an examination of their nature and their relationships build up a picture of that complex and highly structured condition. For only by proceeding in this way can we, I believe, get a full and precise grasp of the constitution of that condition, rather than merely referring in the account of it to more elementary phenomena whose nature remains not fully explained. At this point, however, I wish still to establish the general nature of this undertaking; and my detailed investigation will begin in chapter 2.

A little further on in Book 2 of the *Ethics* (1106a 10), Aristotle says that virtues are states of character (see also von Wright 1963: 144 and chap. 7). And this does appear to be correct. When we speak of a man's character we speak of his virtues (and of his vices); of his being, for instance, brave, honest, generous, fair-minded, conscientious; or of his being cowardly, deceitful, mean, prejudiced, irresponsible; and so on. (Cf. Aristotle, E.N. 1103a 4–10.) Thus, an inquiry into what the possession of a certain spirit and its articulation in action comprises connects directly both with an inquiry into what the possession of certain states of character comprises and, finally, with an inquiry into what the possession of certain virtues or vices comprises. Thus, we are inquiring into the elements and structure of a man's soul that comprise his possession of virtues (or vices – I shall not endlessly add this). And this I understand as an investigation of the moral psychology of virtue.

A number of small points may be mentioned here. First; whilst Aristotle says that all virtues are states of character, he does not say that all states of character are either virtues or vices.[1] And it may be asked if there are any states of character which would normally be thought of as being neither virtues nor vices. I cannot think of any. It has been suggested to me that curiosity or the desire to find things out might be such a case (C. Hookway, pers. comm.). But as soon as we reflect that this desire, if excessive, becomes nosiness or intrusiveness (particularly if exercised upon the affairs of others); and, if defective, becomes inert indifference to the way things are and work, we realise that we need to specify the desire as being of a proper kind, of appropriate strength exercised on appropriate subject-matter, if we are to have anything which might look like a state of character which is neither a virtue nor a vice. But then, so far from appearing as neutral, it appears as a virtue, having a proper degree of interest in finding out about and understanding appropriate things. So this does not seem to be a counter-example. It is no objection to say that we do not have a single word to refer to such a state of character; that we do not only show that we have felt no need for one, not that there is no such state. Aristotle points out that certain states of character have no name (e.g. E.N. 1119a 10; 1125b 26). In default, then, of a clear class of counter-examples and a principle for identifying them, I conclude that not only are all virtues (and vices) states of character, but also all states of character are virtues or vices.

Secondly, we make, I think, some very uneasy distinctions between people's states of character and matters of their temperament, personality and general disposition of their feelings. And it will be useful to try to see how things stand here. Someone's exuberance or optimism is thought of as a temperamental characteristic rather than a character-trait, at least typically. And someone's being of a very affectionate nature would be thought of as a feature of their personality or of the general disposition of their feelings. However, if someone remains optimistic, looking always for the best in men and affairs, in spite of much personal disappointment and unmerited misfortune, then we may think this shows 'strength of character' on his part and that his optimism betokens a praiseworthy effort not to become embittered or cynical.

---

1 Of course, Aristotle denies that continence is strictly counted as a virtue (and it is, presumably, not a vice either). But perhaps also it is not a 'state of character' in the intended sense. See Aristotle: E.N. 1128b 35.

Clearly the rôle of choice and self-direction in the face of difficulty or pain makes an important difference here, and I shall be explaining the significance of this more fully later. A man's temperament comprises, perhaps, the 'given' material of his desires, feelings and objectives, which, by the growth and stabilisation of character, may come to be put to good or ill use.[2] Public schools are said to be concerned with 'character-building' and this is, I would suppose, connected with inculcating a certain determination to carry on in the face of hardship. 'Personality-building', if it means anything at all, seems to signify either boosting one's self-confidence or building up a picture of oneself as having a large and expansive *persona*, a dramatic rôle to play. 'Temperament-building' means nothing at all. 'Strength of character' – referred to already – imports something quite different from 'strength (or force) of personality'. The latter seems to signify a certain natural prepotence of being and manner; the former, a certain resoluteness and determination to push through to one's chosen purposes in the face of difficulties or inducements to weakness, to turning away. Of course, the effect of either of these in an argument, say, may be pretty much the same.

Obviously differences of a general kind exist here, but it is very hard indeed to give any systematic explication of them. For this reason, rather than spend a lot of space on problems of demarcation, I shall instead be concentrating on what are certainly central cases of states of character. And it would be by comparison and contrast with these that we would expect to be able to find general principles of differentiation here, if there are any. It is often the best way to grasp the order in complicated phenomena to place slightly differing cases side by side, rather than to attempt to give an abstract general statement of principles of likeness and difference between cases. The systematic 'placing' shows differences which often can only be said very cumbersomely. One related contrast, between 'virtue in the strict sense' (see Aristotle, E.N. Book 6, chaps. 12–13; Beehler 1978: chap. 5) and 'natural virtue', which possibly provides one source of the distinction between character and

---

2 On character and temperament, see Bradley 1927: 238–9. 'And dispositions or natures vary indefinitely: some are more harmonious than others, and some again are more chaotic and lead inevitably to jars and painful contradictions. The material of some men offers more resistance to the systematizing good will . . .' See also Ayers 1968: chap. 8.

11

temperament, will occupy me a good deal in what follows. And if this throws some light on the differences between the notions, this is all to the good.[3] I return to these matters in chapters 6 and 7 below.

Another problem of 'demarcation' lies in differentiating traits of character from other admirable or deplorable qualities, particularly of an intellectual or executive kind, that a man may possess. Aristotle, of course, distinguishes 'intellectual' and 'moral' virtues, and says it is only of the latter that we speak when we speak about a man's character (E.N. 1103a 4–10); on this subject see Anscombe 1968: 186–7 and *passim*. This is not to say that 'moral' virtues do not require 'intellectual' virtues, as Aristotle fully emphasises, but only that they do have a different nature. But it is Hume who presents the most far-reaching case here, insisting that it is only a 'verbal' issue whether or not a ready and capacious memory or inventiveness, for example, should count as among a man's 'moral' virtues. These, he insists, are as much excellences of his and redound to his credit as do his honesty or courage. (For Hume on virtues, talents etc. see *Treatise*, Book 3, pt 3, sect. 4; *Enquiry*, App. 4; see also Attfield 1971; Dent 1976b).

I would not dispute that these are excellent qualities for a man to possess, but I would argue that virtues and 'talents' or 'natural abilities' can be materially, and not simply verbally, distinguished. The most substantial difference lies in this. Whereas a man's talents enable him to do exceptional and outstanding things if he wishes, his virtues and vices pertain to the goodness or badness of what he is apt to wish. A man's virtues and vices relate to the quality of the ends for which he is disposed to employ his talents; his talents only to his degree of capability of accomplishing the ends he sets before himself, the powers he has at his disposal. Furthermore, whilst a man's talents enable him to pull off certain distinguished tasks (if he will), his virtues are not a matter of setting himself to achieve certain tasks (or only indirectly), but of standing in a proper relation to what is good, of giving certain values a proper governing place in the overall direction of his life. Finally, and I say this in spite of Hume's polemic against the view, the rôle of our choice and will is much more central to the acquisition and retention of virtues and vices

---

3 Is temperament like 'natural virtue'; or is it a matter of 'faculties', that is, of 'the simple capacity of feeling the passions' (E.N. 1106a 7)? There is, I think, simply no clear answer to these questions. On the notion of 'personality', see Geach 1977: 75ff.

than it is to the acquisition and retention of talents. Talents cannot, logically, be acquired. And though talents may be lost, old age as much as bad living may be the explanation of their disappearance. Whereas bad living does not explain the loss of virtue, it *is* the absence of virtue, the presence of vice; and old age need not affect one's virtues at all. Virtues may be, as we shall see later on, in a substantial measure acquired and retained by choice, and are also characteristics of the nature of a man's habitual choices. Talents are capabilities merely, not achieved by choice, nor modes of choice.

So although we quite properly admire a man's excellent memory, we need have no anxiety that such-like qualities cannot be distinguished from his virtues or vices. It is perhaps worth remarking that what may be put down to a 'poor memory' can quite often be a symptom of vice. Someone may be so wrapped up in himself that he simply fails properly to attend to others and pay sufficient attention for the necessary matters to 'register' with him so that they might later be recalled. Or he may be too lazy to think hard enough about what he has been told to do. Conversely, what may be put down to someone's having had merely the good fortune to be blessed with an excellent memory may in fact be a matter of his being sufficiently mindful of and attentive to others that he clearly and properly registers and understands the needful points. And this argues to his generosity and thoughtfulness towards others. More forgetfulness and stupidity is possibly indifference and laziness than we care to realise (see Edgley 1964).

It may here be objected that there is a class of virtues, sometimes called 'executive' virtues, which are more like talents than I have allowed to be possible. Courage, for example, is sometimes discussed as if it were primarily a matter of stopping oneself from being deflected from one's purposes by the impulses to self-preservation aroused in fear. As such, it constitutes a kind of capacity, for a certain kind of voluntary self-control, which better enables a man to accomplish his purposes, rather than being a mode of choice of better or worse purposes. Thus it lacks that relation to choice of good or evil I was stressing in the case of virtues, whilst being for all that a paradigmatic virtue. Hence, it seems, I cannot maintain the distinction between virtues and capacities as I wish.

This argument is, however, a weak one. For, just to the extent that

13

courage is taken only to be a useful form of self-control, it loses its title to be regarded as without exception an excellent state and hence a virtue. For a man can as well show such self-control in his pursuit of evil ends; and, as employed to those purposes, courage itself is not to be admired. Schopenhauer, for one, clearly drew this conclusion (*Essays*, 134). In order to have it that courage is, as such, an admirable quality we shall have to say that 'true' courage is shown only in the pursuit of admirable ends.[4] Or, if this seems to be too much of a merely verbal manoeuvre, we shall have to say that the resolute determination to master fear is of itself something to be fitly chosen and admired. That is, in choosing to become the sort of man who can master fear one is as such choosing something estimable. So although from courage we do not directly choose some better or worse purpose, seeking to become courageous is, itself, a good purpose. Then on either account courage is not merely a capacity which may be put to good or evil use. Either it is such a capacity as is always put to good use; or it is a capacity which is, itself, one which it is good to choose to acquire and to exercise. And thus, though not so directly a matter of the character of a man's choice of ends, it bears still a close and inextricable relation to that. (On the relations between courage and what are often called 'executive' virtues, see Taylor and Wolfram 1971; Wallace 1978: chap. 3; Williams 1976: 316.)

Such a variety of relationships between virtues and the choice and pursuit of certain ends is only to be expected. For although we have generic terms such as 'state of character' or 'virtue', we would be over-optimistic in supposing that one single, simple, account would match the features of all instances. I shall, in fact, be insisting that there are important differences of a general kind between the elements and structure of such virtues as temperance, generosity and conscientiousness, quite aside from the special features of the case of courage we have just cursorily examined. There would be no profit in trying to provide a single form of account for all of these, but we should recognise that there may be difference and variety which does not amount to random inchoateness.

4 Aristotle distinguishes 'true' courage, which is 'for the sake of the noble', from five other kinds of state; in the case of the 'citizen soldier' the motive for his conduct is fear of penalties and reproaches and the desire for honour. See E.N. Book 3, chaps. 7–8. See also Dent 1981; Geach 1977: 160.

14

I have suggested that states of character, which are what virtues and vices are, comprehend such things as a man's feelings, desires, purposes and the reasons he has for acting one way rather than another, for seeking one end rather than another. I shall be concerned above all to explain how each of these kinds of thing is involved in and contributes to the nature and direction of a man's conduct, although, remembering the caveat entered at the end of the last section, we shall not expect the involvement and contribution to take quite the same form in the case of every virtue. It will be as well, therefore, to specify some of the reasons for saying that all these sorts of elements are involved here. We shall notice, also, that it is not only the diversity of elements that come into the case that produces complexities and confusions. It is also the subtlety and diversity of the inter-relations and interdependencies between them that makes a great deal of difference in different cases.

I shall show these points not by an abstract argument, but through a brief discussion of a variety of cases which will serve to highlight first this, then that, aspect of the constituents and operations of virtues and vices. These 'exemplary' cases will provide the concrete 'data' of which any convincing theory must make good sense. And I shall, therefore, have them very much in mind throughout a great deal of the subsequent theorising, as providing a criterion for its cogency.

The first case to be considered is one suggested by the opening discussion of the glad or grudging spirit in which someone may act.

First case: a number of people are comfortably seated in a bus when a woman with a heavy load of shopping and a tired and crying small child gets on. One of those comfortably seated is immediately sympathetic to her need and feels an immediate desire to help. He gets up and offers her his seat. Another person is aware that she needs help, but feels no ready impulse to offer it. However, he is well schooled in the 'duties of a gentleman' and, guided by the thought that it is his duty, he gets up and offers her his seat. This he may do with a good grace, or perhaps in a somewhat wooden or truculent fashion. Either way, it is no kindly impulse that prompts his action. He is more apt to think: 'I suppose I have to help';

or, 'I really ought to help' rather than, 'I would like to help'.[5] And he may resent this 'having to', since, independently of it, he really feels no inclination to move from his comfortable place. Finally, there could be a third person whose prompting to help comes only from the thought that other people may criticise him, look upon him with contempt, if he makes no gesture of assistance.

In terms of this rough sketch, I think we should be very apt to say that the first man's action displays a kindly and sympathetic character, for although one kindly impulse doesn't make a kindly man, it goes the right way towards making this. The second man is more aptly called conscientious, one well prepared to do what he takes to be his duty, rather than kindly, for the impulse of sympathetic concern is absent in his case. The third man evidences only a fear of censure. And though the fact that he is not immune to the prospect of that shows some sensibility on his part, he would hardly be taken to be either kindly or conscientious.

We may suppose that in an 'idealised' case the outward demeanour and behaviour of these three men could be indistinguishable. But once we have been made privy to the differing states of mind from which their behaviour respectively issued, we see that there is a great deal of difference between the moral state of the agents, at least in the particular case and quite possibly more generally. This would, of course, properly affect the valuations we make of them, over and above what they did; but in this context that is not my concern. The point of the example for my purposes is that it clearly shows that certain feelings and impulses are involved in kindness and sympathetic concern and not merely, if at all, the thought that something is what one ought to do or is what is incumbent upon one. This thought is, however, more centrally present and determinative in the case of conscientious conduct. Thus we see here two things. First, that some virtues do include as at least one of their component elements certain feelings and desires on the part of the possessor of the virtue. And secondly, that we have here a significant contrast of a quite general kind between virtues, and thus that the claim

5 Williams (1976: 315 n.6) claims that the 'basic representation in deliberation' of a virtuous disposition takes the form 'I want to . . .', rather than the form 'I ought to . . .'. It is, however, worth noting that 'I must . . .' can express both the urgency of strong desire as well as a sense of (perhaps unwelcome) constraint. See also Foot (1972: 311).

made earlier that a simple, single, account would not do for all cases is already being borne out.

Second case: in the example just considered, I drew a rough contrast between kindness and conscientiousness, on various grounds. One ground was that whilst conscientiousness involved undertaking to act in recognition of something as one's duty, it appeared that acting out of kindness or sympathetic concern involved no such thought. It might then be concluded that it was sufficient to be a kind person to have a general disposition to have and act upon (other things being equal) spontaneous impulses to help arising in response to the perception of another's need. But this would be a mistake, as can be seen by considering this further case.

Imagine someone who has become convinced of a pseudo-Nietzschean idea that one should be a hard, strong man uninhibited by life-paralysing pity and compassion for the weak and needy. Such a man may, for all his conviction of this, still be touched quite regularly by feelings of sympathy for the needy and moved by impulses to help them, upon which, indeed, he acts pretty often. We might say he exhibits a 'fortunate' kind of weakness of will (see Aristotle, E.N. 1151b 18). However, when he has thus betrayed his ideals, he subsequently berates and despises himself for being so soft as to be ensnared in this way. He regrets having these feelings and acting on them, for all that he remains liable to this.

Can we say in a case such as this that the man is compassionate and kindly? At best we could say that he was 'at heart', but it would be misleading to say he was 'the soul of kindness' or 'kindness incarnate'. And this is obviously because he is divided against himself, and whilst liable to the feelings and impulses proper to one who is kind, he fights against them and deplores his liability to them. Thus, whilst a general tendency to have and enact sympathetic feelings and desires is evidently very material to determining whether someone is kindly, it seems that we are bound to consider more than this in order to reach any properly final judgement on the case. In particular, we must consider what might loosely be called the person's attitude towards his having this general tendency, whether he accepts or endorses these feelings and impulses to which he is liable or whether he regrets and deplores them. As a first

17

approximation to registering this point we might say that a man must 'identify himself' with these feelings and impulses, with what they suggest to him to do, if we are to find a secure basis for the ascription of the quality of kindness to him. And what goes for kindness goes also for all those virtues which include an element of spontaneous feeling and desire. The point is not special to this one case, but applies to a general class of cases.

What precisely goes into this 'identification', and how such identification might concretely manifest itself in the stream of an agent's life, are matters which I will consider later in detail (see also Davis 1979: chap. 6; Dent 1974; Frankfurt 1971: 16–17; 1976; Körner 1973; Neely 1974). At this point it is sufficient to see how such a matter arises and its general rôle in determining what the possession of certain virtues comprises. But we can ask here whether this 'identification' that a kindly man must make with his sympathetic feelings and impulses to give help will take the form of his taking it that he has also a duty to help those in need. For that was the point of contrast between kindness and conscientiousness we began with – kindness not apparently involving that thought, conscientiousness essentially doing so; and nothing said so far appears to soften this particular contrast. I do not think that the idea of duty is quite the right notion to introduce here, but that it is along the right lines can be seen by means of a further case.

Third case: I shall begin with an illustration intended to give an analogy for the point I want to make.

Many people, from time to time, feel a desire to have a glass of beer; and, if then offered one, would gladly drink it. But it would be ridiculous to say – in the absence of some very special considerations – that if I don't feel like drinking a glass of beer I ought to accept one, or accept it in preference, say, to a glass of cider if that is what I presently feel like drinking. There is simply nothing about the act of drinking a glass of beer which would make doing it incumbent upon one regardless of one's inclination to do so. It is something to be done if one feels like it; and something to be forgone if one doesn't. Beer has no claim upon one to be drunk which could override the absence of any actual desire to drink it.

Consider now someone who is moved from time to time by sympathetic feelings to help this or that person in need, and who acts upon

18

these feelings. We might, in the light of this, be inclined to say that he was a kind man (as discussed in relation to the previous case). But suppose another closely comparable case of need presents itself to him by which, however, he is entirely unmoved; and being unmoved by it he pays no attention and simply carries on with whatever else he may be doing, without a second thought. In this case he shows a regrettable indifference, and its occurrence has important implications for the interpretation we should place upon his former behaviour.[6] For now it appears that he never saw anything in relieving the needs of others beyond its being something to be done if he feels like it, and as something he may omit to do if he does not feel like it. This is where the case of beer-drinking provides an analogy. That indeed is an activity to be undertaken or forgone just as one happens to feel at the time. But someone who behaves as if relieving the needy is something to be undertaken or omitted just as one happens to be sympathetically involved or not at the time surely cannot be thought of as a kindly man. For clearly he attaches such marginal importance to doing this that he behaves as if the decisive factor relative to his undertaking it is only his 'mood of the moment'. Whereas it seems plain that one who is really possessed of the virtue of kindness does, and must, recognise helping the needy to be something that properly befits or claims his attention and work, to be something it is good that he should do. And this recognition precisely involves accepting that this is work not to be done or omitted simply as and when feeling prompts one to it; it is something that requires concern and does not wait upon its adventitious presence. None of this is to say, of course, that it is the only, or the over-riding, requirement which a man may lie under at any moment. It is only to say that, being a requirement of any weight at all, it makes a claim beyond the casual influence of occasional feelings. For if that were all there were to the performance or its omission, that would be to say that there was no requirement in the case at all, at least in this respect. It is then but a short step to saying that to recognise and accept that there is in the need of others a claim upon one, which the kind man must do, is to recognise and accept that one lies under a duty, of more or less stringency, in this direction.

6 Of course, this indifference is only regrettable other things being equal. No one is expected or required to do all possible kindly things; but even allowing for this, some non-offerings of help are still unkind failures to offer help, and it is such cases I have in mind.

19

Someone who acts only as the mood of the moment takes him may, if his moods happen to be amiable and generous ones, do good and generous things for others. But so long as he remains only one who so acts, he cannot be properly thought of as possessed of kindness. To possess such a quality in one's character does involve appreciation of a claim or fittingness in the undertaking, which registers it as calling for a response on one's part and not as just waiting upon the fortunate occurrence of a suitable response.

If this be granted, it appears now that I am on the point of quite removing the contrast I have been employing between doing something 'as a matter of duty' or something 'one has to do', and doing something out of kindness and sympathetic concern. However, it is in seeing that the virtue of kindness consists *neither* in simply occasional feelings and impulses (nor, indeed, general tendencies to have certain feelings and impulses) which prompt action, *nor* in simply having a clear perception of one's duty and the willingness to carry that out, that we find one of the cruxes of this inquiry. It has to be seen both that, and how, such a virtue comprises a certain complex structure of feelings, and feeling-based desires, and the recognition and acceptance that something is good and befits, requires, our undertaking. Neither of these alone comprises kindness. Nor – though this is a more difficult point – does their merely accidental congruence comprise kindness. Nor, finally, is kindness to be found in something else altogether. Rather, the possession and exercise of such a virtue as this involves the co-ordinate assent and work of the 'heart' and of the 'head' to what we do and aim for. Identifying and explicating the nature and components of this state of co-ordinate assent and work comprises the core of the account of the moral psychology of (many) virtues.

I say only of many virtues, since this will not be true of all; in particular, still not true of conscientiousness, as I have roughly identified that. For, in that case, there are not involved the spontaneous feelings and impulses to act which kindness, and virtues of that type, involve. And hence no comparable assent of the 'heart' will be involved here.[7]

7 This claim needs to be qualified to some degree. First, there can be what Kant calls 'reverence' for the law. But, of course, he insists that this is a 'feeling' produced by a rational concept and not 'received through outside influence' (*Groundwork*, 401 and note). Also, second, a full-hearted assent to some goods very much aids conscientious awareness and conscientious action. See further chap. 6, section vi, below.

Fourth case: the case just discussed concerned particular occasions of being moved by sympathetic feelings and acting on these, and the relationship between this and recognising the claim upon us of helping those in need. We can now consider a closely related point in relation to a general tendency on the part of someone to have and act on such-like feelings. This will serve also to elaborate the second case considered in illuminating ways.

Take the beer-drinking analogy once again. Suppose beer has been my favourite drink for some years but, for some reason, I lose my taste for it or develop a greater taste for cider instead. It would be ridiculous to suggest that, in either case, I should continue to drink beer in spite of the change in my general preferences. We properly gain or lose such preferences without being unduly concerned about it. Possibly we may be a little puzzled about why something we so much liked no longer brings pleasure. Perhaps, too, we reflect with regret upon the pleasures we once enjoyed but no longer have any taste for. But that is about as far as it will normally go.

But now suppose that someone regarded his general liking for relieving the needs of others in much the same sort of way as this. That is, if for one reason or another he simply lost any sympathetic concern for the weal and woe of others; or if he became generally rather more preoccupied with his own private concerns; then he simply noticed this as one way in which his preferences happened to have changed over the years and took no further thought about it. If this were the case, surely we would be quite justified in saying that he never saw (or, if he did, he has lost the perception of) any claim upon him in the need of others to be relieved. His indifference to his losing any natural promptings to offer help testified that, for him, offering help was always something to be done whilst one was 'in a helping mood' but not otherwise. I do not mean that this was his conscious policy; but only that this was how the pattern of his behaviour was actually structured.

The fact that for some time he was one who was apt to experience, and to act upon, benign and attractive sentiments and impulses certainly gives much of the appearance that he is a kind and considerate man. It would never be the case, of course, that A, who is in reality kind and considerate, would feel and do less than he. But A will be apt, certainly, to do more than he, in two somewhat different ways. First, he will be apt to act to help those in need even when, for some cause, no sympathetic impulse prompts him. For such a man recognises and accepts a certain claim incumbent on him in this. But secondly, and another way in which the acceptance of this claim will be manifest, A will make due efforts, as and when appropriate, to try to cultivate and retain a general tendency to sympathetic responsiveness in feeling and impulse to the needs of others. He will try to check any clouding or obstruction of such feelings and his liability to them, appreciating that if he were to allow this to happen this would be allowing at least one part of himself to grow indifferent, or even hostile, to this demand. By 'one part of himself', I mean, of course, his feelings as they are caught and moved in response to various situations. It might still be that, out of a sense of requirement alone, he scrupulously met the demands of the cases he came across. But then it would be that he was primarily conscientious in his efforts, rather than kind and considerate.

So here, as before, we see that there must be a complex inter-relation of, crudely, desire and duty in the motives of one who acts from kindness or sympathetic concern. Neither of these by itself captures all that is essential in the case. And we have glimpsed, also, one of the forms that this inter-relation may take, in the cultivation and reinforcement of general patterns of feeling and desire, motivated by the thought that what these feelings and desires cause one to be concerned with is something that befits and warrants concern.

It is, I am sure, some idea of this need for the interdependency of desire and recognition of demand which leads Aristotle to define virtue as a state of character concerned with 'choice' (E.N. 1106b 36), rather than simply a state concerned with feelings, desires or actions (not that these are exclusive, but they are not equivalent). For by 'choice' we must understand at least the desire and pursuit of things for reasons which relate to the merits and demerits of such desire and pursuit and not solely, if at all, to whether you happen to have such desires, be interested in such pursuits. But it will be some while before it will be possible to say at all precisely what the relevant notion of 'choice' imports. Enough has been said already, however, to see how misleading it would be to suppose that whenever and wherever we have some action done which represents a man's 'choice', he must there and then have deliberated about the pros and cons of the proposed action and acted upon the results of his deliberation. For the recognition and heeding of the pros and cons of various kinds of action can be manifest in the way a man regulates, inhibits or reinforces certain of his liabilities to various feelings and desires. And this can take place over a long period of time and need not consist in the premeditation of every deed. Should such premeditation be necessary, it would in fact suggest that the person has in some way failed duly to regulate his feelings and desires, and hence failed duly to heed the relevant pros and cons which would order his life appropriately. For had he fully succeeded in doing this, there would very often be little occasion for premeditation. He would have proper cause to trust the promptings of his feelings. I shall return to this point in later discussion.

One caveat must be entered here. Just because the recognition that there is a demand upon one to help others implies that one has reason to do this over and above what one happens to feel like doing, it does not follow that kindness towards others is centrally or essentially shown by helping them when one does not feel like doing so. For, in such a case – as I have said before – one's action betokens principally one's conscientiousness rather than one's kindness. As I have tried to make clear, whilst kindness *does* involve the recognition of the importance, the claim, of the need of others, this recognition does not at all involve acting *only* on the basis of that thought. It will with equal importance involve the effort to acquire, retain, stabilise, facilitate patterns of sympathetic, emotionally involved, concern and interest. And thus, when one acts, one's act will express one's emotional commitment as much as one's recognition of what is due and appropriate. This recognition, though it involves more than an emotional commitment, need not, and typically does not, exist wholly apart from that. Rather, it is in good part embodied and articulated in a certain ordering of one's emotions and the actions expressive of them.

As I have, in effect, claimed already, the recognition and acceptance of a certain demand which kindness involves is the recognition and acceptance that one has certain reasons for acting. This then vindicates my statement that states of character, the possession of virtues, involve reasons for action, as well as spontaneous desires, feelings, purposes, etc. The notion of 'reason' in relation to action (and also to desire) has at least two aspects, which may be called its 'explanatory' and its 'justificatory' aspects (see Dent 1976a: 167–70). As explanatory, inquiry into

23

the reasons for people's actions is inquiry into the reasons why they acted as they did, that which will provide an explanation of how it came to be that they did what they did, into what will account for their behaviour. As justificatory, inquiry into the reasons for people's actions is inquiry into their reasons for acting as they did, that which (as they took it) gave them (sufficient) reason to do, ground or justification for doing, what they did, that which they will give in account for their behaviour. It is the 'justificatory' use of reasons which is important here. In this use, the idea of a good, sufficient or whatever reason for doing something is the idea of what comprises a merit, value, claim or require-ment in what is going to be undertaken. Thus, seeing (some measure of) requirement in helping others simply is seeing (some measure of) jus-tifying reason for helping them.

We can, incidentally, readily see why the notion of reason in relation to action should have these two 'aspects'. For it is the normal case that a man's taking himself to have (as he believes) good reason for doing something is at least a central part of the reason why he does that thing. Of course, this is not always the case; and sometimes when it is not we speak of a man's reasons for doing what he does as mere 'rationalis-ations' of what he was doing in fact for some other reason, perhaps one of which he was not fully aware. I shall be considering some further aspects of this issue in chapter 5, section ii below. (See also chapter 7, section i.)

iii SUMMARY OF RESULTS

The purpose in presenting these illustrative cases has been to show *prima facie* justification for saying that the possession of virtues comprises the possession by someone of certain tendencies of feeling, desire etc., and of his having (as he believes) certain reasons for acting one way rather than another, for seeking one end rather than another. And for saying that these must be inter-related and interdependent in various crucial ways. Of course, little has yet been said in detail about the exact nature of these various components of virtues, or about the precise ways in which they inter-relate. Most of the rest of this study will be devoted to these issues. However, the leading points of concern displayed by the cases discussed can be summarised as follows.

First, the virtue of kindness, and any virtue which includes having certain spontaneous feelings and desires as one of its elements, does not comprise simply doing something because one thinks it one's duty, something required of one or incumbent upon one. At most, this form of motivation will be paradigmatic of dutifulness or conscientiousness. And though these are clearly virtues also, they do not provide a model for the understanding of the character of all virtues.

Secondly, occasional feelings and desires, or general tendencies to have certain feelings and desires, do not comprise all that virtues such as kindness involve, for all that they are an essential part of what they involve. For such feelings and desires may be disowned or regretted; and it can be that they are unrelated to any recognition of the value, importance or claim that the activity to which they prompt a man may have. The former point is simply a special case of this latter, more general, one. And in the absence of the recognition and acceptance of this claim, someone's behaviour is simply a matter of his doing what he feels like doing just as and when he feels like doing it and not otherwise. But this is not sufficient to the possession of a virtue, which requires an established commitment to the relevant activity as something meriting our undertaking.

Thirdly the possession of a virtue such as kindness does not, however, consist in some quite other phenomenon, or set of phenomena, than patterns of desire and feeling and the recognition and acceptance of certain reasons for action. Rather, it is in a certain integration of these that the possession of such virtues consists.

Fourthly not all virtues have precisely the same general, or formal, character. Most obviously, dutifulness and conscientiousness do not relate to patterns of spontaneous feeling and desire in anything like the way kindness or generosity do. And we shall properly expect other cases to exhibit differences of formal character from these also.

In my attempt to provide a systematic explanatory account of these points, I shall first treat separately of the several kinds of elements which go to make up the possession by someone of a virtue. But since it is no mere fortuitous agglomeration of these elements that comprises a virtue, but a thorough-going integration and interdependency of them, it will be of equal importance to examine the ways in which they may be related together. And I shall consider this in the light of the account of the nature and workings of the several elements. The final result will then be an account which does justice both to the character and oper-ations of the component elements of a virtuous state, and also to the way in which these are co-ordinated and collaborative in making it the case that when a man, say, offers help in kindness this is an unequivocal expression of his whole self, an undivided articulation of his character in action. The divisions made in the course of analysis must not remain as divisions in the activity of a virtuous man, which, as much as any human activity can be, is marked by its being the integrated expression of a unified self.

Before beginning this programme of account, I shall conclude this chapter by saying a bit more to 'place' the study of the nature of virtue in relation to other, generally more familiar, approaches to the understanding of moral action. It is worth doing this for two reasons. First, because although there are welcome signs of a renewed interest in the nature of virtues (see, e.g. Geach 1977; Wallace 1978; the best short account remains Laird 1935: Part One), their rôle in moral life and activity is still very much neglected in current moral philosophy. And, secondly, because this will enable one to achieve a more solid and secure appreciation of the distinctive rôle and contribution that the possession and exercise of virtues can and does play in our lives. The importance of reflection on the way in which the spirit is expressed in action will then be better understood.

iv MOTIVES, PRINCIPLES AND CONSEQUENCES OF ACTION

Recent moral philosophy has concentrated very largely on two aspects of human action. First, on the issue of the principles by which such action should be regulated, morally speaking. Secondly, on the issue of what ends, objectives, such action should be directed to, morally speak-ing. Clearly these issues are not necessarily independent. It may be said that those principles of conduct by which a man's action should be regulated are those which procure, or are likely or intended to procure, certain ends which are those that ultimately should be procured. Or it may be contended, on the other hand, that there are some principles of conduct – and some of these will be moral principles of conduct – by which a man's action should be regulated irrespective of the actual, likely or intended results of adherence to those principles. Or perhaps it

26

will be said that amongst the ends which should be procured is precisely the conformity of an agent's activity to those principles.

But however things stand in regard to these claims – familiar from the disputes between 'consequentialist' (or utilitarian) and 'deontologist' moral philosophers – it is clear that the character and motivation of the human agent will take a very secondary place in the discussion. If it is considered at all something along the following lines may very well be said: it must not be forgotten that we predicate moral goodness of agents. An agent will be morally good if he knowingly, willingly and consistently intends either to adhere to the required precepts of conduct, and/or to pursue the required objectives of conduct. If a man's conduct expresses such a knowing, willing and consistent intention, then we may say that he did not merely do what he should, but that he did it as he should; that he did not merely do the right thing but did it well; that his act is not only right but morally good.[8] That is, the moral excellence of agents is made dependent upon their recognising and adhering to rules or values whose excellence is primary and ultimate, from the excellence of which such value as a knowing, willing and consistent adherence to them has is derived (cf. Laird 1935: 27).

A little reflection is sufficient to show that so to view the source of the value in the moral goodness of agents gives rise to a very distorted picture. Consider the view that the moral goodness of an agent consists in the agent's knowingly, willingly and consistently adhering to certain precepts of morally required conduct, conformity to these as such being the ultimately valuable thing. On this account it follows that the sole, or at least the supreme, human excellence in the field of morality, the sole or supreme virtue, is dutifulness or conscientiousness.[9] Considered as the sole virtue this is scarcely credible; considered as the supreme virtue, it is at least disputable. Before saying why, let us consider the alternative popular view – that moral goodness reposes in the knowing, willing and consistent intention to pursue certain good or desirable ends which –

8 See, for example, Mill, *Utilitarianism*, chap. 2. 'Utilitarians', he says, are 'of opinion, that in the long run the best proof of a good character is good actions; and resolutely refuse to consider any mental disposition as good, of which the predominant tendency is to produce bad conduct'.

9 This is commonly thought to be Kant's view. But Kant derives the fitness of certain principles of action from the excellence of the 'good will' and not vice versa. Kant is not, in fact, a 'deontologist' in the customary sense given to that term. See Kant, *Groundwork*, chap. one.

with the supplement that the foremost, or even the only, desirable end is the general well-being (this being the view of 'classical' consequentialist utilitarianism) – has the result that the sole, or at least the supreme, virtue is either benevolence or beneficence (the wishing or doing of good for others). Again: considered as the sole virtue this is scarcely credible. And considered as the supreme virtue, it is at least disputable.

My reason for making these adverse judgements is that in neither case is there any apparent recognition of the enormous, and diverse, range of human qualities which we normally regard, and need very good reason if we are not to continue to regard, as morally excellent human qualities, admirable in others and much to be wished for in ourselves. For example, such qualities as generosity, sympathy, patience, fortitude, kindness, love, gentleness, tact, discretion, candour, responsiveness, reverence and so on, in addition to such qualities as dutifulness and benevolence or beneficence. The thoughts to set against giving equal place to these qualities may be that though they are, in their ways, excellent and admirable qualities, their excellence is not moral, and thus they form no part of an agent's moral goodness (see Baier 1970; Frankena 1970). Or that, again granting that they are in their way excellent qualities, they are always liable to break the bounds of morally right action, and thus they must be subordinated to and regulated in their exercise by the 'higher' virtues of dutifulness, or of benevolence (Baier 1970). Or again (a thought more plausible only if the supreme virtue is taken to be benevolence and not dutifulness), it may be said that these qualities really are only special cases of this supreme virtue in particular departments of its activity. However, any of these counter-claims would need extensive support to over-ride the *prima facie* appearance that things stand otherwise; and this is not readily obtainable.

To take a specific illustration. Consider the virtue of generosity in its relation to action. A generous man is evidently concerned to promote the well-being of others. But generosity is not so closely tied to procuring others' well-being for that endeavour to exhaust its content. Nor is the substance of generosity to be spelled out in terms of its comprising some set of acts to be performed, even if it be added that these should be performed in a certain spirit, with a certain motive.

Consider the first, counter-consequentialist, claim concerning the character of generosity. Generosity is no mere matter of giving of one's time and money and efforts to others, for the sake of their well-being, over and above the call of duty. A man's generosity is as much comprised in the thoughts he has regarding people, their aspirations and endeavours; in the interpretation he puts upon their actions (especially those which appear to obstruct his own life); in his emotional reactions to their demands etc. Generosity fundamentally comprises a certain general *attitude* towards others' well-being, and *actions* intended substantially to advance that well-being are only *one* of the elements that go to make up that attitude. Attitudes comprehend, in addition to purposive, result – procuring, actions, also thoughts, desires, feelings, reactions, hopes, fears etc., all forming a certain definitely ordered and integrated whole. And we value in generosity not only the good procured to us or others by a generous man's active endeavour, but also the concern, care and regard he has for us or them which, first, adds so much to the real significance his beneficent act holds (cf Irwin 1977: 162, 281) and, secondly, means that we still love and are grateful to a man who bears for us a generous interest even when circumstances may make it impossible for him to give it material effect in his conduct (perhaps he is a friend in a distant country). He wishes us well, and this matters very much in itself – not to be alone in the world, uncared for, quite apart from his wishes taking effect in his gifts, his money or acts of assistance. The manner in which a man regards us, the love he bears for us, is a centrally valuable element in human relationships, over and above the material benefits such love may bring. And a loving regard – in some measure at any rate – is essential to the constitution of generosity. We miss much of the inestimable worth of the virtues which have regard to men's relations one with another if we see the value in these as reposing only in the intent to procure, or the actual production of, benefit for another through action. The loving care they contain is, in itself, every bit as significant, and this comprehends more than deliberate acts alone (see Dent n.d.).

On the second, counter-deontological, claim regarding generosity, this may be considered. Even should we look at generosity *only* in its active good-producing aspect (which, as I have just contended, we really should not do), it is not possible to set down a class of act-kinds by performing which, even with the right motive, a man shall have exemplified the virtue of generosity. For generosity is an ever-inquiring,

29

ever-developing, creative attitude, seeking new ways of helping and giving to another as chances occur or can be contrived. It comprises no set forms or formulas, but transcends all such, spilling over the customary pathways which are 'standard' ways of giving and helping. Giving money is, possibly, a standard form for the expression of generosity in our times. But withholding money, even from someone in need, can also be generous, if one wishes not to put anyone under an obligation, knowing your recipient will feel obligated to reciprocate even if you think he should not.

It is of no avail to say that these differences between cases can all be 'written into' ever more complex principles specifying acts to be done. For not only would such 'principles' be so complex as to be quite unusable, it really is literally true that the variety of circumstances in which generosity can be shown and the variety of ways in which it can be shown is open-ended and cannot be mapped out in advance. What makes a man able to do the generous thing in this unpredictable variety of circumstance is not his reliance on maxims prescribing actions he should perform, for these would not always apply and then he would be lost for what to do; it is his having a steady and consistent direction of concern and intent, willing and desiring another's well-being and doing, which gives him the firm orientation that keeps him on the right path.

It is true that when, for example, seeking to encourage generosity in a child, or to explain to someone what generosity is, you may say that a generous man, for instance, gives of his time and money to others beyond the requirements of duty; that he does not stint his guests; and that he puts a good construction on people's motives – and such-like things. But reflection makes it clear that we can specify such kinds of acts in these cases only because they are such acts as are *typical of one with a generous heart*. It is not that someone is generous-hearted because he typically does such acts, they giving the substance of what generous-heartedness comprises. It is because someone has a generous heart that we can specify such acts as generous, since they are just such as would be typical of (though not necessary to) one possessed of a generous heart. It is the quality of his heart's desire that centrally makes a man count as generous, not as such what he does. (See Dent 1975; also Hume *Treatise*, Book 3, pt 2, sect. 1, 477–8.) What he does is material only as

30

symptomatic of his having and being actuated by the relevant desire. It is true, of course, that actions – though really not *only* actions – provide evidence of what a man desires. But desires or, at any rate, such desires as generosity comprehends, are not exhausted in dispositions to act. Acts express generosity (if performed in the right spirit); they do not comprise it.

I conclude that it is quite impossible to give anything like an adequate account of what generosity is either in terms of following precepts requiring certain conduct, or in terms of ends to be produced by deliberate action. So unless it is denied the status of being a moral excellence at all, we need to enlarge the scope of moral theory beyond the limits given to it by deontological or consequentialist theory to account for its character and significance. And what goes for generosity goes likewise for kindness, patience, compassion, tact and, come to that, their companion vices. Thus we see a need here to give serious attention to the nature of the virtues.

v ASPECTS OF HUMAN ACTIONS

If we reflect still further on aspects and elements of human action, we can find a second substantial reason for philosophical interest in the nature of virtues.

In any human action we may distinguish at least three significant factors: (*a*) the motive or intent with which what was done was done; (*b*) what was actually done; (*c*) the effects or results (intended, foreseen or otherwise) that what was done had. For example: from generosity (motive), I give you five pounds (act), which makes you very happy (result). Or: with the wish to have you sent down (intention), I tell the professor that you cheated in an examination (act), with the consequence that I am generally hated (result – probably unintended!). Of course, the separation of the act (or act description) from the motive of and result of the act is not straightforward in every case, and the principles of account in use here are very obscure. We sometimes, for example, redescribe, or originally characterise, acts – what someone did – in terms of his motive in acting. Thus: from flattery, with intent to flatter (motive), Smith praised Jones's essay (act), may be put as follows: Smith flattered Jones (act) by praising his essay (manner in which the act was

31

realised). Again, we can re-describe acts in terms of their results. Thus: Smith struck Jones (act) with the result that Jones lost consciousness (result), may be put as follows: Smith knocked Jones out (act), by striking him (manner in which the act was carried out). There are many very difficult problems about the identity and individuation of acts (see, e.g. Anscombe 1963: sect. 23ff; Davidson 1971; Goldman 1970: chaps. 1–2; and many others). But these do not deter us from making the distinctions I have indicated, in a rough-and-ready way, all the time. In so doing, we are often enabled to say that the same act was performed by different people, or by the same person at different times, with different motives or intentions. And that the same act may, in different circumstances, have different consequences. And these differences, in motive and result, of the same act may, of course, very much affect the desirability of that act being performed at some juncture.

This granted, we may go on and ask: why is a certain sort of *act* morally required? Why is it desirable, morally speaking, that acts of a certain kind should be performed? We can identify three possible general approaches to answering this question. One general line of approach would be to say: because it is the sort of act typical of a certain excellent motive, an act of the sort that it would be natural to a good man to do. This sort of answer derives the desirability of the act from the desirability of the motives or traits of character of which such an act would be the typical embodiment, unfolding or expression. And this we may call an *aretaic* approach to the obligatoriness of acts, since the obligatoriness of the act is said to be derived from the *ethike arete*, the excellence of character, of which the act is, or would standardly be, a token.[10]

The second general line of approach would be to say: because it is the sort of act required for conformity to some binding precept or law of conduct, which prescribes the performance of such acts. This sort of answer derives the desirability of the act from the desirability of observation of those precepts which demand the performance of such acts. And this we may call a *deontological* approach to the obligatoriness of acts,

10 I derive this illuminating classification of standpoints in ethical theory from Laird (1935). He distinguishes 'Virtue; or the Theory of Aretaics' from 'Duty; or the Theory of Deontology' and from 'Benefit and Well-Being; which in the Form of Well-Doing may be called Agathopoeics'.

since the obligatoriness of the act is said to be derived from its being *deon*, a needful or binding mode of action.

The third general line of approach would be to say: because it is the sort of act which would (be likely to) produce desirable results, to bring into existence states of affairs which it is good or needful should be brought into being. This sort of answer derives the desirability of the act from the desirability of certain states of affairs that the act does (is likely to) produce. And this we may call the *consequentialist* approach to the obligatoriness of acts, since the obligatoriness of the act is said to be derived from the *con-sequo*, the things that follow along with, the performance of the act.

These 'lines of approach' may be illustrated at work in our moral thinking in some simple cases. To illustrate the 'aretaic' approach consider this case: someone asks: why should one say 'thank you' to someone who has given you a gift? The answer given may be: because such a response would be a token of the desirable response of gratitude towards one's benefactor, which is a response a good man should have and act upon. For the 'deontological' approach consider this: someone asks: why should one return a book one has borrowed? The answer given may be: because doing that is required for conformity to the binding precept of returning to their owners things that have been borrowed from them. For the 'consequentialist' approach consider this: someone asks: why should one take out life assurance? The answer given may be: because doing so would result in those dependent upon you enjoying security in the event of your death, which is a state of affairs it is desirable should be procured, as being beneficial.

Of the aretaic theory of the source of the moral requirement of certain actions it is clearly in place to go on and ask why the motive or trait of character, from which it said that the kind of action in question derives its value, is itself a desirable or obligatory motive to have, act on, or perform the acts typical of. And parallel questions arise for the deontological and consequentialist theories. Why, it can reasonably be asked, is such and such a precept, conformity with which requires the performance of some action, binding, such as should be complied with? And, again, why are such and such states of affairs, the production of which necessitates certain actions, desirable, such as should be produced by human endeavour?

The point of expounding these different 'lines of approach' to the question whence an action acquires its moral desirability is to show that each is at any rate *prima facie* cogent and workable, and that there is no reason *a priori* why one should be given less weight and attention than the others. In particular, there is no reason why the approach through the excellence of virtue to the excellence of actions typical of (let alone actually expressive of) virtues should be given a smaller place than the others. Of course, I am not contending that we are likely to be able to provide a comprehensive account of the moral necessity of all kinds of action on this basis *alone*. Clearly each of these approaches has pretty evident limitations and pretty evident strengths. Each, it seems natural to conjecture, has a field of moral activity to which it best and properly applies. But, if this is right, it will be equally misplaced to seek to provide a comprehensive account of the moral necessity of all kinds of action on these *other* bases alone. So far as the appearances go, at any rate, there is every reason to consider each approach with the same seriousness and thoroughness. And this means, in the present state of things, particularly to emphasise the approach through the virtues to this question. Because this approach has the same *prima facie* cogency there is the need to give to it the same full treatment as the other approaches customarily receive. It has equal claim on our attention. It is not, or not evidently, a poor relation to be passed over quickly or made a mere dependent appendage.

2

The active powers of man:
(A) sense-desire

i INTRODUCTION

The examples discussed in chapter 1 section ii showed that the possession of such a virtue as, for example, kindness towards others involved at least two elements, a tendency to be touched by feelings of sympathy for their plight, to be moved by their need; and also a recognition of a claim or demand upon one to relieve this need. Neither of these alone, it seems, constitutes the virtue of kindness; nor does their un-coordinated compresence in a person. Rather, when someone possesses the virtue of kindness, these two elements are in a certain way related and integrated. It is my ultimate purpose to characterise clearly and in detail the nature of this state of integration. But in order to do so it is necessary first of all to secure a firm understanding of the respective natures and operations of each of these contributory elements, so that it will become clear in what ways they are capable of being integrated, mutually inter-related. To this end, I shall try to give, in the next three chapters, an account of the relevant contributory elements to the constitution of virtuous dispositions, treating them as more or less self-contained, discrete, elements in the human psyche. However, it is always important to realise that the possession and exercise of virtuous dispositions does not consist in a mere agglomeration of these elements. The 'integration' of them, their fusing into one, that I have spoken of, is intended to imply that they are capable of thorough and deep-going inter-relation and inter-dependency, and that this is essential to the character of an established virtuous disposition. So although I shall initially discuss these elements in independence of each other, this is done only with a view to preparing the ground for seeing how they may come together in that complex structured state which comprises the possession of a virtue, not with the thought that they retain their separateness in that finally achieved state, in which they are merely externally conjoined. Aristotle uses a striking metaphor when he speaks of the 'obedience' of the 'irrational element' to the 'rational principle' in the brave and temperate man: 'in him it speaks, on all matters, with the same voice as the rational principle' (E.N. 1102b 28; see also E.N. 1139a 25). And I want to try to present the detailed facts which justify the use of the metaphor of 'speaking with the same voice'.

I shall consider the nature of three contributory elements to the constitution of the virtuous state, which I shall refer to as 'active powers'. By an 'active power' I understand a source for human activity, a capability for acting in certain ways in relation to certain things. I shall not attempt to show *a priori* that there are only three such powers of relevance to the constitution of a virtuous state; nor to show *a priori* that they have the character I ascribe to them. My accounts should be judged by their capacity to highlight salient features of familiar experience, to introduce a coherent and perspicuous order into the range of phenomena under consideration, and by the fruits they bear in the resolution of problems of understanding and interpretation. In these ways I hope to vindicate the conceptualisation I make of the patterns of human interest and activity, and I do not want to argue that one is somehow necessarily committed to classifying the phenomena in the way I have. I would not suppose that alternative classifications are impossible; but I would hope that they are less perspicuous and fruitful than those I employ.

The accounts I shall give of these powers are by no means novel in their general outline, and are not intended to be. In particular, I have been very much influenced, positively, by the moral psychologies of Plato and Aristotle, that is, by Platonic and Aristotelian accounts of the capabilities and dispositions of men which contribute essentially to the determination of their moral character and activity; and I have been influenced equally, though negatively, by Hume's moral psychology, by the need to argue against the treatment he gives to reason, passion and desire in his accounts of the genesis and direction of human conduct. But my discussion is not intended as a commentary on these writers, rather to utilise ideas which I have found in them (or, possibly, imagined I found in them). It may be useful, none the less, to say that in proposing a tri-partition of the human soul as that is articulated in a person's virtues and vices, I am closer to the Plato of the *Republic* than to Aristotle, although I generally find Aristotle the more perspicuous writer on these matters. (On the issue of bi-partition or tri-partition of the active powers of the soul, see Fortenbaugh 1975: chap. 2 and *passim*.) The specification Irwin gives of the nature of the 'parts' of the tri-partite soul in the arguments of the *Republic* serves very well to give a pointer to the general form of the characterisations I shall offer.

According to Irwin, there are, for Plato, three kinds of desire in the human soul:

(*a*) The desires of the 'appetitive part', which are entirely good-independent and non-rational, unrelated to beliefs about goods (at least in origin).
(*b*) The desires of the 'emotional part', which are partly good-dependent, are influenced by beliefs about some kinds of goods.
(*c*) The desires of the (practically) 'rational part', which are entirely good-dependent, influenced by beliefs about over-all good. (Irwin 1977: 192. I have modified his wording slightly. See also Dent 1976a)

Whether this classification be just as an interpretation of Plato is not, as I have said, my concern here. The value of this summary is that it provides a good general indication of the kinds of distinction between active powers, varieties of desire, that I want to make, and which I shall proceed to discuss more fully. It outlines effectively the general framework of my account. I shall begin, then, with a treatment of the desires of the 'appetitive part', which desires are entirely good-independent, whose genesis is unconnected with any belief the subject of them may have about what is good (or evil) in particular or overall – at least originally so unconnected. I shall refer to such desires as 'sense-desires' and I shall explain my choice of this term in a moment (for the notion of 'sense-desire' see Aquinas, *Summa Theologiae* 1a, QQ 80, 81; 1a 2ae, Q 13, Article 2; 1a 2ae, Q31, Article 1, and following).

ii   THE NOTION OF SENSE-DESIRE

The notion of a sense-desire I shall employ is this. To experience a sense-desire is to experience an inclination to secure, for oneself, the enjoyment of some sense-pleasure, some pleasure which comes from, or reposes in, the gratification of one (or more) of the five senses. This is not intended as a 'definition', but as an initial approximate statement to be amplified and refined in what follows. There is a parallel notion of sense-aversion, which is to experience an inclination to avoid the suffering of a sense-pain, some pain which is comprised in the exacerbation of one (or more) of the five senses (most prominently the sense of touch) (see Hobbes, *Leviathan*, Pt 1, chap. 6; Hume, *Treatise*, Book 3, pt 3, sect. 1, 574; Book 2, pt 3, sect. 9, 438ff). But sense-aversion has no special features, so I shall not refer to it again.

Three aspects of sense-desire will be considered in more detail. First: the nature of the occasions and objectives of such desires. Second: how such desires originate, are engendered, in a man. Third: how such desires, once possessed, determine someone's behaviour. I take up this first point directly.

iii   THE NATURE OF SENSE-PLEASURE

There is a thesis made popular by Butler that there can be no such thing as a desire for pleasure alone and for nothing other than pleasure. This claim is one strand in his arguments against psychological egoism and hedonism. Butler contends, in a famous passage, that all pleasure depends upon desire reaching its appropriate objective; and, since this is so, there must be a desire for this object(ive) to provide the occasion for the occurrence of the pleasure. Thus, he writes:

Besides, the very idea of an interested pursuit necessarily presupposes particular passions or appetites; since the very idea of interest or happiness consists in this, that an appetite or affection enjoys its object. It is not because we love ourselves that we find delight in such and such objects, but because we have particular affections towards them. Take away these affections, and you leave self-love absolutely nothing at all to employ itself about . . .[1]

Strictly speaking, Butler is here discussing 'interest or happiness' rather than pleasure. But that this is also at issue is manifest from Sermon 11, to which the earlier quotation is a preface. Butler there writes:

That all particular appetites and passions are towards *external things themselves*, distinct from the *pleasure arising from them*, is manifested from hence; that there

---

1 See Butler, *Sermons*, Preface, sect. 37. The passage continues with a claim about an asymmetry between pleasure and pain in respect of their dependence on desire. This claim is, I believe, mistaken; but it would take us too far afield to pursue the matter here.

could not be this pleasure, were it not for that prior suitableness between the object and the passion . . . (Butler, *Sermons*, Sermon 11, sect. 6)

Thus, I take Butler to be saying that if we desire pleasure for ourselves we must necessarily, and more basically, desire something other than pleasure (and whatever that may be need not be desired for ourselves, though it may be). For, if we did not, there would be no occasion of pleasure, for there would be no 'appetite or affection' which was enjoying its object.

Butler is clearly correct that we do come by pleasure in this way. If I have wanted to own a Mercedes and I then acquire one, this is likely to bring me pleasure, although getting what one wanted is not always pleasing to one. But it would be wrong to think that this is the only way in which we come by pleasure for ourselves. A simple example to suggest otherwise is given by Plato, of a pleasure which can 'come quite suddenly without any previous pain' (i.e. without the pain of unsatisfied desire, of 'depletion'), namely the pleasures of smell – a point developed by Burke (see Plato, *Republic*, 584b; Burke *Philosophical Enquiry*, pt 1, sects. 2–4. The following quotation is from sect. 2):

If in such a state of indifference, or ease, or tranquillity, or call it what you please, you were to be suddenly entertained with a concert of music; or suppose some object of a fine shape, and bright lively colours to be presented before you; or imagine your smell is gratified with the fragrance of a rose; or if without any previous thirst you were to drink of some pleasant kind of wine; or to taste of some sweetmeat without being hungry; in all the several senses, of hearing, smelling, and tasting, you undoubtedly find a pleasure . . .

It surely need not be the case that I must have wanted to smell, for example, the scent of a rose, or any scent, for it to be a smell pleasing to me. There need not be a desire here that 'enjoys its object' in order that the object, the scent of the rose or smelling the scent of a rose, be pleasurable to me.

It has been suggested (A.W. Price: pers. comm.) that the case could be interpreted in a way congenial to Butler's general thesis, as follows. Smelling the scent generates a desire for this experience to continue which, providing it does continue, 'enjoys its object' and is thus gratified and brings pleasure in the way Butler suggests. In this way we can explain why satiety should set in; the desire can be sufficiently gratified and wane, and we then no longer wish to continue to experience the smell so it is no longer pleasing to us. But this interpretation seems to me more ingenious than convincing. For, first, it can hardly account for fleeting or momentary pleasures which are over before we have time to wish the continuation of the relevant pleasing experience. But there are such pleasures. Secondly: it fails to explain why such experiences *should* generate a desire for their continuation. The most plausible explanation would surely be because they are pleasing to us, and what we wish is to continue to enjoy this pleasure. Third, the phenomenon of satiation permits other explanations, as I shall indicate below. So there seems little reason to be resistant to recognising that we may have experiences which are pleasing to us without this pleasure being connected with, and hence not derivative from, the satisfaction of a desire to have that, or any similar, experience.

Plato's example was of a pleasurable olfactory experience. We may take a lead from this instance to suggest that there is a whole class of experiences which can yield pleasure in a comparable way, that is, experiences which are gratifying to any of the five senses. The appropriate stimulation of any of these is very typically pleasurable. Certain smells are immediately pleasing; others are offensive, nauseating and repugnant. Likewise, seeing certain colours, hearing certain sounds, having certain tactile experiences (such as result from being stroked) can be directly pleasurable.[2] There are marked variations between individuals, and in one individual over time, about which of these experiences gives pleasure and how intense a pleasure. But this is not important. Nor is there anything question-begging about describing the stimulation as 'appropriate'. For all that I am claiming is that we can come by these pleasures in a way that is independent of our having any desire satisfied by the having of the relevant experience. And there is no plausibility in suggesting that the criterion of 'appropriateness' of the stimulation would be its 'suitableness' (to use Butler's word) to a pre-existing desire. Why one degree of pressure in the rubbing of the skin is appropriate to cause a pleasurable experience, whereas others do not (but hurt or tickle), presumably has a physiological explanation, and does not at all derive from the agent's prior desire to have just the

---

2 On pleasurable sounds, see Shakespeare: *The Tempest*, Act III, Scene 2:
    Be not afeared: the isle is full of noises,
    Sounds and sweet airs, that give delight, and hurt not . . .

experience that that degree of pressure produces. I do not imagine, in fact, that any description of the nature of the experience is available to the subject other than that it is a pleasurable tactile experience, and it could not then be the object of a desire which made no reference to pleasure.

It may be asked why it is that certain experiences involving the five senses are found pleasing at all, if they do not answer to an existing desire. If the question supposes that there is something more problematic about this than there is about why it should be that a desire's attaining its object should be found pleasing, I have to say that I do not see any such difference. That we make reference to the fact that someone is pleased, and to the degree and duration of their pleasure, when they get what they want, as one way of judging how much they wanted whatever it was, shows only that getting what one wants does (sometimes) please, and does not explain *why* it does. If we seek an explanation here, the best route is through noticing a very common feature associated with being pleased, namely an increase in vitality, an upsurge of a sense of well-being, a certain quickening of one's life. This may be, of course, only very temporary, limited in scope; but none the less it is very generally present.

With this in mind we can suggest why getting what one wants brings pleasure. For when we are in a state of unsatisfied desire our natural energy, which is expressed in cleaving to something as an object of desire, is stopped up, arrested, for the lack of the object into which we have put our concern and which forms the focus for the onward movement of our life's activity. When the object of desire is secured, our arrested energy is released, and we now move to the state which was the projected pathway for the unfolding of our active life. The movement into the desired state is, thus, the release of arrested onward movement, an embodiment of the vital activity of the agent as that was projected forward into the desired object. This line of thought would also help to explain why the permanent impediment of fundamental desires typically leads to a general inertia, depression and loss of vitality. For in this case the release of arrested energy, projected into future activity in desiring, never takes place, and the subject's life is never quickened in fulfilling movement to the end and its achievement.

If this sort of picture of the connection between satisfying desire and

41

vital activity is at all plausible, it can be seen that it applies equally well to the stimulation of the five senses. For although it is true that in the absence of such stimulation there need be no arrested projection of energy in desire, it will be that our sensory powers lie unexercised and inactive. And appropriate matter for their exercise 'brings them to life', quickens them into activity. The deprivation of appropriate sensory stimulation can just as well lead to general depression of the spirit as the frustration of desire does. In both cases the quickening of activity is absent. (On the depression of spirit due to deprivation of sense-gratification, see Lawrence 1960: 158–9.)

None of this speaks directly of pleasure. But the connection is easily made, in one of two ways. Weakly, by the thought, mentioned above, that it is generally the case that where we have a quickening of vital activity we find pleasure attending this. Or, more strongly, by suggesting, in the manner of Hobbes, that pleasure is the perception or awareness of an 'increase in vital motion'. Hobbes writes: '. . . therefore such things as caused delight, were not improperly called *jucunda*, *à juvando*, from helping or fortifying; and the contrary, *molesta*, *offensive*, from hindering, and troubling the motion vital' (*Leviathan*, Pt 1, chap. 6, 33). Again, Aristotle's conception of pleasure as the unimpeded activity of our faculties, states and dispositions suggests a similar picture (E.N. Book 7, chaps. 11–14; e.g. 1153b 10); and it is likewise prominent in Spinoza (*Ethics*, Pt 3, Proposition 11, Scholium; Pt 4, Propositions 42–3; Proposition 60; and elsewhere).

Whether anything along these lines withstood critical examination would need extensive further discussion. But two points are made sufficiently clear by it. First, whatever difficulties there may be in accounting for the pleasurableness of experiences of sensory stimulation they are no greater than those in accounting for the pleasurableness in attaining what one desires. There is no reason to think the former case is more problematic than the latter. Second, connecting pleasure with the unimpeded activity of our powers and dispositions goes some way to explaining why pleasure should be desired and thought desirable. For it is clear that pleasure is then associated with the active fulfilment of human capacities and potentialities and these clearly contribute essentially to human well-being. A defect in recent accounts of pleasure in terms of freely given attention to or absorption in some experience or activity is that it is not made clear why such absorption should be desired or desirable. But if that absorption is seen as related to the active life of some power or disposition it can be seen as related to our being more fully and amply alive, quick with vitality, and this is clearly central to being well and doing well as a human being. And such a thing is central to much of what we naturally and properly desire and take to be good.

None of this shows, nor is intended to show, that pleasure is the only good or the highest good. Indeed, so far as pleasure derives from the unimpeded activity of some power or disposition, the good of any pleasure will depend very largely on the value of the activity of that power or disposition which is bringing pleasure. And that may be only of marginal importance (see e.g. Spinoza, *Ethics*, Pt 4, Proposition 60; also Aristotle, E.N. 1153b 7ff).

There is, then, no reason to doubt the existence of a large class of pleasures, the occurrence of which is not dependent upon our having an antecedent desire for them, or for anything else, the procuring of which brings pleasure in its train. This is the class of pleasures of the senses. I do not wish to say that this is the only category of such pleasures, though I do think it is the most important class (see Frankena 1973: 22–3, commenting on the views of John Clarke made in criticism of Butler). It can be seen, by reference to this, why it is that theories of psychological (or ethical) hedonism are so often taken as theories of psychological (or ethical) sensualism, despite the protests of their proponents.[3] For, if we take hedonism to be the claim that, for one reason or another, we desire always and only pleasure for ourselves, this immediately excludes our having desires for anything other than pleasure, even although there might be a pleasure attendant upon the satisfaction of these. Butler, as we have seen, is inclined to say that this renders hedonism, thus understood, impossible, as having 'absolutely nothing at all to employ itself about'. But I have argued that this is a mistake; we can and do desire the pleasures of the senses, these being pleasures not themselves dependent upon the satisfaction of desire. And since, generally speaking, it is the pleasures of the stimulation of the sense of touch that are the most intense, a desire to enjoy the maximum of pleasure will become

---

3 Mill, of course, made this protest. In *Utilitarianism*, chap. 2, he writes: 'To suppose that life has ... no higher end than pleasure ... they designate as utterly mean and grovelling; as a doctrine worthy only of swine ...'

the desire to enjoy the pleasures of fleshly stimulation, that is, become sensualism. What is wrong with such a conception of the ends of human desire is not that it is in some way logically impossible to have such an end, but that it is simply false that all men do, must or should desire only such pleasures. There is no credibility in the idea that fleshly pleasure is the sole end of human endeavour.

Of course, hedonism permits of other interpretations, for example that we desire pleasure and such other things as we suppose are means to pleasure. This might then lead us to acquire, or, if we have them anyway, to retain, desires for things other than pleasure if we learn that the satisfaction of these desires is very pleasurable.[4] This conception would not tend to devolve into sensualism. But now we have a view which, so far from being one which Butler would object to, comes very close to one he endorses (at least at times) – a kind of 'second-level' hedonism, whereby we choose to satisfy those desires the satisfaction of which is, as we learn, more pleasurable than is the satisfaction of other desires.[5] It would be beside the present point, however, to pursue this matter further.

My argument has been for the existence of a class of pleasures the occurrence of which is not derivative from a desire (for something other than pleasure) being satisfied. It needs no separate argument to show also that the occurrence of such pleasures is not derivative from our placing some value (moral or otherwise) upon something, upon having a certain experience. For although getting something we value, just as much as getting something we want, is typically pleasing, it is not essential to being pleased that what we get (or what we experience) be valued or desired in order that it be pleasurable to us, in every case. It is not essential to finding the scent of roses pleasing that we value smelling that scent. But the question now to be considered is not whether such experiences need to be valued in order to be pleasurable, but whether in

---

4 An amusing instance of this is given by Laclos, *Les Liaisons Dangereuses*, Letter 21. Valmont writes: 'I was astonished at the pleasure to be derived from doing good, and I am now tempted to think that what we call virtuous people have less claim to merit than we are led to believe.'
5 A form of 'second-level' hedonism appears to be proposed by Hume, *Enquiry*, App. 2, 301. Such a view surfaces occasionally in Butler: see Sermon 1 sect. 7; Sermon 11, *passim*; and elsewhere.

order to *come to desire* such pleasurable experiences we must attach some value to having them. For it is only if it can be shown that this is not so that we have here a 'good-independent' kind of desire, that is, a kind of desire for something not originally dependent for its existence upon our knowing or believing that what it is a desire for is of any value to us (of a moral or any other kind). And this is what I am anxious to determine.

iv   THE ORIGIN OF SENSE-DESIRES

I have argued that there are pleasurable experiences we may have irrespective of our desiring them or anything other than them. But, once we have experienced them, it is common enough that we do come to desire to experience them again; we come to desire to taste such pleasures again. How is the genesis of such a desire to be accounted for? In particular, is it a necessary condition for having any desire to undergo such pleasurable experiences again that we come to attach a value to undergoing these experiences, in relation to which valuation we form a desire to have them? For, if it were, the desire of sense-pleasure would be 'good-dependent', that is, would not exist in the absence of some value being placed by the subject of the desire upon his having sense-pleasure, even although the occurrence of the pleasure itself may be 'good-independent'.

It seems to me that the generation of a desire for sense-pleasure is not good-dependent, but is a natural response of the human organism to having had such pleasurable experiences. The naturally engendered sense-desire need not be pressing or omnipresent; it may be for some sense-pleasures rather than others; and so on. But these differences seem to depend on the natural constitution of each individual and upon his past experience of such pleasures, and not upon differences between individuals, or in one individual from time to time, in the kind and degree of value attached to the enjoyment of such pleasures, at least in the first instance. *Of course*, people very generally do come to attach value (or disvalue) to having such pleasurable experiences; and, doing so, this will very much modify the character of their original interest in having them. But this does not at all show that having such an 'original

45

interest' is *itself* dependent upon some value of some kind and degree being placed upon having these experiences.

Nor would the case be much different if my argument of section iii were not accepted. For suppose it were said, contrary to the claims made there, that in order that a certain sensory experience should be pleasing one must have desired that experience (or one like it) and it is having one's desire gratified that is what is pleasing in the case. It still would not follow that one need place any valuation upon having that experience in order to desire it; nor, crucially, place any valuation upon enjoying the pleasure that ensues upon the gratification of that desire in order to desire that pleasure. For instance, Irwin cites hunger (a 'basic biological drive for food') as a case of a good-independent desire, which is surely plausible (1977: 193). The way one desires food when one desires it from hunger does not at all depend necessarily upon one placing a value upon eating food, though one of course may do so, and may do so precisely *in consequence* of one's being hungry. So one's desire to eat is good-independent in the required sense. And if, as we may expect, eating food when one is hungry is pleasant in so far as it is satisfying to one's hunger (if for no other reason) one may also desire this pleasure, the pleasure of relieving one's hunger. But there is no reason again to suppose that the desire of that is good-dependent. Just as the desire of food was good-independent, so likewise may the desire for the pleasure, attendant upon satisfying that good-independent desire, also be good-independent. So, strictly speaking, one need not accept my account of sense-pleasures, as not dependent upon desires being satisfied for their occurrence, in order to accept that there is a good-independent desire for such pleasures. However, since I suppose my account to be correct, I suppose also that one class of good-independent desires is the class of desires for sense-pleasures of one kind or another with the character I have ascribed to them, which class of desires I call 'sense-desires'.

I have said that 'it seems to me' that the desire of sense-pleasure is good-independent; and that is not, clearly, to provide an argument that it is. I have nothing like a strict proof that it is a good-independent kind of desire. As I said earlier, the acceptability of this claim must ultimately depend on the overall coherence and clarity of the final account which results from it. And for the present I am only assembling the components for the final account. But I hope to be able to show that this conception of the nature of sense-desire does make the best sense of the case overall. Even if we do, as we typically do, come to acquire a good-dependent interest in the enjoyment of the pleasures of sense (such as is central to the life of the voluptuary), it is far from obvious that our desire for such pleasures is entirely dependent for its existence *ab initio* upon our placing some value upon the enjoyment of them as an element in our lives.

I mentioned above another good-independent desire, namely the desire one has, in hunger, to eat. It is important to get clear about the likenesses and differences between the physiologically based 'drives' for food and drink and the desire of sense-pleasure. For although these are both kinds of good-independent desire, there are important contrasts between them (see Hobbes *Leviathan*, Pt 1, chap. 6, on appetite and desire). Our ordinary use of terms does not register the differences here clearly: one speaks as well of an appetite for one's lunch and of someone having a hearty appetite for work. If one calls the latter a metaphorical use, this only shows a sense that there are differences here which call for closer examination.

Hunger and thirst normally recur periodically as physiological changes dictate. As a result of these changes someone comes from time to time to be desirous of eating or drinking, perhaps looks forward with pleasure to eating or drinking, or on these as at least providing a relief from the unease that accompanies hunger and thirst. If he then eats or drinks this will typically relieve that distress and he will cease to be hungry or thirsty until the relevant changes in food or water level take place once again and the desires reassert themselves. This return to the neutral state may be, as said, simply a relief or it may be positively pleasurable (cf. Plato, *Republic*, 585a).

How, then, does this roughly described pattern of appetition and satisfaction differ from that involved in sense-desire? The most obvious difference is that whereas sense-desire is evoked by the belief that some-thing would be pleasing to the senses, when one is hungry it is pleasant to eat because one is hungry and one is not 'hungry for' the pleasure of eating. Hume brings this out very well when he writes:

Beside good and evil, or in other words, pain and pleasure, the direct passions frequently arise from a natural impulse or instinct, which is perfectly unac-countable. Of this kind is . . . hunger, lust, and a few other bodily appetites.

These passions, properly speaking, produce good and evil, and proceed not from them, like the other affections.[6]

The 'good and evil' they produce is the pleasure attendant upon satisfying them or the pain attendant upon their non-satisfaction. They are not themselves, therefore, directed towards, nor do they proceed from, pleasure or pain.

A second difference between the cases is this: eating at the prompting of hunger ceases when hunger is allayed, when relief is secured. However, one typically eats beyond this point if one is directed by sense-desire (if one is fortunate enough to be faced with tasty dishes). Thirdly: hunger and thirst occur and recur as physiological changes dictate; one's sense-desire, on the other hand, may be a permanent disposition of one's interest. And sense-desires for this or that pleasure are elicited by the belief that they are available to one. Whereas one need not be caused to be hungry by the thought that food is available. Hunger is, indeed, belief-independent in a very strong sense, being a 'biological drive'. Sense-desire is not, being dependent upon beliefs about where pleasure may be obtained.

Aristotle points out (E.N. 1113b 25–29) that 'there is no gain in being persuaded not to be hot or in pain or hungry or the like, since we shall experience these feelings none the less'. These things are, he says, 'neither in our power nor voluntary', and hence fall outside what we may be praised or blamed for (cf. 1109b 30, and Book 3 chaps. 1–5 generally). But we are praised or blamed for the extent and intensity of our desire for the pleasures of sense, which implies that, in one way or another, it is in our power and voluntary. In what way, I shall examine when I come to consider the virtue of temperance.

These are, then, some of the contrasts between sense-desire and hunger and thirst (as instances of good-independent physiological drives). If some of them seem strained, two observations will serve to confirm them. First, it is not remotely plausible to suggest that our interest in the seasoning of dishes or in completing a meal with a sweet

---

6 *Treatise*, Book 2, pt 3, sect. 9, 439. The words omitted from the quotation are: 'the desire of punishment to our enemies, and of happiness to our friends'. It seems to me strange that Hume should have thought the origination of such desires 'unaccountable', and that they were wholly 'good-independent' (and even 'pleasure independent' in relation to Hume's own theory).

or savoury is dictated by hunger. These interests display a desire to enjoy gustatory pleasures quite over and above anything which might be needed to allay our hunger. It is true that we have the saying: a good appetite is the best relish. But this is only to say that a person with a keen appetite may get pleasure from plain food in allaying it. It does not suggest that hunger alone can account for all our interest in the variety of flavours. Second, though there may be disorderly (excessive) hunger or thirst, such as is manifest in boulimy or dipsosis, these are medical disorders which call for medical treatment and have nothing to do with greed. Whereas an extreme degree of desire for the pleasures of the table is an essential element of greed. One is neither a gourmet nor a gourmand on account of the extent of one's hunger. It is clear, therefore, that hunger and a desire for gustatory pleasure are quite different kinds of desire.

The point, taken from Aristotle, made above that one is not praised or blamed for feeling hungry, and hence that hunger does not come under consideration when treating of virtuous or vicious dispositions of desire, should not lead one to conclude that *acting* at the prompting of hunger may not be praised or blamed. For even if being hungry is not 'in our power nor voluntary' acting to allay one's hunger is; and someone who ate his fill when there were only 'starvation rations' available would have acted wrongly. But the wrongness in this case lies not in the fact of his having the desire to eat, but in his acting upon that desire without due regard to other considerations which bear upon the appropriateness of so acting; that is, the fault lies in the determination of action, not in the hunger. Whereas someone who has an excessive desire for gustatory pleasure has a 'wrong desire', which is over and above any wrong action he may perform if he heedlessly acts upon that desire. There is no vice of 'wrong hunger' or 'wrong thirst', although there may be right or wrong ways in which and occasions on which to allay one's hunger or thirst.[7]

Thus there is no difficulty in making a real and effective distinction between sense-desire and hunger and thirst, even although both are

---

7 There is a weak sense to be given to 'feeling hunger wrongly'; for example, when someone has omitted to have a meal at an appropriate time and now, inconveniently, feels hungry. But clearly the wrong in this case lies in the lack of foresight, not in the character of the state of hunger itself.

good-independent desires. Also, we have seen why hunger and thirst do not pertain to virtue or vice directly but only indirectly in that, as potential sources for action, they may lead us to act wrongly if we are not mindful of other considerations which may be pertinent. But there is never anything wrong (or right, come to that) in feeling hungry or thirsty as such. So I shall make no further direct reference to hunger and thirst, as being immaterial to this discussion. (See, however, the discussion of Fortenbaugh's views, below.)

The picture of sense-desire I offer, then, is this. As a result of having had pleasing sensory experiences we are caused to desire to have suchlike experiences again. That such a desire should be engendered in us is a natural feature of the human constitution. In Hume's words, it is an 'original instinct' of the mind to unite itself with pleasure. (*Treatise*, Book 2, pt 3, sect. 9, 439). Sense-desire may be present in a man in a number of different ways: he may have a strong, persistent, hankering for sense-pleasure which leads him actively to seek out sources of it. Or it may be simply that when the prospect of enjoying some sense-pleasure is presented to him, he feels a desire there and then to take it, and so on. This variety in the ways in which someone may be possessed of a certain desire is quite familiar, and does not present any special problems. (On 'dispositional' and 'occurrent' desires see Ryle 1963: chap. 5; White 1964: chap. 6.)

For later reference, it is important to stress certain features which are *absent* from the pattern of generation of sense-desire. First, as I have insisted, sense-desire is good-independent. It arises, originally, without the subject of it needing to place any value of any kind upon the enjoyment of sense-pleasure. Secondly; there is no sense in which it would be true to say that one chooses, decides or determines after deliberation to have a sense-desire (at least not originally). That I shall or shall not feel a sense-desire for this or that pleasure is something that happens or does not happen to me; such desires are evoked in me, a desirous response is called out from me. My coming to have such a desire neither depends on nor derives from any conscious plans or purposes I may have. As we shall see later on, I may indeed form a deliberate desire to secure the enjoyment of sense-pleasures for myself; but such a desire is not a sense-desire for them, for sense-desires do not depend upon deliberate judgement for their occurrence, but only upon the belief that sense-pleasure is obtainable from a certain object. I may indeed go further and deliberately order and stabilise my tendency to feel sense-desires for this or that. And then it may be said that, on some particular occasion, my desiring this or that pleasure does depend upon my conscious purposes in a certain way. But this does not go to show that sense-desires are themselves the product of deliberative judgement, only that deliberative judgement may modify one's tendency to have them in some way by, for example, 'shaping' one's proneness to experience them. These points will be made out more fully when I discuss the structure of temperance.

The significance of the facts that sense-desires are good-independent and are not chosen or decided upon will become apparent when I come to consider more closely the character of deliberative desires in chapter 4. Whereas the temptation is, I dare say, negligible to model the character of sense-desires on the pattern of deliberative desires the opposite temptation is, it seems, very much stronger and many writers have, wittingly or unwittingly, succumbed to it. But it is essential to recognise that neither assimilation would be correct, and that is why I draw explicit attention to these points now.

v   SENSE-DESIRES AND ACTION

Just as it is without reference to deliberation or decision that we come originally to be desirous of enjoying a certain sense-pleasure, so it is that such desires, once evoked, tend to move us towards securing whatever provides that pleasure without reference to deliberation or decision about whether to do so, in the basic case. I may indeed need to deliberate about *how* to secure what will, as I judge, bring me the pleasure; but I shall ignore this point for the present. I am claiming now only that one does not deliberate about whether to seek that pleasure. In the primitive case, the arousal of sense-desire is at one and the same time the generation of an inclining towards, a 'tipping over' towards, securing the pleasure of which it is the desire.[8] The arousal of the desire is the first moment in a continuum which unfolds into seeking something and engaging in directed behaviour towards procuring it. Of course, this

8 White 1964: 93: 'As the word hints, what is "inclined to" something is already on the way to it or about to fall over into it.'

51

continuum can be interrupted, and that will sometimes be essential if we are to behave properly. But it is a continuum which is not originally constituted by a decision to act upon the desire, but simply by the natural press of desire towards its own fulfilment through producing behaviour tending to secure its fulfilment.

I would not wish to deny that a translation of impulse into action of such pristine simplicity is rarely found in adult life. One who, for example, on the spur of the moment helps himself from a box of chocolates is likely to have the conversion of his impulse into action covertly informed by the thought that the chocolates are his to take, or that he is not allergic to sugar, or whatever. But the direct, unregulated, translation of desire into behaviour is very obviously central in the lives of young children, and it is out of this simpler structure that the more complex modes of adult behaviour develop. They are the elaboration of a simpler form, not the original structure of that form.

As before, the importance of remarking upon the unmediated conversion of desire into action in this case lies not so much in what is present in the phenomenon itself, but in what is absent from it. What, as I have suggested, is most prominently absent from it is any rôle for deciding or choosing whether to pursue what one is desirous of pursuing. Such decision comes in, I suggest, only when we employ our powers of practical rationality in the assessment of the good or evil of certain ends and actions and in our determination of ourselves in the light of that assessment. Further, it will be precisely by interrupting the continuum of unfolding of desire into action that we will be able to effect the regulation of our action upon sense-desire. So the use of our powers of practical rationality in deliberation and direction of action cannot form part of the original structure of that continuum. It may be objected to this that the continuum I have spoken of may be checked not by deliberative determination but by the irruption of some contrary desire. For example, a child tempted by some sweets may not eat them for fear of a beating. But it would not be true to say of this case that the child has been determining whether or not it is worth risking a beating for the sake of the pleasures of eating the sweet. The conflict he suffers is resolved by the preponderance of the attraction over the aversion he feels, or vice versa, not by his assessment of the relative benefits and costs of the alternative courses of action he might take, and action undertaken on the result of

52

that assessment. Here too the child's action is not ordered through a deliberatively made decision, but is still the 'overflow' of a desire state into behaviour, although now a complex and conflict-ridden state of desire. There remains the absence of deliberative determination to enact desire. I shall consolidate later (in chapter 4) the considerations which lead me to saying this. But I would hope that it can already be seen as having some plausibility.

vi   SENSE-DESIRE AND PASSIONAL DESIRE

I have argued that sense-desire, the desire to enjoy some pleasurable sensory experiences, is good-independent. Our having such a desire is not originally conditional upon our placing any value upon, seeing any good in, our enjoying such pleasures (even although they may be good and we may also believe this). The question I now wish to discuss is whether all desire can be conceived of as good-independent, that is whether the pattern of the genesis of sense-desire provides the definitive model for interpreting the character of all desire. To make this at all plausible, one would have to suppose that the range of things we could desire in a good-independent way extended far beyond sense-pleasures alone. But nothing I have said ruled out this possibility, nor was it intended to. So, let this supposition be made, and it be considered if all desire be good-independent. The gain in simplicity and generality of account that would result would be enormous.

I shall, however, argue that this cannot be made out. I have already indicated this with reference to what I have called (with little explanation as yet) 'deliberative desires' (see Aristotle E.N. 1112a 15; 1113a 10; *Eudemian Ethics*, 1226b 20ff). But rather than consider this claim more fully directly – I shall come to it in chapter 4 – I want to look at the second kind of desire Irwin characterised, the desires of the 'emotional part' of the soul, desires which are partly good-dependent, are influenced by beliefs about some kinds of goods. I prefer to call these 'passional' desires, since this name usefully suggests that these are desires rooted in our passions, states we suffer or undergo as patients, as being acted upon, rather than desires which exemplify our agency, our being the active instigators of our ends and purposes. For this is a conception of them I shall consider in some detail later on. The question I want to consider is whether passional desires really are good-dependent or whether, like sense-desires on the account I have given of these, they are good-independent. I shall claim that passions and passional desires do depend upon their subject holding certain things to be good or bad, do depend upon value judgements being made, and thus cannot be understood as good-independent in the way that sense-desires are. So far as I am aware, it has never been suggested that we feel passions in relation to things we *neither* think to be good or evil, *nor* think to be pleasant or painful. It is, therefore, only the thesis that passions derive, in a good-independent way, from pleasures and pains that I shall consider and attempt to refute. My question then is this. Granting that there are many more pleasures and pains than just the sense-pleasures and pains discussed earlier, do passions and passional desires arise directly from these pleasures and pains; or do they only arise if the subject makes certain valuations, has beliefs about some kinds of goods (and evils)?

I shall discuss this question through the consideration of an example. I would suppose anger to be a central case of a passion the onset of which involves the occurrence of a certain desire, normally the desire to inflict an injury or harm upon the person who provokes one's anger, one's antagonist. It is *prima facie* plausible to say that anger is occasioned by the opinion that one has been unwarrantably injured or abused in some way (at least roughly; more exactness of specification of this occasioning belief is not here called for). Clearly, taking oneself to have been unjustifiably ill-used in some way is not a sufficient condition for the onset of anger; one could quite well remain unmoved even though one believed this. But it appears to be a necessary condition for becoming angry that one takes this to be so. Now, can this belief that one has suffered an unjustifiable injury be given an account such that it involves only the belief that one has suffered an evil-independent pain, that is, a pain the occurrence of which is wholly independent of the subject's beliefs about what it is bad or undesirable that he should suffer? If this were so, anger could be understood as a response to an evil-independent pain. Clearly some pain, the pain of a cut or abrasion, is evil-independent. But, unless the subject of such-like pain thought his suffering it was unwarranted, its occurrence would not be a possible occasion of anger. Further, people may be angered by, for example, criticisms of their professional competence or innuendoes about their character, when these are construed as injurious. Now, in these cases it is natural and proper to say that these remarks are hurtful, that someone is pained or wounded by them. So perhaps in this case suffering an evil-independent pain provokes anger. But a moment's reflection shows that these 'hurts' are not evil-independent. One is 'pained by' someone's remarks precisely because one finds in them something one takes to be damaging or injurious to what one values, holds dear, for instance one's self-esteem or repute in the eyes of others. To be pained in such a case is to respond to damage to what one values, to one's evaluative integrity, as one might say that physical pain is a response to damage to one's physical integrity. It is this damage to something one values which occasions the pain or hurt, so it will be that damage which occasions one's anger also (if one is angered). The 'pain' is *itself* a consequence of the (believed) damage and cannot, therefore, itself be the sole basis for the angry response.

So where there is an evil-independent pain, such as physical pain, that cannot alone occasion anger without the thought that suffering it is unwarranted; and that thought essentially imports a value judgement. In other cases, besides this point also applying, the 'pain' in question is already evil-dependent, that is, is a 'pain' the occurrence of which depends on the subject holding something to be of value, believed damage to which occasions the hurt or pain suffered. So, in either case, it looks as if it is impossible to conceive of anger as a passion had in re-sponse to suffering an evil-independent pain. Such a passion does appear to be evil-dependent; the possibility of its occurrence depends on and derives from its subject holding certain things to be bad (in some way or another). It could now be said that anger is an exception in this regard in relation to other passions. But before considering this possibility, I want to look at two more immediate objections to what I have just said.

First, it might be claimed that my account of the occasioning situ-ations of anger is entirely superficial. For it needs to be asked why some-one attached value to, for example, the repute he enjoys in the eyes of others such that he is angered when that reputation is damaged. Is it not reasonable to suggest that he does so because it is a basic source of pleasure to enjoy the good favour of others and a basic source of pain to suffer rejection by and contempt from others? So, whilst on the surface anger is occasioned by suffering what one believes to be evil, a bad thing, more deeply one's anger is a response to the pain of rejection and contempt, and these are 'basic' pains, evil-independent pains.

How plausible is this objection? I think it is weak for the following reasons. First, since this line of thought is intended to apply not merely to the sources of anger but to the sources of all passions, it implies that all the valuations which appear to be involved in the occasions of passions are utility valuations, that is values or disvalues we attach to things because they conduce to or detract from our securing some value-independent pleasure or suffering some value-independent pain. And this is to say that the notion of something being good or bad as an end or in itself has no application in relation to these phenomena; no application because the pleasure we care about or the pain we dislike is good- (or evil-) independent. And although such a view has economy and generality, it does not have much plausibility.

Secondly, such an account does not provide any ready explanation of why some damage to one's reputation should need to be thought of as unwarranted if it is to occasion anger. For warranted damage to one's reputation is likely to be every bit as painful. And I see no way whatever in which this thought could be given an account of in terms of (a complex of) value-independent pains. To give its content one must necessarily refer to conceptions of what is due, or fit, in the conduct of others towards one, and these conceptions embody evaluations of how men should stand and behave in relation to others. Thirdly, some people are little susceptible to anger. If anger were at root a reaction to suffering a value-independent pain, how would this be explained? In terms of some kind of congenital anaesthesia to 'spiritual' suffering? Or what? Whereas if we see anger as dependent upon someone's 'value-system', variations in susceptibility to anger permit of a ready explanation in terms of variations in the weight different people attach to different things, to their self-esteem, to the regard of others, etc. It is not a matter of some temperamental or acquired sensitivity to damage to the spirit (construed on analogy with sensitivity to damage to the body) that is involved here. It is the development and possession of varying conceptions of the importance of certain kinds of treatment and reception.

Finally, it can readily be explained why it might be supposed that bare 'pain' is essentially involved in anger, by reference to my earlier remarks. For one may be 'pained by' damage to one's reputation, and perhaps one necessarily is so whenever one is also angered by that damage having been inflicted. But as soon as it is realised that such a 'pain' or hurt is itself value-dependent, it will be seen that anger is also value-dependent, even if it necessarily involves suffering this kind of 'pain'. The picture of there being a 'pain' involved here of a kind analogous to physical pain as being value-independent is an illusion. But it is relatively easy to see how this contrast might have been overlooked, and why therefore the idea that anger was derived from a value-independent pain might have come to be held.

I may seem to be labouring the obvious in defending the conception of passions as value-dependent, since it is now very widely held that emotions do depend upon their subject's holding certain things to be of value or disvalue. But this view is usually defended only in contrast with an 'atomistic' picture of emotions, in which these are presented as being unique *sui generis* inner experiences, either unconnected with or only contingently connected with any other mental states (see Hume, *Treatise*, Book 2, pt 1, sect. 2, 277). It is not typically defended against the claim that whilst indeed emotions are necessarily related to other mental states, it is only to value-independent pleasures or pains they are related, and not the subject's valuations. So this further point needs attention. Also, the notion that the passional and desiring life of human beings is exclusively and exhaustively dependent upon being susceptible to having value-independent pleasures or pains remains central to generally empiricist accounts of the ultimate sources of desire and feeling, a tradition of account deriving from Hume (if not from earlier sources). Hume, for example, writes:

'Tis easy to observe, that the passions, both direct and indirect, are founded on pain and pleasure, and that in order to produce an affection of any kind, 'tis only requisite to present some good or evil. Upon the removal of pain and pleasure there immediately follows a removal of love and hatred, pride and humility, desire and aversion, and of most of our reflective or secondary impressions. (*Treatise*, Book 2, pt 3, sect. 9, 438. Cf. Bentham *Introduction*, chaps. 1, 3, 4, 5)

It is important to recognise that when Hume, in this (and other) passages, speaks of 'good or evil' he does not at all have it in mind that there may be good-dependent as well as good-independent pleasures, or evil-dependent as well as evil-independent pains. Here, as elsewhere, for Hume 'good' is just 'pleasure' 'in other words', and 'evil', 'pain' 'in other words'.[9] So the category of the good reduces to the category of the

---

9 See, for example, Hume, *Treatise*, 276; 399; 439; and elsewhere. Of course, that pleasure or pain that denominates something morally good or evil is, according to Hume, of a 'peculiar' kind; see *ibid*. 472.

pleasant and of the evil to the painful. So we have here what is not a negligible theory which can be passed over in silence; it must be responded to effectively.

The second general objection which may be levelled at my account of anger as dependent upon valuations being made is this. Is not anger ascribed to animals and infants? But yet it would be absurd to credit them with making valuations of themselves and their circumstances of a kind I have suggested are appropriate to anger. Either, therefore, anger cannot properly be ascribed; or the anger must be a response which possesses a simpler source than I have said. And what more likely simpler source than suffering a value-independent pain?

My response to this objection is two-fold. First, when anger is ascribed to infants this is always done as part and parcel of ascribing to them (not necessarily very convincingly) some rudimentary and inchoate idea of what is due or owed to them by 'the world', so that pains and deprivations are experienced by them as improper denials of their legitimate demands. Thus such ascriptions do not go counter to my claim, but serve to support it, since the relevant evaluative beliefs for anger are always co-ordinately ascribed.

On the other hand, it is not always obvious that the ascription of anger in such cases is justified by the phenomena. It is easy to call what is an aggressive response to frustration or to pain 'anger'; but this would be a mistake. The 'frustration–aggression' reaction, as I shall call it, can be governed by a value-independent pain, and thus can be ascribed comfortably to animals and infants. But is not it simply special pleading to make this distinction? I do not think so. Consider the following case. I am trying to hammer a nail in an awkward place, and time and again the nail bends over. Anyone who has experienced this will know how maddening it can be. But does this 'maddening' amount to anger or is it the frustration–aggression reaction? Surely not the former, unless I am in a way angry with myself for my ineptitude, or for a moment absurdly think it unfair of the world to inflict such a misfortune upon me. But both of these cases import the relevant evaluative opinions necessary for the ascription of anger. Without these one need not, of course, experience nothing: frustration, aggressive desires, being maddened – all of these occur. And because they can still occur, that suggests their occasions are simpler in character than is required for anger, and thus they can more properly be ascribed to animals and infants.

However, is this now not in effect to allow that there are some passions, for instance, frustration and aggression, which may be dependent only upon suffering value-independent pains? And does this not defeat my general thesis that passions are value-dependent? And thus it may be that anger is, after all, a special case, not at all exemplary of a kind. It would clearly be impossible to go through every instance of a putative passion to determine whether or not it is value-dependent. I shall consider, therefore, one further instance only, which will serve to highlight the fundamental issue here, namely the contrast between value-independent and value-dependent desires. This further instance is fear.

We do often ascribe fear to animals and infants as well as to adult humans, and that already suggests that only a primitive apprehension is necessary to experiencing this reaction. So perhaps fear is simply a reaction to the prospect of suffering a value-independent pain, not involving the subject placing any disvalue upon this suffering, but only being naturally averse to it. If we grant this, we must also grant that fear does not remain confined to the prospect of suffering value-independent pains, but in adulthood is extended so that we come to fear, for example, disgrace, or making fools of ourselves, which are 'painful' to us as being damaging to what we value.

This gives rise to a problem. It is not simply that the range of things that can arouse fear in us enlarges as we grow older and understand more; that is not problematic. It is that the character of the sources of fear changes, from being only the prospect of suffering some value-independent pain to including that and also the prospect of suffering damage to what one values. And thus we have two quite differing kinds of occasion for our reactions, and we should wonder how and why they can so easily be classified under one head. I suggest the reason is this. Even though it be granted that fear may be a response to suffering some value-independent pain, such pains as are naturally apt to inducing fear are those that are in fact, though not necessarily in conception, associated with conditions of fundamental disvalue to the organism, for example, pains of physical injury. Or in cases where there is not even physical pain involved, yet fear is present in infants, as in the fear of heights, this also connects with physical injury, since falling from a height causes that. The idea of physical injury being a disvalue is simply

59

this, that it detracts in obvious ways from the viability and well-being of the organism.

The point is now this. When a child acquires the notions and attitudes appropriate to attaching value and disvalue to anything, he naturally and properly recognises as basic disvalues for him these pains (or situations) to which he reacted in primitive, inchoate, fear. Such primitive fears attach to pains which have just such a rôle in the economy of viable life and well-being as to make them apt objects for conscious and articulate disvaluation, when this becomes possible. And if, as I judge, animals never do attain to this level of articulate comprehension, none the less *we* recognise the pains they suffer as having this general rôle in their lives. We recognise how these pains are connected with what are basic threats to their existence and hence are fundamentally disvaluable to them, and, being so, are proper objects of fear. We have, then, one concept of fear here, one concept for a reaction to something which is an evil as being a threat to our existence or well-being, a reaction which may occur primitively to what are in fact such disvalues and threats, and also more sophisticatedly to what are in conception such disvalues and threats. And, once the conception of such disvalues is attained to, their potential range of sources will enlarge. So even in this case it does appear that the emotion of fear is dependent upon a valuation.

If this argument does not convince, it does not deeply matter. It will simply then be that the notion of fear covers two different patterns of response, one dependent upon a valuation being made, the other not, and we shall have to reckon separately with these. And if this shows that not all emotions are dependent upon valuations, I do not think it can be denied that some are. And that would alone be enough to necessitate the recognition and explanation of the nature of passional desire, desire coming from passions which do depend upon valuations, by contrast with sense-desire, or more generally value-independent desire. The main point is to see that the character of passional desires cannot simply be assimilated to the character of value-independent desires. And to see this it is, possibly, not necessary to insist that *all* the desires involved in passions are value dependent, though I do think this is so and have tried to argue that it is. I shall bring forward some further points which bear on this in the next chapter. But I hope enough has here been done to vindicate the integrity of passional desire as a distinctive kind of desire.

60

It may be complained at this point that my argument for the good-dependence (or evil-dependence) of passional desires omits a crucial step. For it is one thing to argue, as I have, that the *pleasures and pains* which occasion passions are value-dependent pleasures and pains. It is another to argue that the *desires* which are engendered, as an element in the passions, by experiencing these value-dependent pleasures and pains are themselves dependent upon a value judgement being made, namely of the good of enjoying this value-dependent pleasure or of the evil of suffering this value-dependent pain. It looks as if judgements of value may come in at *two* points: at the point of experiencing the pleasure or pain, *and* at the point of experiencing desire or aversion as a result of doing so. Only if I argue that they come in at this *second* point as well have I succeeded in showing that passional desires (or aversions) are themselves value-dependent, and not just that their occasioning pleasures and pains are value-dependent. Indeed, a point I argued earlier in the chapter about sense-desires seems to show the need to mount this extra argument (see the end of section iii, and the start of section iv above). For I pointed out there that it is one thing to show that sense-pleasure does not arise from the gratification of desire, or from achieving something valued; and quite another to show that we can come to *desire* sense-pleasure without placing a value upon enjoying it. This latter point needs a second argument. Why then have I not given a second argument in the case of passional desire, to show that we shall come to desire value-dependent pleasures only if we place a value upon having them (or to show that we will be averse to value-dependent pains only if we place a disvalue upon having them)?

My reasons for not mounting this second argument here are two. First, it seems to me quite unnecessary. If you are 'pained' by someone's unwarranted coldness towards you, you necessarily interpret that coldness in evaluative terms (as your suffering an evil) – or so I argued. If you then feel an angry desire to return injury for injury, how could it be made out that this *desire* was not equally value-dependent? It would be quite artificial to say that suffering the 'pain' was a value-dependent suffering, but that the 'pain', once experienced, merely 'naturally' engendered the vengeful impulse, although there is room, so to say, to put the matter like this. The originating cause of the 'pain' is the coldness, perceived by you as evil; and it is for that *coldness* you desire to revenge yourself. There is no occasion for saying that the desire arising from the

61

'pain' is caused merely 'naturally' by the 'pain', and is not caused by your value judgment (perception) of the coldness. How is the causal effect of the latter supposed somehow to terminate at a certain point? This is to make a notional and not a real distinction.

Secondly, were I to have incorporated this point into the body of the preceding discussion, it would have made what is already a complicated structure into an intolerably confusing one. Mapping out the value-dependencies and independencies of pleasure and pain, desire and aversion, is complex enough as it is, without introducing – only then to withdraw – possible multiplications of such dependencies and independencies.

A further point may here be noted. Very occasionally the following kind of situation can arise. Someone feels absolutely tortured, is terribly distressed, by the neglect or rejection they experience. And, goaded by their anguish, they may lash out at anyone and everyone. Here it seems to me plausible to say they are goaded into angry destruction by their pain, as a simply 'natural' reaction to its intolerableness. Somehow they hope to assuage their pain; that is the function of, though not, I think, their purpose in, their destructive rampage. Indeed the orgy of destruction is often curiously intense but aimless. The pain is within them, not out 'in the world' so that it can be destroyed. This, I suggest, is not at all how it is in the more 'normal' case. The relief of the 'pain' is not the purpose of the angry retaliation; the purpose is to get your own back, to give back evil for evil suffered, thus to re-establish your dominance (or equality) of position or power, or some such thing. Relief of your 'pain' does not come to be a 'secondary' (let alone primary) target for your angry impulse. That focusses on your (supposed) aggressor, and does so as mediated by the value judgement you have made upon what he has done to you. The object of your desire is its primary instigating cause.

Finally, it is briefly worth considering whether or not the converse assimilation to that I have just discussed could reasonably be made. Could it be argued that there is no such thing as a desire for pleasure independently of a valuation being placed upon the enjoyment of that pleasure, but only ever a desire for pleasure dependent upon coming to value having such pleasures? Clearly some pleasures depend upon valuations; and the desire of some pleasures depends upon valuing them. But the question is whether this is always the case. That it is seems to be the view of Fortenbaugh, when he writes: 'Bodily pleasures may be the object of acquired desires whose efficient cause is cognitive and open to reasoned persuasion . . . The temperate man . . . has acquired . . . loves and hates which are rational appetites obedient to reasoned argument.'[10] However, he holds this view apparently because he thinks the only alternative to it is to suppose that what interests us in bodily pleasure are our 'non-rational appetites caused by physiological changes', namely, hunger, thirst and sexual desire. And then, as he rightly points out, we would have the strange result that a temperate man is disposed to desire the right bodily pleasures on the right occasions etc. 'because his bodily processes have developed some miraculous rhythm'. This does, however, neglect the possibility, which this chapter has sought to show is an actuality, that standing between 'bodily appetites' and 'obedient rational appetites' (that is, in my terms, (ordered) passional desires) there is a natural inclination to the enjoyment of bodily pleasures, the having of which is not dependent upon the judgements of practical reason. Not that I at all wish to deny that we can and do come to love (or hate) bodily pleasures, and hence have a further kind of interest in them. But I have wanted to deny that it is absolutely necessary to having a desire for such pleasure that we place a value upon the enjoyment of it.

Is there, though, any decisive counter to this attempt at a converse assimilation? I cannot think of one, any more than I suppose that my arguments against assimilating the character of passional desires to that of sense-desires are altogether decisive. In both cases it is a question of the overall explanatory power and perspicuousness of the position that results. And I think that in order to achieve this we should resist this generalising attempt as much as the former, more common, one. The 'loves and hates' that Fortenbaugh speaks of are indeed central to the state of temperance; but they bear indirectly upon our desire of sense-pleasure and do not constitute its original character. I shall discuss this fully in chapter 5.

I have, then, attempted to show that there is a kind of desire, passional desire, different in character and structure from sense-desire. I turn now to a more careful consideration of its nature.

---

10 Fortenbaugh 1975: 84–5. I took a similar view to this (as I now believe) mistaken one in an earlier draft of this essay. It is not without its attractions.

3

The active powers of man:
(B) passional desire

I have argued that the character of passions or emotions must be distinguished from the character of sense-desires in at least one basic respect which is relevant here. The having of passions is dependent upon one's making valuations, whereas having sense-desires is not. It is necessary now to explain more clearly the character of passional desires, their relation to passions and the nature of their dependency upon valuations being made. I shall first set out the relation between passions and passional desires.

A sub-class of passions include as part of their onset the arousal of an impulse to act towards a goal, some desire to secure an objective, on the part of the subject of the passion. Anger and fear, for example, to which I referred in the last chapter, are cases of such passions. Normally the onset of anger includes the evocation of an impulse to injure or harm one's antagonist or, at the very least, the wish to see him suffer. Normally the onset of fear includes the inducing of an impulse to remove the threat to one either by removing oneself from it or by attacking and destroying it (flight or fight). It would be unintelligible for someone to say, for instance, that he was angry with someone but felt no wish to see him suffer or to pay for the injury he caused (as one believes). I shall call such passions as these, 'active passions', for their onset typically includes the arousal of a propensity to engage in directed activity. Along with anger and fear, such other cases as envy, hatred, pity, resentment are cases of 'active passions'.[1]

Not all states normally thought of as emotions or passions are 'active' passions as I have identified these. Joy, gladness, elation; sorrow, misery,

---

1 Compare Aristotle E.N. 1105b 21: 'By passions I mean appetite, anger, fear, confidence, envy, joy, friendly feeling, hatred, longing, emulation, pity and in general the feelings that are accompanied by pleasure or pain . . .'

despair, are not, because although these do prompt their subject to behave in various ways which are expressive of these states – to an exuberant manner or to laughter in the case of delight, or to withdrawal or tears in the case of sorrow – their onset does not include a prompting to engage in *directed* behaviour, the inducing of a desire directed to attaining some goal. These are rather emotions in which we celebrate our attaining, or mourn our failure to attain, some goal we have; or, more generally, celebrate the well-being and faring of something we hold dear, or mourn its ill-being and faring. They come in at the point where desire has found its objective, not where some objective is being established for someone and he becomes set upon undertaking it. Their place will be more exactly specified later.

I am not concerned here to give a complete account of the nature of emotional states, but only to emphasise those features of them which are material to characterise the moral psychology of the virtuous state. For this reason there are several questions about emotions, for example, about how we have knowledge of them, about their related sensations (if any), which I shall not consider.

ii THE GENERAL CHARACTER OF ACTIVE PASSIONS

The active passions I have mentioned so far exhibit a general similarity of character which may be described thus. Some feature of a person's situation, or something that (as he supposes) has happened or will happen, is believed by him to be in some way and to some degree bad, undesirable. (Believed *by* him to be undesirable; not necessarily believed to be undesirable *for* him. Consider the instance of pity.) This belief induces in him, not after deliberation, but as an immediate unpremeditated response, a desire to modify the situation in just such a way as to rectify it in the respect in which he believes it to be undesirable. And in the simplest case this induced desire prompts the subject to behave in ways which tend to the procuring of this result, this remedy to the evil in the situation. It is not necessarily under the description, 'bringing about a modification of my situation which will rectify it in the respect in which it is (as I believe) undesirable' that, for example, a frightened man desires to flee and flees; indeed, it is doubtful that it is ever under that description. But the end of putting a safe distance between himself and what he takes to be presenting a threat to him, which end he desires, does in actual fact rather obviously have this character. In the onset of active passions of the kind I have mentioned is included a desire, on the subject's part, to change the situation in which he finds himself from a bad to a better or good state, one better or good in a respect strictly co-ordinate to the original bad character he believed his situation to possess when he reacted to it in passion. The value to the human species of being moved to desire to remove undesirable features of their situation in this unpremeditated, spontaneous and often peremptory way should be obvious.

There are several features of this general pattern in active passions which I shall clarify further.

iii THE SOURCES OF ACTIVE PASSIONS

All the cases of active passions mentioned are of passions experienced in connection with the subject of them making a value judgement upon some feature(s) of his situation; in their case, a judgement that it is a bad, undesirable feature in some way and degree. It is a necessary condition of undergoing such passional responses as these that such a negative valuation is made. In the absence of such a valuation being made it would be logically incorrect to say that, whatever reaction the subject may have, his reaction should be classified as the undergoing of one of these passions. Of course, placing this negative valuation upon some feature of one's circumstances is not a sufficient condition (causally or logically) for undergoing a passional response to it. Someone may, for example, recognise that he has been insulted and find this offensive, but yet not be angered by it. Or, someone may recognise that someone is favoured before him by someone whose favour he wishes, but not be rendered jealous by this. I have no clear idea what might constitute a sufficient condition of the arousal of a passional response in someone, for getting him to respond emotionally to his situation. This would seem to be an empirical question, not one to be uncovered by conceptual reflection. I shall simply take it for granted that sometimes, at any rate, a passional response is evoked by the belief that some evil is present (or has occurred or will occur). Sufficient conditions could, no doubt, be given for saying that such a response has occurred, but that is a quite different question and one it is not material to settle here.

The kinds of undesirability which are associated with the various passions mentioned are very diverse. In anger, the undesirability has the form of something one holds dear suffering an unwarranted injury (as one believes) – at least roughly. In jealousy, the undesirability takes the form of being less favoured than another in relation to the affection of one in whose affection one wishes to be central. In pity, the undesirability takes the form of someone suffering some ill, and so on. These differing kinds of undesirability the subject of the passion believes to obtain are, indeed, one central criterion for the differentiation of passions (cf. Scruton 1971: 40ff and *passim*; Wilson 1972: chap. 5 and *passim*). But, however diverse these kinds of undesirability may be, in all cases some conception about something being bad about the situation is necessarily involved.

I have tried, in chapter 2, section vi, to defend this view that passions are dependent upon valuations being held and applied to the situation against the view that they are responses to enjoying value-independent pleasures or suffering value-independent pains. To those considerations, the following may now be added further to support the claim that this is indeed a necessary dependency against other objections to this. For instance it may be objected as follows. Cannot someone be terrified of spiders and yet sincerely deny that he believes them to be destructive, harmful, threatening or intelligibly undesirable in any way? Is not this kind of response not at all uncommon? In which case no disvaluation is necessary to experience fear.

To the points made in the previous chapter about fear, the following can be added. First, it is perfectly possible to suppose that for such a man a spider is associated with or symbolises something he really does believe to be harmful or threatening, but that he has forgotten, is unaware of or even has repressed this. We are not always able to be specific, or explicit, about the way in which some situation strikes us as adverse, whilst it is still true that it does. It is a quite general truth that our thoughts, especially about anything disturbing to us, are not always quite readily available to us; opinions may be operative in ordering our feelings yet 'buried', not present to consciousness nor easily made so (see Foot 1968: 243).

Secondly, when someone experiences fear in a case like this, they typically feel violated by and estranged from their response, which appears to them as an alien, unaccountable irruption into the stream of their lives. This is altogether different from the case where, say, some-one threatens you with a knife and you are frightened, where the nature of the case is quite lucid to you and you are entirely 'at home' in your response as flowing naturally from the interpretation you give to the situation. It would be quite wrong to take as the definitive case for an account of passions instances of these self-estranged and alien emotional responses. These are deviations from the norm and do not serve to establish it. Thirdly, we typically call such-like reactions to spiders, to open spaces, etc., which are apparently radically dissociated from the scheme of values of the subject of these reactions and through which he has a sense of the value saliences of his situation, phobias, matters of an inchoate dread. Our having this distinctive conception of them marks our recognition of their special character. Treatment of phobias may take several forms. It can be effective simply to treat them as aberrant affective and motor responses, and to inhibit these by drugs or de-conditioning, irrespective of whether or not their subject thinks of his situation in any peculiar way (see Neu 1977: Pt 3). But equally one may proceed by trying to bring some buried opinion of value 'to the surface' and attempt to relieve the subject of it by discussion and so modify his reactions. This is not necessarily the most efficient thing to try to do, but it is not absurd. In a small way we are already doing this sort of thing when we think over more carefully the way we assess our relations with someone we thought we liked if we find, strangely to ourselves, we deeply resent their advancement. I think the 'rational' treatment of phobias is only an elaboration and extension of this kind of process.

I conclude that there is nothing in this point which presents any further serious challenge to the view that a valuation must be placed by the subject upon some feature of his situation if it is to be possible that he respond in passion to it. That we can respond in passion without this being at all obvious is not to be denied. But typically we do not, and there is no reason to take these other cases as central.

A different point about the character of the dependency of passions upon valuations which deserves notice is this. Our passional responses occur in relation to valuations we happen in actual fact to make of our situation. It is not within the scope of our passional responsiveness itself to consider and determine the justness or otherwise of these valuations; our response is simply 'in obedience' to them, and occurs (if it occurs) regardless of this further point.[2] Some of the valuations which govern our passional responsiveness may possibly have been arrived at, or 'vetted', by due and just deliberative reflection. How this may be so I shall be considering later on. But it is equally possible that other valuations may well have been taken over from parents or peers with little or no independent, let alone just, judgement of their true soundness. Someone may be extremely sensitive to slights and to signs of indifference to himself, and this might very well betoken an excessive value being attached by him to receiving the good regard of others. But it is without reference to whether the value placed upon this is excessive or appropriate that he responds with anger, resentment or misery. He will undergo these reactions simply if this is an opinion of value he holds, its rightness or wrongness not coming into the case.

This is one clear reason why it would not be satisfactory to trust to one's passions in living one's life (see Aristotle, E.N. 1095a 4–11); not that, in response to this point, one should seek to live a passionless life altogether after the manner of the Stoics (cf. Aquinas, *Summa Theologiae*, 1a, 2ae, Q 24, Articles 2–3, and elsewhere). Since our passional responsiveness is simply dependent upon whatever evaluative assessments we happen to hold, it is liable to lead a man to react and to act wrongly, since he would be proceeding regardless of the appropriateness of those assessments. On the other hand, this feature indicates one of the major places at which the right ordering and regulation of passions may possibly be made. For it makes quite clear, as Aristotle insists throughout the *Nicomachean Ethics* about the passions, that the 'irrational' element in a man's soul 'shares in a rational principle' (see, for instance, E.N. 1102b 13ff). Hence the right activity of the 'rational' element, which would originate right rational principles for conduct, could order the operations of passions through the very components and structure of these. If we could come to a just sense of what is truly desirable or undesirable in what measure, to what extent, our passions could come to be rightly elicited, by what they should be, in the measure they should be, when they should be, etc. This is of course not primarily a matter of correcting errors of empirical fact such as, for example, the

2 Compare Ross's note to Aristotle: E.N. 1102b 34: 'Aristotle's point is that the *alogon* (the faculty of desire) can be said to have *logos* only in the sense that it can obey a *logos* presented to it by reason, not in the sense that it can originate a *logos* . . .'

error of thinking that it was a real and loaded gun one was threatened with when it was really a water pistol and hence no threat at all. It is rather a matter of correcting errors of evaluative estimate, of the sense of the importance of things, such as, for example, the error of supposing it to be so awful not constantly to be in receipt of marks of esteem from others (as in the case of excessive proneness to anger), or of supposing it to be of such great import that one receives the full, foremost, attention of the person on whose love one counts (as in the case of jealousy). Passions are not blankly a-rational affective and motor responses, utterly unconnected with a man's conceptions of what is good and evil, what is important and what trivial. They rather depend upon, embody and enact, such conceptions; and if these conceptions are sound one's passions may also be, not by any fortunate accident merely but by design, reasonable and appropriate. I shall, in due course, be looking carefully in later chapters at the character of this 'in-forming', moulding of internal structure, of passion by true judgement of good and ill.

I should not be understood as saying that we can, just like that, cease to be jealous, cowardly or irascible people by concluding that it is not so bad a thing to be less favoured, to run the risk of harm, to suffer slights. But the intransigence of patterns in our passions is badly misrepresented if it is represented in terms of a conflict between reason and passion, as if these were altogether disparate powers capable of only an external confrontation. It would be closer to the nature of the case to represent it as a division within (practical) reason itself – though one the implications of which extend beyond reason alone: a division between our having become deeply wedded to, and having our feelings governed by, certain opinions as to the values of things (which we could think of as prejudices, prior to judicious judgement); and our coming, upon deliberative reflection, to conclude that these are misconceived opinions (our 'postjudices', if there were such a word). This is a division in our practical judgement itself, between considered and deliberative and unconsidered and unreflective judgement; it is not a judgement of reason set over against something altogether different in character. To come to be able to live by what is truly good, understood as such and because so understood, cleaved to, is very much a matter of becoming conscious of, and prising ourselves loose from, pictures of what matters which are in various ways infantile, neurotic, deformed or just plain ignorant, which are carried in our passions. This is essentially the work of greater understanding, albeit an understanding that must extend itself into and shape the whole of a man's soul. (Aristotle insists on this latter point (E.N. 1144b 17–30).) How this may take place I shall, as I have said, be considering later on.

This concludes the discussion of the sources of active passions, or at least of those I have so far referred to (but see also section vii below).

iv   PASSIONS AND INDUCED DESIRES

The position reached so far is then this. It is the central mark of the 'active passions', in distinction from other passions, that their onset includes the evocation of a desire to bring about some change in their subject's situation. In their occurrence is incorporated the arousal of an interest in procuring some result thought of by their subject as desirable. (I shall return to the character and rôle of this attendant thought.) This is what principally sets them off from, for example, gladness, sorrow etc., as noted before. I have suggested, specifically, that one who undergoes an active passion is caused to desire to rectify his situation in the respect co-ordinate with that in which it was believed by him to be undesirable, which belief occasioned the occurrence of his passional response with this incorporated desire.

The point I wish to emphasise about this incorporated desire is that it is one its possessor is induced to have; it is a desire evoked in him, called out from him, and he is likewise made to think of bringing about some change in his situation as desirable or good in at least one respect, namely as remedying the evil of his situation (as he thinks obtains in it). The subject of the passion does not formulate this desire; he does not elect or decide upon wanting to change his situation in this way. Rather, this change is established as an objective for him, as something he would like to bring about, in the very onset of his passion, as something provoked in him.

For example, one whom the prospect of danger causes to be fearful is induced to desire refuge from that danger, this being the change in his situation which would remedy the evil he finds in it. He may be caused to think: 'I must, at all costs, get out of here', as a dominant, all-

71

absorbing idea. He does not decide upon this as the thing he should be best advised to be doing and hence determine upon doing it. Again, one from whom another's suffering evokes pity is moved to desire to relieve that suffering, this being the outcome which would rectify the situation in what is, as he believes, its undesirable respect. And likewise in other cases. A certain purpose is established for the subject of the passion in the elicitation of the passion itself. The subject does not decide upon having this as his goal. And this is, I believe, of central importance.

The elicited desire incorporated in an active passion need not be overwhelmingly intense or uncontrollable, for all that in no case does the subject instigate this desire himself, but it comes upon him. Even if only a slight interest in procuring a certain end is engendered, this end has not been decided upon as a desirable one by the subject. This is a good part of what is meant when it is said that we suffer or undergo passions; *patio* means 'I suffer' or 'I am acted upon'; I am someone who is a patient, or is moved from outside, as the term 'emotion' also suggests. By the onset of a passion, itself a way we are 'acted upon', we are induced to desire certain things, a second way we are 'acted upon'. Certain things hold our interest and in a measure we are in thrall to them, under their influence and direction and we are not entirely self-directing, masters of the placing of our concern. I shall be considering these contrasts more carefully in the next chapter.

A few further points about the nature of the desires incorporated in active passions may be noted. First, the desire evoked in the onset of such passions is primarily a desire that the subject of them himself bring about the rectification of his situation, not simply a desire that his situation be rectified through some agency or another. But in some cases when, for example, the subject of the passion believes himself incapable of rectifying his situation, his desire may become merely a wish that the evil in it be remedied in some way or another. For instance, if on a television programme someone abuses something I hold dear and I am angered, I shall be caused to desire that he suffer for this. And if someone in the studio audience is likewise angered and goes ahead and strikes the man, I shall have my own desire to a degree assuaged. It is still, however, natural to say 'I wish *I* could have got my hands on the man for all that I am thankful that he got what was coming to him.' It would, however, not be correct to infer from such cases as these that whenever

I desire that I myself rectify my situation when prompted by passion, I do so in the light of judgement about whether it is possible for me to do this. The passional desire is originally and primitively a desire for the subject of that desire himself to be bringing about a certain result. It is by modification of this that the other case results. The primitive case does not result from supplementation of the desire that some change occur by assessments of the practicality of my bringing it about, leading to the formation of *my* desire to act for that end.

Secondly, as I indicated above, the evocation of a desire in the onset of an active passion will typically be accompanied by the evocation of certain thoughts about the objective of that desire. Bringing it about will be dwelt on with pleasure, and the occurrence of the change will be thought of as desirable, for example. It is not only the direction of attention and of the propensity to action that is modified in passion, it is also the content of the subject's thoughts that is subject to influence. This is a central way in which passions deform judgement. It is not simply that when in the grip of a strong passion one is generally agitated and unsettled so that one cannot think clearly or steadily; it is that one is caused to think certain particular thoughts, perhaps almost obsessively, for example that something is unendurable or that life is worth nothing unless a certain change occurs. And these thoughts can be quite out of proportion to the real significance of the case, for all that they dominate one's mind and assessment of one's circumstances. Just as the adverse judgement in relation to which an active passion is evoked may be misplaced, so correspondingly the evoked opinion about what it would be desirable to bring about may be disproportionate. We have in this a further aspect of the case for saying that it would be a mistake to trust heedlessly to our passions as a guide to what to be doing. For what we shall by them be caused to think of as worth seeking is in direct relation to that assessment which, without regard to its appropriateness, engendered our passions. We have a great need to consider the justness of the opinions of desirability which we are induced to hold. And this will crucially involve the exercise of practical reason, as I shall try to show.

Related to the point just considered is the phenomenon which may be called the 'single-mindedness' of passion. That desire I have as part of an active passion is a desire directed only towards rectifying my situation in relation to that *particular* respect in which I take it to be undesirable. This is the single concern I have through my passion; and if it is at all intense this concern can easily dominate my attitude to my circumstances to the exclusion of awareness of or responsiveness to any other practically significant features of it. But it would be a rare thing for procuring that change to be the sole relevant factor which bore upon what to do in some situation, for all that someone may be heedless of any others. If, then, we are to be in a position to give due and appropriate weight to all the factors which may bear upon the situation, we need to acquire and to employ in a steady and consistent fashion the capacity to 'bracket' any particular passionally induced purpose, in order to attempt to determine what overall good there would be in securing that purpose. This capacity is, I should say, not so much an exercise of reason in relation to action as such, but is a precondition for the possibility of bringing such reasoning to bear upon what we are to be doing. No particular passion can, of itself, do the job of making an assessment of the overall good of that purpose it suggests to its subject as a good; for the passion itself is that which presents this purpose as a good in the first place. The comparative estimate of the importance of goods and evils which deliberation involves cannot be made through particular passions, since each passion is, so to speak, mindful of only one good or one evil and gives that a hold on the subject. Some overarching power of judgement is required for this and that is contained in the employment of practical rationality.

Many would contend, of course, that no such thing as an assessment of the overall or true importance of the purposes which each of our several passions suggest to us as good is, in the nature of the case, possible. For to speak like this implies that we could establish and employ something like a scale of the value of ends with which to moderate those 'suggestions' as to the value of ends put to us in our passions; and that we could finally adopt or reject ends as suitable to our pursuit by reference to this 'scale', and order our ultimate undertakings accordingly. But, it will be said, that something shall be of value to us can *only* be for us to have some passional responsiveness to it, some passional involvement with it. So all that can happen here is that one passion predominates over another on a particular occasion or more generally and pervasively. That *is* what it will be for some end to be more important to us, for the desire for it to exert a stronger, more persistent, hold over us.

It will be clear already from many observations I have made that I think such a view mistaken, at least as a matter of theory; in practice I dare say we quite often follow our passions blindly, not moderating their influence by true judgement or even reflective judgement. I shall be defending my view fully in chapter 4; but it will be useful to spell out here some of the consequences of the conception I oppose, in order to see its ramifications and hence where it might be called into question. Consider a case where someone is beset by conflicting passions. Different features of some situation attract and repel us; or possibly we are alternately attracted and repelled by the same features. So we experience conflicting inclinations in regard to our circumstances, have conflicting views about what it would be good to be doing in relation to them. The question then arises: how might this conflict be resolved? I believe that we would take it that there are, in general, two possible forms of resolution. Either one of these inclinations comes to have such a degree of predominance over the other that the latter is overborne and one is moved to act accordingly. In this case, the subject would not be said to have selected which of these purposes to give paramount weight to; simply one of them draws his concern progressively more forcibly until it asserts a dominant hold. Or else, on the other hand, in such a case as this the agent falls to consideration of which of these purposes which have some appeal to him as good would be overall most desirable for him to actualise, and on the basis of his judgement he endorses one and rejects the other as a fit purpose for his endeavour. Or it might be that he determines upon some other objective altogether.

Now if it be denied that the possibility of any reasoned evaluation of the good in passionally suggested purposes exists, this second outline account of how a resolution of conflicting inclinations might occur simply has no application. For all that could ever take place in any case would be that one inclination finally has a more forceful hold over a man and thus the objective of that becomes his final purpose (see Hobbes, *Leviathan*, Pt 1, chap. 6, 37–8; Schopenhauer, *Essay*, 36–7. I discuss these passages in detail in chapter 4).

Is not this conception of the necessary character of the case open to objection? For, first, it would be extremely surprising if we should have, and use with apparent success, the conceptual resources for characterising two different forms for the resolution of the conflict of inclinations if one of these forms of account is entirely spurious. Such a widespread error calls for a deep explanation, and it is by no means clear that one has been offered. (It should be noted that it is not any general thesis about the determination of action by desire excluding the power of directing behaviour by deliberative choice of ends (if indeed it does) that is in question here. It is the much more limited claim that the idea of making a reasoned judgement of the worth of ends, and of according action, does not make sense, does not describe a possible state of affairs, and the larger issue does not come in.)

Secondly, the conception of conflicts of desire being resolved, or resolving themselves, only by the superior force of one desire over another, is quite false to experience, gives an interpretation of our experience of such cases which is very strained. Some cases, indeed, match that account quite closely, as one can see the play of aggression and fear in the changing posture and expression of someone until he finally strikes out or flees. But in very many cases we represent the matter to ourselves as involving an effort to look at what we might be involved in doing if we do one thing or the other, and as trying to form a considered assessment of the real merits of what, because of our passional involvement, appears worth doing to us. One takes oneself to be involved in trying to make an active determination of what it would be best to do and in trying to order one's conduct in accordance with this, and not as simply becoming possessed of a gradually predominating inclination. Also, it is an implication of this view that it is only if something arouses a passional response from us that it is capable of having any rôle in the governance of our activity. There are, however, many things which, perhaps wrongly – though that is now neither here nor there –do not work on our feelings but which yet we can and do see merit in, and in the light of this recognition can be mindful of in the direction of our conduct. It might well be true that people are more likely to give to Oxfam if moved by compassion for the suffering of starving children. But it can also happen that one determines upon giving convinced by an argument about justice or fairness. Quite generally, the notions of the strength of feeling in favour of something and of the strength of argument in favour of it are not identical. And someone can surely be convinced by the strength of an argument when he has no strength of feeling; indeed, be dissuaded by argument even when he has a strong feeling.

I shall be elaborating many of these points in the next chapter, and supplementing them with others also. But they provide, I hope, already a *prima facie* case for saying that we can deliberatively adopt ends aside from their drawing out a passional response from us; and that we can deliberatively assess the purposes our passions set before us, and be governed in our final determination of what to do by this assessment. It might be that we do not direct ourselves thus all that often; but to argue from that to what it is possible should occur would be mistaken.

Finally, and further by way of preparing the ground for more detailed later discussion, it will be useful to say a little about the justification of passions and passional desires. A man may be, and know himself to be, quite justified in being angry, afraid, jealous. Quite generally, in so far as the evaluation of the situation which governs someone's passional response is just, so far his response and the purpose he is moved to desire to achieve are just also. And, as I said, a man might know this to be so about some particular passion he feels on an occasion. However, we must be clear what rôle a man's knowing (or even believing) himself to be justified in responding as he does plays in relation to his responding, his growing angry or becoming afraid or feeling jealous. Growing angry, to take that case, is not a conclusion that one draws in the light of reasons for growing angry, however good these may seem to one. Believing oneself to have even decisive reasons for being angry is neither necessary nor sufficient to being angry; one does not 'form anger' on reasons as one might form an intention or formulate a resolve on reasons – although one may allow, for reasons, one's anger to form by not stifling a nascent vengeful impulse. So what, then, can the rôle be for taking oneself to have good reasons for being angry? It is in assessing the occasions of anger one experiences, reflecting upon the kind and degree of evil that they contained so as to order one's liability to being angered in other situations. The way having what one knows to be good reasons for anger, knowing one's anger to be justified, operates in relation to one's anger is through ordering one's apprehension of situations so that, when anger comes upon one, it does so as and when it should. It remains a response that comes upon one, a reaction one has to the situation. Whereas, as I have hinted, when one takes oneself to be justified in having a certain intention, this would be absurdly misrepresented as so ordering one's assessment of reasons that, when intentions come upon one, they do so as and when they should. In the one case it is a question of moulding a response to which one is already liable; in the other case it is a question of forming a response. The fact that one may have every reason to be angry and, in a certain way, not be angry unless one thought one had every reason to be, must not lead to a picture of the rôle of reasons and reasoning in the formation of passions which would underestimate our passivity in relation to them. The difficulty is to do justice both to the degree to which passions incorporate and are amenable to rational judgement and to the way in which they are not alone 'creatures of reason', judgements we form, but ways in which we are moved, acted upon. Generally one aspect of them is sacrificed to the other, typically the former to the latter;[3] but both need to be acknowledged and understood. Again, I shall try to expand on this point later.

v INDUCED DESIRES AND ACTION

I have argued that the onset of the active passions I have instanced includes the arousal of a desire to bring about a change in their subject's situation which would rectify the evil supposed by the subject to be present in it, which belief occasioned the passion. I want now to say a little about how this desire, once aroused, governs the subject's behaviour in relation to bringing about the desired change.

Just as one does not deliberatively elect a certain objective as one worth pursuing when that objective is established as desirable to one in the onset of a certain active passion, so in the basic case, when one acts out of a passionally induced desire this is not in the light of a deliberative election to translate it into action, of a decision to bring about the change one desires. I am not denying that one can decide upon doing this; it is important for my overall account that one can. I am only saying that, primitively, this translation of desire for an objective into action directed to securing that objective is not mediated by any decision to 'take action', as if wanting this and seeing nothing against it I then determined upon doing what I wanted. In this respect, the basic mode of enactment of passional desires is parallel to that of sense-desires. Having them and acting them out are steps along a continuum which is not con-

3 The over-assimilation does not always take this form. For an over-reaction see Solomon 1977: *passim*.

stituted by any decision or choice of their possessor but is constituted simply by the natural onward movement of desire into its behavioural expression.

This is most clearly seen in the case of those passional desires which have a 'natural expression'. Striking out in anger, running away in fear, hiding one's face in shame are unpremeditated, spontaneous, behavioural embodiments of desires, to hurt, to avoid harm, to escape ridicule. One does not determine upon these as suitable ways of achieving what one desires; they have a primitive aptness to procuring that rectification in the subject's situation which he wishes. They have an inherent teleological appropriateness without their expressing the agent's own conscious design to achieve this end. However, precisely because their aptness is primitive, uninformed by any deliberative control appreciative of the varieties of circumstance, they can turn out on occasion to be ill-adapted to bringing about the agent's purpose. An angered seven-stone weakling may much better secure the revenge he wishes by some more devious plan than by flailing in impotent rage upon the manly chest of Charles Atlas.

Suppression of these natural behavioural expressions of certain passions, and substituting for them some calculatedly effective course of action judged fit to secure the desired end is, I should maintain, one aspect of the work of practical rationality. For even if we do not deliberate over *whether* to seek revenge for some hurt received, but are unhesitatingly borne along by the tide of our angry wishes, if we do deliberate about *how best* to revenge ourselves then we are ordering our actual conduct, our eventual undertakings, by reference to some reflection on good or ill, even if only on the effectiveness or ineffectiveness of certain methods of revenge. It will be in recognition (as we take it to be) of the good in a certain course of action, as being for instance the safest way to secure our end, that we determine ourselves upon undertaking it. We are heeding a requirement of reason for the direction of action when we thus direct our conduct, and we are not merely enacting the immediate promptings to action of our desire.

What is primarily of note about the relation between passional desires and directed behaviour dependent upon them is, as was true of sense-desires, not what is present in the structure of that relation but what is absent from it. In the primitive case neither the transition from

79

desiring to bring about a certain change to actually proceeding about procuring it, nor taking the particular means by which one shall proceed in one's endeavours, are dependent upon one making some deliberative choice, whether to take this desire as the one worth enacting or whether to take this way in enacting it. Where even so minimal a deliberative ordering of one's conduct comes into the case as is involved in selecting the best way to secure an end, to the worth of securing which one does not give any consideration but simply assumes, there we have an added complexity of structure which is not the product of passional responsiveness alone.

vi THE ACHIEVEMENT OF THE END OF DESIRE

If the subject of an active passion is successful in achieving that change in his circumstances that he desired to achieve he will normally experience pleasure, joy, delight, elation to some degree at doing so. If he is unsuccessful, he will normally experience distress, dismay, sadness at this. The intensity of such responses is often taken as a measure of the magnitude of the agent's desire. And there is nothing especially problematic in this. However, three points about such responses as these are worth observing. First, it is at this point of the agent's attaining his desired objective that we find the proper place for the occurrence of those passions the onset of which does not include any inducement to engage in directed behaviour, to desire an end to be secured. These I called the 'celebratory' or 'mourning' passions, in which we celebrate our achievement of, or mourn our failure to achieve, what we desired. Though these passions have characteristic behavioural expressions, they do not include behaviour directed towards securing any further objective.

Secondly it is, of course, not only when we have achieved or failed to achieve some objective we thought desirable that we are apt to experience joy or sorrow. More generally, we are liable to experience such reactions when anything we hold dear fares well or ill, even if their faring ill or well has nothing to do with what we ourselves have done or been unable to do. The cases where its faring well or ill depends on our activity are simply a sub-class of cases of this more general kind. I mentioned this earlier. Thirdly, it is in connection with the delight felt at

80

securing some desired state of affairs, and/or delight felt at thereby rendering something held dear to fare well, that Butler's point, discussed at length in chapter 2, applies. For it would obviously be a mistake to say that because when our desire attains its objective this is attended with delight, the objective of that desire, or indeed of any desire, was to secure that delight. There *can*, however, be a 'secondary interest' in fulfilling only such primary desires as we learn are productive of great and enduring delight to us upon their fulfilment. This, again was discussed in chapter 2 (see p. 44). Certain distinctions are worth noting here, however. I argued that there could be a desire for sense-pleasures, and that such pleasures occurred independently of there being a desire for having a certain sense-experience which, being had and thus satisfying one's desire, brought pleasure. Presumably, though, if a certain sense-pleasure *is* desired and secured, we shall enjoy both that pleasure and the pleasure of satisfying our desire for it. And this pleasure of satisfying our desire seems to be common to sense and to passional desires. But there is a distinction between the pleasure *of* satisfying a certain desire and the pleasure *at* satisfying a certain desire. This latter seems to me to occur only when the agent attached some value either to the very act of satisfying the desire itself or to whatever he has done in satisfying it. And thus it seems that this 'pleasure at' would be absent in the case of satisfying a value-independent desire for some sense-pleasure unless and until the agent has come to attach some importance to satisfying such desires and/or to enjoying such pleasures. I think joy and delight are most naturally associated with 'pleasure at' something, and thus betoken the agent's recognition that something of evaluative significance to him has been achieved or has occurred. 'Pleasure in' doing something, or the pleasure of doing something, is very often less or not at all dependent upon this kind of apprehension of the meaning of the situation to the agent. So, to the extent to which the gratification of passional desires brings joy or delight this suggests, once more, that passional desires depend upon valuations, for their satisfaction represents the attaining of something of value to their agent (see Scruton 1975: 159; Wollheim 1975: sect. 3). These passions are much more cognitively dependent, derive from a more complex understanding and interpretation of what has occurred, than is the pleasure in or of doing something.

81

The active passions I have been considering, those such as anger, fear, jealousy, pity, etc., have all been responses to features of his situation which their subject takes to be undesirable, bad, in some way and to some degree. It would not be correct to infer from these instances, however, that all passional responses are occasioned by their subject's negative valuations. This is obviously not the case in relation to 'celebratory' passions; but there are also active passions occasioned by positive valuations, and it is these I want now to consider. I have deferred the discussion of these because, as we shall see, they all relate to a kind of interest we have which has a basic, structural, rôle in relation to all passions of whatever kind; and it is easier to show what this is after having explained the character of other cases first.

Active passions which relate to positive valuations include friendly feelings, maternal love, patriotism etc; and all of these can easily be seen as particular forms of love for something or someone. It is the centrality and fundamental rôle of 'love', of cherishing and holding dear, in relation to all passions that I want now to try to show. What draws a loving regard out from us in relation to something or someone is the perception (as we take it to be) of good, beauty or worth in them, and it need not be initially evoked from us in response to something we regard as evil as, for instance, when we come to love the thought of avenging ourselves when we are angered by an injury.[4] Love is, I suggest, a response to the perception of positive value, and underpins all our other emotional responses, as I shall explain. First, though, I need to say a little about what I am here understanding 'love' to involve.

In the sense I intend it, 'love' is not so much a particular passion as the basic source of all passions, which are specific ways in which our love manifests itself, as the object of our love suffers various vicissitudes. Rather than speaking of love, one might more colourlessly speak of being 'attached to' something or someone, of being 'involved with' them. Most fundamentally, it is the investing of concern or care in something as being something of importance, value or good to one in

4 See Vlastos (1973: 8 n. 20). Aside from love of the Good, Plato appears to have thought that all other loves were responses to things we judge evil (especially deficiencies in ourselves), moving us to remedy these. See also Annas 1977: 535ff.

one way or another. It is that kind of interest which one speaks of when one speaks in general of someone having 'a passion for' something, whether it be for justice, for medieval paintings or for fish and chips. It need not be an elevated or edifying attachment – nor need it be particularly strong or permanent, as perhaps is typically implied when one speaks of someone's 'passions' in life. This rough indication of my meaning will become clearer if I now show what rôle I think such love(s) play in relation to the passions I have previously discussed.

I contended that active passions such as fear or jealousy were occasioned by their subject's opinion that some aspect of his situation was undesirable. A moment's reflection will, however, reveal that what underlies this opinion about the undesirability of something is a more basic opinion of the subject's about what is *desirable*, what is good or dear to him. And it is some threat or damage to that which is what he is judging to be undesirable. For it is as and when objects to which we are attached in love are under threat or are suffering damage that we react with fear, jealousy, pity, resentment or whatever it may be, depending on the nature of what is loved and the nature of the imminent or actual harm. Thus, in fear, it is some threat to one's well-being, or the well-being of someone one holds dear, which occasions this response, this being seen as an evil in that it portends harm to oneself or them. In jealousy, it is the deprivation of the special favour of someone whose concern for one is specially significant to one that is seen as an evil. And so on in other cases. And by the onset of such passions we are moved to desire to remove this evil, and thus restore what we love, hold dear or important, to its previous satisfactory state; we are moved to wish to relieve the loved object of the evil it is threatened with or suffers. (I am using the term 'object' formally here, to signify whatever it may be that I hold dear; it need not be a material object but may be a state of affairs, as in the case of jealousy where 'what' I love is my being the foremost object of concern; and so on.) It is our loving attachment to these objects which therefore stands as the ultimate source for these active passions, as providing the occasion for a negative valuation to be made of our situation which is of a kind that is apt to arouse our feelings. In the absence of a loving involvement, even although we may make a negative valuation of aspects of our situation, this will not be liable to occasion a passional response. In saying this I am not going back on my earlier

83

claim (chap. 3, sect. iii, above) that we cannot give sufficient conditions for the onset of active passions of the kind that depend upon negative valuations. For although one could formally say: if Henry loves Ethel, then if Ethel suffers what Henry takes to be some evil, Henry will react with anger, pity or whatever may be relevant, one still cannot state a sufficient condition for the formation of a loving attachment to Ethel on Henry's part, and hence not a sufficient condition for Henry's reacting with anger, etc.

Those passions which derive from negative valuations do in fact embody and express our loving concern in a certain fashion . This is well brought out in a short note by Whiteley, when he writes: 'Loves and hates . . . are dispositions to respond to a variety of kinds of situation with a variety of emotions and actions . . . Thus if Jack loves Jill he will experience anxiety when she is in danger, anger when she is insulted, joy when she returns his love, pride when she achieves a success, despair when she dies' (1979: 235). (I should not, in fact, place love and hate on a level as Whiteley does. Hate derives also, I believe, from love; one is moved to hate what damages what one loves (cf. Suttie 1963: chaps. 1–2 and *passim*). But no doubt hate is also a 'generic' sentiment in some way also, more particularly manifest as resentment, envy, anger and so on; hate is the *genus*, perhaps, of those active passions occasioned by negative valuations. But love makes possible the tendency of those negative valuations to arouse passions, for it is as they adversely affect what we love that we respond feelingly to these evils.)

If this line of thought is right, various points of importance follow. First, there must be a prior loving attachment to something before active passions, which are dependent upon negative valuations, shall be possible, as just indicated. This is not to say that we may be aware of the formation of a loving attachment to someone prior to experiencing such-like passions when certain things happen to them. It may be the first sign one is aware of that one has fallen in love with someone that one realises that one is jealous when they give preference to another, is distressed when they are ill, etc. But it is precisely because of their linkage to the formation of a loving attachment that these passions can be understood as having this sort of significance.

Secondly, it should clearly occasion no surprise that a loving attachment to something or someone should not only be manifest in passions and passional desires in which we are reacting to its faring ill, but should express itself directly in desiring the well-being and faring of what is loved and in being moved to act for this end. In this case, there is a spontaneous direct expression of care for the good of what is loved, not an indirect expression of that care in response to the thought that it suffers or may suffer harm.

I am claiming, therefore, that the following structure exists in the passions. Basic to all of them is the establishing of a loving attachment to, a concern for the good of, something or other. This attachment may be called friendly feeling, maternal love, patriotism etc. depending upon the character of what is loved, one's relation to that and the particular kind of concern for its good that one feels for it; and in such an attachment the subject desires the well-being of what he loves, in whatever shape or form that may take, and is moved to act to ensure that well-being. If and when what we wish well is well, whether through our own efforts or not, we 'celebrate' this in our feeling elation, joy, delight at this. If and when what we wish well fares ill then we shall be apt to respond with anger, fear, envy, pity etc; which particular passion is involved will depend upon what is loved and how its well-being is threatened or suffers. By these passions we are moved to wish to remedy the ill, and to act to procure this remedy. If and when we are unable to procure the appropriate remedy, then we shall be apt to respond with the 'mourning' passions of sorrow, despair, melancholy etc., wherein we mourn the damage to what is loved (and, sometimes, the damage to ourselves in the loss of or hurt to something we feel 'bound up with' in our love; see Freud 1957: 243–58). This seems to me to provide a plausible and perspicuous account of the implicit order and relationship between these various passions.

It is clearly important to say something about the formation of a loving attachment to something, about how and why we might come to care for its good, since this is now seen to be of fundamental importance. The formation of such an attachment is something that happens to us, occurs in us; we cannot choose or decide to be attached to something or someone, although we may, by choice, try to facilitate or to impede the possible growth of any loving concern and, by choice, endorse or dissent from such loving attachments we have formed in some way and at some time. But such attachments, if and when they are formed, are responses to

85

what we believe (possibly mistakenly) to be desirable, good, important or valuable in some way or another. Not that having such a belief is sufficient for the formation of a loving attachment, but it is necessary. And through our loving attachment we incorporate these values into our lives, embody them in the stream of our feelings, desires and activities as the focus of these. This is part of what is meant when it is said that, in love, we identify ourselves with what we love and feel its well- or ill-being and faring as our own well- or ill-being or faring (cf. Aristotle, E.N. 1170b 5 on one's friend being 'another self'; and Book 9, *passim*). For, in being the focus of our desire and endeavour, these things constitute the substantive content of our active concerns and living, comprise the matter with which our living is taken up. Our particular nature, as the individual beings we are, is constituted by the abiding concerns which our course of life embodies and enacts; and these are provided by the objects of our abiding loving commitment. One can only think of oneself as having an existence aside from what one loves if there would survive any active concerns, any possibility of active life, apart from these. And whilst this may be a possibility in relation to any particular object of love (though it is not always felt that it is by people about, say, their children, their 'cause', or whatever), it would not seem possible in relation to everything one loves.

I shall be contending, in chapter 4, that there can be such a thing as right love and wrong love, misplaced or inappropriate love (see also chap. 3, sect. iii, above). There are two ways in which love may be misplaced, inappropriate, one important and one less so (at least in theory). The less important is that in which we may come to have a loving regard for someone because we believe, but mistakenly, that they possess certain excellent or admirable qualities, qualities which, had they possessed them, would have been perfectly proper occasions for our interest and attachment. This kind of error, though it occurs commonly enough, raises no particular problems for theory. More important, but more problematic, is the other way in which love may be inappropriate, wherein one loves to excess, one is disproportionately or immoderately attached to something, taking it to be more important, more valuable, than it is. One example of what I have in mind would be where someone's 'ruling passion' is to receive the acclaim of his fellows, something which is desirable but to which he attaches such importance that all his energies are tied up in this pursuit and all other concerns he may have are subordinated to it. Here I think we might well say that he has a disproportionate attachment, an excessive concern, for this good, attributes to it altogether over-much importance.

It is, I shall argue, the single most important aspect of the exercise of practical reason to make our love intelligent and appropriate, to make the nature and degree of our involved concern with various goods appropriate to their true weight and significance. Practical reason, duly employed, should enable us to form a realistic and stable sense of the relative importance of the variety of goods to which we may be attached, and to regulate our concern for these to the degree to which it is merited, to the degree to which this or that is deserving of our care and commitment. If this is right, we can see how the employment of practical reason and the concerns of passional desire are not antithetical or independent. Rather it is that practical reason takes up, orders, sifts, regulates and extends the often fragmentary and incoherent perceptions of value and concerns for value we possess in our passions, and moulds these into an integrated whole which could enable a man's life to have some overall significance and lucidity to himself. Not that the concerns of practical reason will be, or should be, confined only to those goods with which we are already concerned in some measure. It is still true in such cases, however, that the ultimate concern of our employment of practical reason will be to re-direct our loving involvement to these properly understood goods, and not simply to leave our mindfulness of them dependent upon our deliberative choice alone. If, in our hearts, we are still set upon false goods, then our practical rationality has not yet completed its work of in-forming our feelings. I shall be examining what this involves in later chapters.

It is pretty sure to be objected to my claim that the formation of a loving attachment to something depends upon the supposition of its possessing a certain value or desirability that this is to reify values, to suppose that 'values' exist aside and apart from certain kinds of human concern with things, whereas the attribution of a value to something is simply an expression of the concern we have for it. This conception, given a classic formulation by Hume (*Treatise*, Book 3, pt 1, sect. 1, 468–9; also Mackie 1977: chap. 1), is, in one guise or another, extremely familiar; and there is no short answer to it. I shall, however, try to argue against it in the next chapter, in particular by showing that it has some very implausible implications (some of which were implicitly discussed in my account of the resolution of the conflicts of desire, above). But for the present it is sufficient to say that, quite clearly, I cannot agree with this conception of the kind of attribution to something the attribution to it of 'value' is. For if it were correct, the notions of misplaced or inappropriate concern, of the kind I have spoken about, would have no meaning (or at best, only a very different meaning from that I suppose; for example in terms of a contrast between enduring concerns and discordant temporary concerns).

Setting aside simple errors of fact about whether or not a person or thing possesses the meritorious property in question, mentioned above, we should note that within the class of misestimates of goods (and evils) there are two forms. First, there is taking something for a good when it is not at all such a thing. A possible example might be malicious gossiping (– it does not matter if the example chosen is unsatisfactory). No doubt such an activity can be fun, can realise feelings of power, and so on. And fun and power are (limited) goods. But, arguably, *this* is not the way, the manner, in which to achieve these goods for oneself. Notice that this is a different case from that of supposing that so gossiping would be fun when it turns out that it is not. Rather it *is* fun; but fun in this is no good (cf Anscombe 1965: 155, on smoking). Secondly, there is over- (or under-) estimating the importance, weight, significance of some (real) good; attributing to it more or less priority or materiality than it really bears – as in the example given of the person who attaches too much consequence to the favourable regard of others towards him. (Again, it does not matter if the actual instance is an unsatisfactory one.) Here one might say: someone overvalues or undervalues a value; while, in the former case, one might say: someone finds value where there is none. I have tended to concentrate in my discussions on cases of over-valuation and undervaluation (see also chap. 6, sect. i). Nothing of importance is left out, I believe, by doing this.

viii   SUMMARY

The main theses of this chapter have been as follows. There is a sub-class of passions whose onset includes the arousal of a desire directed towards achieving a certain change in their subject's situation. These I called 'active passions'. Some of these active passions are necessarily dependent for their occurrence upon their subject placing a negative valuation upon features of his situation. In these cases, the subject is caused to desire to rectify his situation in the respect in which he finds it to be undesirable, though he does not necessarily desire whatever it is he is caused to desire under this description. Having such a desire is at one and the same time to be tending towards, inclining towards, securing this rectification. In the primitive case, the subject of the desire does not choose, or determine himself upon, translating his desire into action; he is moved into action without this being involved. In some cases, there is a natural behavioural expression to such desires which has a certain basic aptness to securing the desired end. In some situations, however, this basic aptness will prove unsuitable to the achievement of the desired end, and here the subject may deliberate about how best to secure what he desires. But, when this is so, his conduct is now (in part) structured by his practical rationality and involves more than the primitive cycle of passional arousal and expression.

Those active passions which derive from negative valuations being made derive, themselves, ultimately from their subject's loving attachment to, or care for, something as good or valuable to him. The negative valuation he makes is apt to arouse a passional response in him because it is a valuation to the effect that what he holds dear is suffering, or is likely to suffer, some ill; and by the onset of these passions their subject is being moved to desire and act in the defence of and for the preservation of what he holds to be good. Such loving attachments do not, however, only express themselves when what is loved fares ill; they are also expressed directly in desire of, and activity directed to, enhancing the well-being and well-faring of what is loved. One does not decide or choose to form such loving attachments as one does form, though one may choose to try to facilitate or impede their formation or continuance. They are responses, reactions, called out from one in relation to what are (as one believes) desirable, valuable, meritorious etc. qualities in what is loved.

In addition to active passions dependent upon positive or negative valuations being made, there are also what I called 'celebratory' and 'mourning' passions, in which we respond to the well-being and faring or ill-being and faring of what we love. A central occasion for such passions is where we secure, or fail to secure, the well-being of what we love against some harm. Such passions have a natural behavioural expression which does not, however, include any tendency to directed behaviour. In them we so to speak appreciate the present state of what we love, and are not concerned with changing it.

In addition to presenting these views, I have also mentioned a number of points where the employment of our practical reason may be involved in the arousal and expression of passions and passional desires. I shall give a more complete account of what practical reason is and what its employment involves in the next chapter, and of how it may modify 'the life of the passions' after that. But it will be useful to collect together some of these points I have made to see the kind of contribution practical rationality can make, on my assessment, to these matters. How and why it can make this contribution I shall hope to be explaining.

First, we respond in passion in relation to whatever valuations we happen to hold. These may not be appropriate valuations, but may over- or underestimate the importance of some good or ill. Our passional response occurs, however, without regard to this; passion simply 'obeys' the assessment held. Thus to live 'by passion alone' may be to desire, and to pursue out of our desire, unsatisfactory goals. And it will be part of the work of practical rationality to secure that we respond in passion appropriately, in correspondence with a due assessment of the importance of the good or ill involved. Thus we may come to be able to trust to the promptings of passions for fit desire and action, as and when they occur.

Secondly, not everything that is of value, indeed of great value, moves us, catches our feelings, either at all or to the degree to which it should. We are not, because of this, bound to be indifferent to these desiderata in the formation of our purposes and in undertaking our actions. We can, should and do take them into account and incorporate them into the direction of our lives by a deliberate election to make them our concern and by resolving upon acting for their sakes. This giving of concern, rather than concern being drawn out from us, comes from the exercise of practical reason in self-determination.

Thirdly, each active passion establishes for us only a single purpose, to promote a particular good or to remove a particular ill. Typically, however, there is more than one good or ill pertinent to selecting a particular purpose and pursuing it, and if we are to act appropriately we must be mindful of and responsive to all of these in their respective claims. Some capacity for concern with good and ill other than that contained in passions must be involved in this, in order to make the comparative assessments and to determine action accordingly. And this capacity is that possessed by virtue of the possession of practical rationality.

Fourthly, it will often be the case both at the point where a certain purpose occurs to us as desirable, and also in the course of carrying through that purpose (if we do), that we may be beset by conflicting inclinations which, if enacted, would lead us away from our original purpose. If we are to retain and execute that purpose, we must have the power to order our conduct by reference to its merits, and we must not simply be governed by the intensity of the feelings of the moment. This mode of resolution of conflict in desire is achieved through the use of the power of practical reason in deliberation, and in the deliberatively based determination to proceed in the way projected.

Fifthly, we are moved to have an interest in and to set about the pursuit of certain ends by the onset of passions. We are, thus, not instigators of our own purposes and activities. To make ourselves so, authors of our own destinies, we must come into conscious and reflective possession of those values which have a hold on us in our passions, and of other values to which we may be in that way indifferent, and out of our own understanding of the significance and weight of these determine our interest and activity accordingly. To fail in this is to be one who is acted upon, one whose life embodies certain conceptions of what is good and what is ill, but one who is only the passive vehicle of these conceptions and not their knowing and willing furtherer and sustainer. One consequence of the full and successful employment of practical rationality in the understanding of our purposes, and our governance of ourselves in the light of that understanding, is that we, so to say, take our life into our own hands and make of it what we would best make of it (if we are at any rate fortunate in our circumstances). We become, by this, authors of our own lives, not those who unknowingly carry out the wishes of others, enact the influences that moulded us. (I discuss this briefly in

Dent 1974: 56–9; 1976a: 170–3. It comes up later on here as well.)

These are some of the kinds of features of desire and action in which, I should suppose, we find the marks of the exercise of that power of the human soul called 'practical reason'. These features are many and various, but a certain common pattern is prominent in all of them. The pattern is roughly this: by our power of practical rationality we are enabled deliberatively, reflectively, to apprehend and assess the merits and demerits of ends and actions, and to direct our intent and govern our undertakings on the basis of this assessment, as determined by the merits of the case (as we have, to the best of our ability, established these as being). These two phases in the activity of practical reason, the critical appreciation of good and evil and the deliberative governance of our purposes and conduct by reference to these judgements, will occupy me in the next chapter. I shall try to show what they involve, and why they are important.

4

The active powers of man: (C) rational desire

i INTRODUCTION

By the arousal of our active passions we are moved to pursue or preserve
something that we take to be good in some respect and in some degree,
or moved to avoid or destroy something that we take to be bad in some
respect and in some degree, after the fashion that I have tried to explain
in the previous chapter. I want now to consider whether our beliefs
about good and evil only ever govern and direct our lives and activity
through the excitation of passions and the evocation of passional desires.
Do such beliefs gain admission to the ordering of our conduct only by
working on our feelings and engendering desires, catching our interest,
after the manner I have attempted to characterise? I have already
indicated at several places in the prior discussion that I do not believe
this to be so. In this chapter I wish to defend this view more fully. I shall
try to show that this is not the only mode of access such beliefs have to
the governance of the shape and direction of our lives, and try to explain
in what other mode it is, after what other manner it is, that they can play
a rôle in determining our purposes and in ordering the structure of our
conduct. I shall claim that we can and do *form* desires upon the basis of
our judgements of good and evil, and we do not always need to have
desires evoked from us if such judgements are to direct our purposes and
conduct. Such desires I shall call 'rational desires', in that they are
desires, for example, to do something which the agent has upon the
ground that, for the reason that, it would be best that he do this thing, as
he believes. They are desires based upon and exhibitive of an agent's
judgements of what he has reason to seek or do, based upon and exhibitive of his practical rationality and reasoning about what he should best
aim for and undertake.

For a desire to count as 'rational' in this sense it does not need to be based upon correct judgements of good and evil or to come from a correct weighting of the magnitudes, import, of goods and evils either in general or in the particular case. If that were required for a desire to count as 'rational' the term would be being used as a 'success word' (Ryle 1963: chap. 5, sect. 5), indicating that a man had employed his practical rationality according to the proper norms and standards, perhaps also with the knowledge of them as the proper norms and standards. We should then need another term to describe those desires formed upon the basis of incorrect judgements or in the light of erroneous reasoning, and none readily offers itself. I shall, therefore, use the term 'rational' in the broad sense to signify a desire that depends upon an agent's judgement of practical reasons for and against ends and actions, and upon his deliberation employing those judgements, even if those judgements and that deliberation be faulty. Clearly, if their faultiness becomes too extreme we cannot any longer recognise the case as exhibiting rationality at all; but we can for all that understand some errors as errors that are made by a rational agent and understand his desires as rational, though inappropriate (cf. Dennett 1979: sect. 2).

Going along with the formation of desires upon the basis of reasons for or against seeking or doing something, as the agent assesses these, are such phenomena as making choices, the formulation of resolves, making the deliberate election to undertake this or that and so on. None of these activities can, I shall argue, be understood in terms of desires being elicited from us through our passions having been worked upon. In all these cases we propose for ourselves some purpose upon the basis of its merits as something to achieve, as we believe. And proposing to oneself a purpose, and proceeding about its accomplishment, upon the ground of its fitness to be undertaken cannot be equated with a certain purpose coming to claim our interest and our being moved to its pursuit through the arousal of some passion with its attendant desirous concern. Nagel has written: ' . . . many desires, like many beliefs, are *arrived at* by decision and after deliberation. They need not simply assail us, though there are certain desires that do, like the appetites and in certain cases the emotions' (1970: 29; see also Hampshire 1965: 38). My principal purpose is to try to explicate what lies behind, or what is contained in, the difference between 'arriving at' a desire by decision and after deliberation and being 'assailed by' a desire, so that we can understand the nature of 'rational' motivation in contrast to that provided by sense-desires and emotions. For all that Nagel has, as I believe, very well identified many of the problems which beset the idea that underlying all intentional actions are (in his phrase) 'unmotivated' desires, more work remains to be done here. His own notion of a rational motivation structure is, I think, insufficiently clarified and insufficiently tied in with the other powers and dispositions of agents. It appears too much as a special power conveniently competent to discharge the asked-for explanatory tasks. What I have tried to do is to develop an account of a practically rational motivational structure which is *somewhat* analogous to Nagel's account. But I have tried to do this in a way which displays the continuity within difference between this 'rational' structure and the other motivational powers we, as human agents, possess. I hope in this way to dispel any feeling that something has been *contrived* to meet the needs of the occasion. There are independent reasons for developing the account.

The best way to come to appreciate the differences that are to be found here, and the distinctive characteristics of desiring and acting on reasons, as one takes oneself to have reason to, is through further consideration of the way in which a resolution to conflicts of established desires may occur.[1] I touched on this matter in the last chapter. There I suggested that we would normally suppose that such conflicts might come to a resolution in either of two ways. In the one case this would be by the gradual emergence of a desire of predominant intensity and persistence in relation to the other desires the subject possesses, which then actuates the subject, moves him into according action. In the other case, the subject of the desires makes an assessment of the merits of the alternatives which, through his possessed desires, are attractive or repellent to him, and determines upon the pursuit of whichever has the greater claim or fitness to be realised, as he judges. (Or he may, indeed, determine upon the pursuit of something else altogether which was not an objective which already captured his interest.)

The process of considering the merits of the alternatives, of reflecting

---

1 Hampshire lays emphasis on the possibility of conflict in his account of desire in relation to action (1965: 36, and chap. 2).

upon the real importance they hold, with a view to determining which, if any, to undertake, I shall refer to as 'practical deliberation' or, simply, as 'deliberation'.[2] And I want to consider what deliberation consists in, its elements and structure, in relation to bringing a conflict of desires to a resolution. This I shall do through criticising two accounts of deliberation, found in Hobbes and in Schopenhauer, which seem to me fundamentally to misrepresent its character by assimilating it, in essence, to that kind of process which precedes action in the first kind of case I sketched out.

ii THE NATURE OF PRACTICAL DELIBERATION

Hobbes writes of deliberation thus:

When in the mind of man, appetites, and aversions, hopes, and fears, concerning one and the same thing, arise alternatively; and divers good and evil consequences of the doing, or omitting the thing propounded, come successively into our thoughts; so that sometimes we have an appetite to it; sometimes an aversion from it; sometimes hope to be able to do it; sometimes despair, or fear to attempt it; the whole sum of desires, aversions, hopes and fears continued till the thing be either done, or thought impossible, is that we call DELIBERATION . . . In *deliberation*, the last appetite, or aversion, immediately adhering to the action, or to the omission thereof, is that we call the WILL; the act, not the faculty, of *willing*. (*Leviathan*, Pt. 1 chap. 6, 37–8; see chap. 3, p. 75)

And Schopenhauer describes the matter like this:

By means of his capacity to think, man can present to himself the motives whose influence on his will he feels in any order, alternately and repeatedly, in order to hold them up to his will. This is called deliberation . . . The ability to deliberate . . . yields in reality nothing but the very frequently distressing conflict of motives, which is dominated by indecision and has the whole soul and consciousness of man as its battlefield. This conflict makes the motives try out repeatedly, against one another, their effectiveness on the will. This puts the will in the same situation as that of the body on which different forces act in opposite directions, until finally the decidedly strongest motive drives the others from the field and determines the will. This outcome is called resolve, and it takes place with complete necessity as the result of the struggle. (*Essay*, 36–7; see chap. 3, p. 75)

2 Compare Aristotle E.N. Book 3, chap. 3. Although many of my ideas in this chapter are derived from Aristotle, I have tried to develop them on their own account. Elsewhere (e.g. in chap. 7), I have approached some issues through explicit use of Aristotle's text.

There are, of course, some significant differences in the details of, and in the general background to, these accounts of what deliberation is and of how it issues in action. Despite these, however, it is surely obvious that they exhibit striking similarities. In both the picture offered of what is going on is somewhat as follows: the mind oscillates between various alternative ends or actions, first finding this attractive, then that repugnant, drawn by this, repelled by that, until such a time as a preponderant influence of some desire, or set of desires, establishes itself, a dominant hold over the mind is exercised by one desire or set of desires (or exercised over the will, in the terms of Schopenhauer's account). Being now possessed of a determinate and decisive interest the agent is then moved or prompted by it to according action, whatever that may be.

Are these, as they present themselves as being, accounts of deliberation and of deliberatively undertaken action? It seems to me that they are not. What is signally absent from both of them is anything recognisable as the agent's giving any consideration to the merits or demerits of the objectives which attract or repel him, reflecting upon their importance or lack of importance to him, aside and apart from his desire and aversion being worked upon and aroused; and anything recognisable as his establishing some purpose for himself as that which has the weight of reason to recommend his undertaking it, as he judges. One can only presume that it is supposed that the character of such consideration and its outcome is adequately captured in the picture of the subject feeling first this desire, then that aversion, of his will being 'tried' first by this motive then by that one, as if this succession of propense and averse inclination *were* that very consideration. But this is wholly misconceived. In deliberation it is the weight of the case, the claim to acknowledgement that various possibilities have, and not the intensity of desirous or aversive response that he experiences, that the subject is concerned to determine, to understand and assess.

Further, the emergence of a decisive preference out of deliberation is the formation by the agent of a resolution or intent to do something on the ground of its being the best thing for him to do in the circumstances, as he supposes – or at least a sufficiently good thing for him to do. (I shall not always add this alternative specification of the merit of the elected-upon act.) However, this formation of a grounded resolve is represented

97

in these accounts as the gradual emergence of a more dominant, powerful, concern out of the field of battle of warring desires, one which comes eventually to absorb the agent's consciousness sufficiently fully that he is no longer seriously affected by, no longer has his concern taken up by, the other matters which originally attracted his interest. Finally, action taken upon deliberation is action taken upon the basis of the fact that it is the best action that can be taken (as the agent believes), that it is the action for which the weight of reason speaks. But this is represented as the agent being moved by the force of his finally dominant desire, carried along by the pressure of his last desire.

Schopenhauer's revealing analogy of the will with a body 'on which different forces act in opposite directions' displays very well how distorted his account is if offered as an account of deliberation and deliberative determination of action. It presents the deliberating subject's will as entirely a passive 'object', solely acted upon by certain influences, inclining it to this or repelling it from that; as wholly devoid of any capability of initiating any response to these influences, of shaping or directing their impact in any way, as if the 'will' were entirely inert, not possessed of any active propensities of its own but only the plaything of forces to which it is subjected. We may notice that it is simply not true in mechanics that the 'decisively strongest' force 'drives the others from the field'. Rather the body subjected to these forces finally moves in a direction and with a speed which continues at every moment to depend upon the magnitude and direction of the opposing, but weaker, force(s). But what could be the corresponding feature of 'resolve'? That my will only becomes fixed upon something more slowly; or that when I finally move I do so being continually held back in some degree by opposing attractions or aversions, as if running with a ball and chain tied to my legs? Also, if a body is subjected to forces which do not pull it in directly opposite directions, but push or pull it from angles other than $180°$ apart, it finally moves in a direction which is proportional to the magnitude of the forces and their angles of application and not in the same direction as any of the original forces. Are we then to suppose that a person torn between desire for the swings and desire for the roundabouts will finally end up on the helter-skelter, this being the natural 'resolution' of the psychic forces he is subjected to? It is obvious that there is no point of real correspondence here; the analogy is deeply defective. What is distinctive in deliberation is that one ceases to be merely worked upon by certain objects arousing one's feelings; one does not allow oneself to remain in this situation, even if this is how one found oneself to be situated at first. Rather one attempts actively to reckon with the significance and import these matters which have affected one bear, to undertake an appraisal of their weight, their claim to concern, and not just to leave the weight they carry for one to be a matter of the force of the impact they happen to be making upon one's mind or feelings at that time. The 'will', one might say, is the source of this active reckoning and according intent; it is not a merely inert object of impulsions.

The terms from physical mechanics which are unreflectively employed in describing the phenomena of deliberation too easily deceive one into thinking that the deliberative resolution of mental conflict exhibits the same basic patterns and laws as the resolution of the conflict of physical forces. But the 'weight' of reason is not the mass of argument multiplied by the acceleration of desire; it is its cogency, its legitimacy, its fitness to serve as a basis and determinant of purpose and desire. A weighty reason does not, like a weighty brick, fall upon one and impart a certain push to one's body *via* the energy-transmitting medium of desire. It does not stun one into unconsciousness of any other reasons which may, perhaps, 'carry force' in the case. It is that on the basis of which one sees a good case for doing one thing rather than others even if there be yet something still to be said for them. In deliberation we try to 'distance' ourselves from the insistent press of desires to their gratification and endeavour to take the measure of their claim to be gratified and not just to have them claim our interest, command our involvement. We try not to be wholly absorbed by such desirous concerns, to have our place in our situation wholly structured by them, but to retain our self-possession, our power to order them and not they us, to command their direction and effect and not they command us (cf. Watkins 1975: sect. 6).

The descriptions Hobbes and Schopenhauer offer fit reasonably well the state of mind of, to take an example that I have used earlier, a child torn between desire for a chocolate and fear of a beating, or of a dog possessed by the desire for a piece of meat but fearful of attack from its present owner. (Hobbes says explicitly that 'beasts also deliberate';

Leviathan, Pt 1, chap. 6); and, on his conception of what deliberation is, this would obviously be true.) Finally, the child or the dog may grab and run; or else they slink away, cowed, overborne, by their fear. It would be absurd, surely, to present these cases as paradigmatic of what deliberative reflection upon and determination of what to do consists in. If the child were to deliberate he would, in however rudimentary, incomplete, unsystematic and short-sighted a way, consider for a moment the importance that having the sweet had for him if its cost were a beating, an importance which involves considering more than that it now seems such an urgent priority to him while the desire is upon him, while he is possessed by it and sees his life according to its dictates. And if he were to act upon his deliberation he would be guided by this assessment he makes, not just be spurred on by the urgent demanding-ness of his desire. To feel first desire, then fear, back and forth, until one predominates and is 'immediately adhering to the action' is not to deliberate and to act upon one's deliberations. It is only to be drawn and repelled, willy-nilly, as one or the other feeling flows and ebbs, fills consciousness or drains out of it.

Nor is this point affected if the desires to which the person is subject, by which he is possessed, are more subtle and diverse in their effects upon him than is evident in the play of temptation and fear, which can overtly modify posture and expression. A person is just as much under the domination of, for instance, a desire for power or for the acclaim of others if these desires order his objectives and actions without his making any considered assessment of the importance to him of enjoying these things and governing his conduct accordingly, even if we cannot discern in the overt play of his expression and movement the impact of these desires upon him. Someone is still in the grip of these desires and does not have command of their influence upon him, so long as it remains the case that their arousal prompts him to their fulfilment and it is not the judgement that their objectives are fit to be achieved that guides his conduct.

There is one further step the argument may take which needs to be considered at this point. It may be said that the accounts that Hobbes and Schopenhauer give are adequate as accounts of practical deliberation, because to think of something as having importance to one, to think of it as something which merits one's pursuit, just *is* for that thing to excite

100

more or less of an interest in us, for it to engender more or less of a desirous concern in us. (I brought this point up earlier, in chapter 3.) The conceptions we have of things being good or evil, the notion of making a comparative judgement of the weight or significance of these to us; all of these, it will be said, are just 'projections in thought' of the desires and aversions we feel at any particular time in their various strengths (see Hobbes, *Leviathan*, Pt 1, chap. 6, 32: 'Good. Evil.' cf. chap. 3, p. 87). I have been arguing for a contrast between the strength of desire for, and the judgement of the importance of, some objective; but, it will be objected, the supposition that there is a contrast here rests on the mistaken idea that the 'merit' or 'importance' of something as an object for concern and pursuit is an attribute or property of that object whereas, in reality, these 'attributes' are just attributions we make as an expression of our being desirously affected by the object, and they have no more foundation in the character of the object than that.[3] So 'deliberatively reflecting on the merits of the case' would be, in actual fact, nothing other than experiencing the oscillation of desire and aversion, this however being present to the subject in the form of his appearing to think over the excellences and defects of various possible objectives and courses of action.

Such-like accounts of the character of claims that something possesses a value, is good or evil in some respect and to some degree, are of course very familiar. It would be out of the question fully to examine and assess them here. But one point which comes from them should be made. If such accounts are correct, it does *not* follow that what Hobbes and Schopenhauer have given are descriptions of practical deliberation. What follows is that practical deliberation does not, and cannot, occur. For if 'reflecting on the merits of the case' *is* only a roundabout expression of the strengths of the desires and aversions we feel in relation to various items in our situation, then practical deliberation does not take place. With the reality of the contrasts I have been trying to make, between feeling the hold over one of certain desires and assessing their fitness as providing grounds for acting, goes the reality of the distinction between non-deliberated purposing and action and deliberatively

---

3 Compare Hume, *Treatise*, Book 3, pt 1, sect. 1, 469. 'Vice and virtue, therefore, may be compar'd to sounds, colours, heat and cold, which, according to modern philosophy, are not qualities in objects, but perceptions in the mind . . .'. Compare *Treatise*, Book 2, pt 2, sect. 6.

guided purposing and action. If the contrasts I have indicated are denied any real foundation, so then is the notion of deliberatively determined choice and conduct denied any real application. It would be quite wrong to suppose that the difference between action preceded by a conflict of desire and action preceded by no such conflict was the difference between a deliberatively structured undertaking and one which was non-deliberated. The 'reduction' of values to desirous or aversive states of the agent removes the legitimacy of continuing to think that practical deliberation is possible. It does not entitle one to think that practical deliberation amounts to the play of such desirous or aversive states, in the fashion described by Hobbes and Schopenhauer. Practical deliberation, if it occurs, is something other than that. If nothing other than that occurs, then practical deliberation never occurs.

None of this proves, of course, that it *does* occur. All I have intended to point out is that we should not accept as an 'equivalent' of practical deliberation what is not that, even if, on certain accounts of the nature of values, what I have characterised as practical deliberation would be impossible. It may be appropriate to consign the notion of practical deliberation to the scrap-heap, as devoid of legitimate application. But it would be better to do that than to accept as practical deliberation some process which lacks its essential characteristics. However, the situation is not so drastic as this may suggest. I shall hope to show, in the next section, that practical deliberation is indeed possible, and hence that the accounts of the nature of values which would exclude its possibility are mistaken. But I shall do this without exploring the full range and implications of such accounts; I shall concentrate upon them only as they apply in this particular area. And for the present, I wish to consolidate a bit further the conception of what practical deliberation involves as I have been presenting that.

We can gain further insight into the contrasts between deliberative and non-deliberative resolutions of conflicts of desire by considering some points of Frankfurt's, in a well-known paper (1971; see chap. 1, p. 18). Frankfurt describes a kind of creature he calls a 'wanton', whose actions 'reflect the economy of his first-order desires, without his being concerned whether the desires that move him to act are desires by which he wants to be moved to act' (1971: 12). (By a first-order desire is meant a desire whose object is something other than to have or to lack a desire.)

Again, Frankfurt writes:

> There is only one issue in the struggle to which his first-order conflict may lead: whether the one or the other of his conflicting desires is the stronger. Since he is moved by both desires, he will not be altogether satisfied by what he does no matter which of them is effective. But it makes no difference *to him* whether his craving or aversion gets the upper hand.
>
> (ibid.: 13)

What these descriptions capture very well is the absence from the life of the 'wanton' of what might be called 'taking one's desires in hand' and controlling and determining the influence they shall have upon one's conduct. Frankfurt's notion that the actions of a wanton 'reflect the economy' of his desires presents clearly all that could be involved in the determination of the action of one who was possessed only of sense- and passional desires. For all that disposes a man to act upon them is the strength of the hold they happen to have upon him.

Frankfurt himself believes that a crucial difference is made to the case by the possession of second-order desires or second-order 'volitions', these latter being desires not merely to have or to be without certain first-order desires but desires that one or another of one's first-order desires should be effective, should actually order one's action. He locates the possession and efficacy of second-order volitions as being central to what it is to be a person. I am not convinced, however, that this notion will do all the work he requires of it. For a man's second-order volitions may, for all that Frankfurt says of them, simply 'reflect the economy' of the strength and range of his second-order desires. And just because someone's ultimate action may 'reflect the economy' of a combination of both second- and first-order desires this does not seem fundamentally to change the character it had when dependent upon first-order desires alone (similar queries about Frankfurt's views are raised by Watson 1975: *passim*). Frankfurt addresses himself briefly to this issue when he speaks of 'decisive identification' with one of one's desires; but he does not really explain what this involves (1971: 16–17; also 1976: *passim*). I shall return to this point in chapter 6, section iii. However, this doubt does not affect the perceptiveness of his descriptions as serving to identify what would be distorted in any account of the origination of human action out of a conflict of desires which made no reference to the evaluation and control of those desires that their subject makes. Such action could be nothing but a reflection of the magnitude of the influence of the several desires and subject possessed; and one whose action was of this character would be a 'wanton'.

In contrast, for one who deliberates there is more than 'one issue in the struggle to which his first-order conflict may lead: whether the one or the other of his conflicting desires is the stronger'. To the deliberating agent, so long as his deliberative inquiry continues without check or distortion, the strength that any of his desires happen to possess at any moment will either be of no significance to his decision about what to do, or will be at most one desideratum among many to be taken into account. He *may* decide that he would secure peace of mind and freedom from an insistent unsatisfied longing if he were to gratify an intense desire that he feels. But, even in this case, it would still not be the intensity of his desire that made his undertaking any other course of action impossible to him. (Compare Schopenhauer: 'the decidedly strongest motive drives the others from the field and determines the will. This outcome is called resolve, and it takes place with complete necessity as the result of the struggle'.) It would rather be that he elected, on grounds which he takes to be cogent, to gratify his longing, perhaps only with the thought that he may thereby rid himself of it and not at all because what he longs for seems to him particularly worth pursuing. Presumably, too, if what he longed for seemed to him actually undesirable, he might think it better to put up with his unsatisfied longing and not to gratify it, possibly seeking some other way of ridding himself of it by, for example, seeking distraction in some other concerns altogether. For a wanton, on the other hand, action is determined, and necessarily determined, by his strongest desire, the one that, in the circumstances, 'gets the upper hand'.

The idea that action *must* be dependent on the 'strongest' desire at the time is, I am sure, compelling in part because of uncertainty over how the 'strength' of desire is to be determined. If the strongest desire is so identified by reference to its being whichever desire is the final determinant of a man's action in the circumstances, then, of necessity, a man's action is determined by his strongest desire. On this account, however, it could well be that a man's 'strongest' desire is that which he has formed upon deliberative consideration, and it need not be any of those first-order desires by which he was beset and about the fitness for gratification of which he deliberated. If, on the other hand, the 'strength' of any desire is given by reference to the pain of its denial, the liability it has to absorb one's attention, or some such 'subjective' criterion, it is obvious that we often do act on less intense desires if, for example, we conclude that our more intense desires are for unacceptable things.[4] Also, it is wholly unclear whether, in this second sense of 'strength' or 'intensity', deliberatively formed desires have such attributes at all. It is not clear what sense it might have to say that there would be 'pain' at the denial of such a desire. Such desires do not beset one in the way that sense- or passional desires do; there is no obvious way in which it might be supposed to be distressing to have to suppress or deny them gratification. The terminology of 'strength' and 'intensity' loses any clear application once we move beyond cases where it is plausible to speak of 'being in the grip of' desires which impel one. It fails to provide an appropriate classifactory and explanatory framework for the interpretation of the character of desires arrived at by deliberation, and for the way such desires issue in action.

It might, perhaps, be sufficient to leave the case here, and rest with having at least outlined the nature of deliberative determination of purposes and action in contrast to how purposes and actions emerge out of an unregulated conflict of desires. For it is hard to see how it could plausibly be denied that we do deliberate and act upon our deliberative decision, at least sometimes. However, as I remarked earlier, the matter cannot be concluded as easily as this. For if, as I have been arguing, deliberation involves reflection upon the merits of the case, involves an assessment of what it would be good to aim for and do, and deliberate action involves acting upon the basis of those merits, as we take them to be, we need an explanation of what such reflection comprises and of how its outcome can serve as a determinant of action. The difficulty is that it seems very hard to understand how any belief, any judgement, about the character of one's circumstances or about the possible courses of action one might take *could* be a determinant of one's action unless this worked upon one's desires, engendered some desire or aversion which

---

4 Compare Edwards 1967: *passim*; also Hume, *Treatise*, Book 2, pt 3, sect. 4, 419 (also 417). Edwards gives a good discussion, in his paper, of 'quasi-mechanical' models of deliberation, also discussing the passage from Schopenhauer I have been considering. Edwards also makes useful reference to some passages in Ross.

could then influence one's conduct. If it does not have this sort of connection with desire, how can it modify, direct, what someone will go on to do? Will it not remain a merely inert piece of information which bears not at all upon what the agent is interested in doing and does? To say that when someone regards some matter as providing a 'reason for him to act', that matter will play a rôle in the direction of his conduct different from that involved when that matter arouses a certain desire in him is no doubt true but is wholly devoid of explanatory power. It offers a phrase for a certain phenomenon, without giving any insight into the precise character of it. It *registers* that some matter plays a distinctive part in the governance of a person's conduct; but it does nothing to display what goes into 'playing that part', reveals nothing about what that rôle actually consists in. And until this is explained, all that has been shown is, at best, that there is something 'special' about regarding something as a reason for action and about acting upon reasons, but it is left opaque what this distinctive way of regarding something comprises, and left opaque how, when we have this form of regard to something, this can enable it to make a contribution to our conduct. It is essential, therefore, that something be done to remove this obscurity, to explain the substantive character of what is involved in taking some matter as 'providing a reason for action', a reason to do this rather than that. To this matter I now turn.[5]

iii PRACTICAL REASONS AND DESIRES

I have been arguing that in practical deliberation we endeavour to reach a judgement upon what we should best do in the circumstances in which we find ourselves, and to direct our conduct according to our judgement. And I have claimed that reaching such a judgement, and acting upon the basis of it, cannot be equated with the emergence of a dominant desire out of a conflict of desires, and with being moved to act by the intensity of that preponderant desire. In reaching such a judgement we consider the merits and demerits of the possible alternative courses of action which are available, we consider the cogency and weight of the

---

5 These remarks echo those earlier made about Nagel's notion of a rational motivation structure. I am inclined to feel that an opacity remains in Nagel's account.

reasons for or against various possibilities; and, when we act upon our deliberations, we act upon those reasons which establish this act as the one we should best undertake, as we assess the situation. The crucial issue which emerges from this discussion is to explain just what it is to regard something as a reason for proposing or doing something such that we can understand how *so* regarding something gives it both a rôle in the direction of our lives, and a rôle which is different in character from that it would possess if it were simply something that worked upon or excited our desire or aversion, by which states of excitation we were then moved to act. We need, that is, to show in what way taking something to be a reason for purposing or doing something is an action-directing state, a conative state; and to show how so taking it is a different kind of state from that state we are in when we have a certain desire or aversion of a certain intensity engendered in us.

Most centrally and fundamentally, to think of oneself as having a reason for pursuing a certain end or for doing something is to see that pursuit or act as making a contribution of more or less significance to one's conducting one's affairs, living one's life, as one believes that it is best that they should be conducted, as one believes it satisfactory or fit that it should be lived. It is to see that pursuit or act as leading indirectly to, or contributing immediately and constitutively to, [6] the realisation of a shape and order in one's life which one thinks appropriate should be realised. [7] What one takes to be a reason for a certain pursuit or act is, in truth, a reason for it if and only if it actually does contribute, indirectly or directly, to the realisation of what is truly the fit and appropriate shape and order that one's life should have. By the same token, there can be reasons for one to pursue or do certain things of which one is unaware, or which one mistakenly thinks are not reasons, or things one mistakenly thinks are reasons. But my concern here is not to try to establish what are in very truth reasons for or against various possible ends and undertakings. My primary concern is to understand the general character of the thought someone has when he thinks, possibly wrongly,

6 For the notion of a 'constitutive' means see Greenwood 1909: sect. II, 46ff; Anscombe 1965; Wiggins 1976a; Ackrill 1973: 'Introduction', sects. 4, 6.
7 See McDowell 1979: 343–4, and *passim*, for an account of the nature and rôle of a 'conception of how one should live'. See also Wiggins 1976a; Anscombe 1965. Anscombe writes (155): 'I suggest that the idea of rational wanting should be explained in terms of what is wanted being wanted *qua* conducive to or part of 'doing well', or blessedness.'

of there being reason for him to pursue this or to undertake that, to understand the nature and implications of such a thought.

My claim is that someone has such a thought about a certain matter if he has some conception of how his life should be lived in order to be satisfactorily lived, and of how that matter has a significant bearing upon the realisation of that conception. And someone thinks a certain matter provides no reason for (or against) proposing or doing something if he thinks it has no bearing whatever on the possible or adequate realisation of his conception of a satisfactory order in his life; and thinks of it as providing a reason against proposing or doing something if he thinks it would detract from the possible or adequate realisation of this conception – or, what comes to the same thing, if he thinks it would contribute to the realisation of an order in and shape to his life he thinks unsatisfactory and unfit.[8]

To think of oneself as having reason to do something is not yet to determine upon doing it. For it can very well be that there are alternative courses of action available which one takes oneself to have a better reason for doing, which have a greater claim upon one's concern, as one assesses the matter. The consideration of this is, as I have already pointed out, a primary concern in practical deliberation. It is not until one has concluded that there is overall a decisive case, or as good a case as is needful or possible, for one particular course of action that one forms the resolution of embarking upon it. By that resolution one endeavours to make one's life assume that shape one thinks it is best that it take. One proceeds as one does with the conception of one's action being of sufficient importance to the well conducting of one's life.

One's capability to be directed in one's desire and action by reasons depends, therefore, upon two principal points. First, upon one's possession of some conception of how one would do well to live one's life, of what shape and order one's conduct of the business of living would satisfactorily take; and of how doing this or that would contribute to the realisation of that conception, to giving reality to it in the actual material

---

8 It is to be noted that I say 'satisfactory' rather than 'satisfying'. If one achieves that life one believes to be satisfactory one may be (one may hope) satisfied (and not merely in that one has achieved it). But there need be no question of having an antecedent notion of what is satisfying to one, and making it the mark of a satisfactory life that it 'maximises satisfaction' (or some such thing) in those terms.

of one's activity. And secondly, upon one's possessing a concern to make it the case that the conduct of one's life will materially realise this conception one has, as it applies in this or that situation one is in.

There are several questions about these two points which call for further explanation, quite aside from the issue of considering what might be a just conception of how one should do well to live one's life which, as I have said, I do not mean to explore further here. First, is it at all plausible to suppose that we do have conceptions of a satisfactory shape for our lives to take? (Cf. Anscombe 1965: 144, 148–50.) Secondly, is it at all plausible to suppose that we have a concern to realise such conceptions in the actual substantive course of our living, even if it can be argued that we do have these conceptions? Thirdly, if such a concern is involved here, how does its nature and rôle in determining conduct differ materially from the nature and rôle of sense- and passional desires in determining our purposes and actions? Is it not just another kind of desire which may or may not be aroused in relation to certain beliefs we have? I shall try to respond adequately to all these questions.

First, then: is it plausible to suppose we do have conceptions of how we should do well to live our lives, pictures of what would be a satisfactory way to dispose our conduct? Let it be noted that the claim is not that we have one permanent, immutable conception throughout all our lives; it may, for all sorts of reasons, change in some or perhaps very many respects during our lives. Also, it could be that someone has conflicting conceptions at some particular time, in some respects; though if the conflict is too extreme the possibility of effective deliberative decision is removed. So the question at issue is not whether we have an utterly complete, comprehensive, consistent, wholly reasoned-out and totally defended conception of the shape our lives should take; it is whether we have some conception, which embraces some set of considerations in some sort of order, which provides at least a partial picture of the proper way in which one should live, as one thinks. Not that having a more complete and comprehensive conception is ruled out; only that it would not show that a negative answer to the question posed should be returned just because few possess such conceptions. With this in mind, I do not think it can be denied that it is very generally the case indeed that humans past childhood do come to possess such conceptions of how best to conduct themselves. We can well understand why this should be by reflecting again upon what is involved when someone is possessed of a certain passional desire.

I argued, in chapter 3, that one who comes to be possessed of a passional desire will also have his thoughts about that which is the objective of his desire modified. The onset of an active passion involves not changes in inclinations to act alone, but also changes in one's judgement and assessment of one's situation. For example, one who is in the grip of fear will be apt to be caused to think that he must get away from where he is, that this is an imperatively necessary thing for him to do. Again, one tortured by jealousy may well think that life is just not worth living if he is displaced as the special object of someone's affection, that there is simply no point in his carrying on with anything. To have such-like thoughts is, for the time for which one continues to be subject to the passion, to be making an assessment of how one should act, or of how the circumstances of one's life should be, if one's life is to be satisfactory, tolerable, worthwhile or whatever. It is to make a judgement about what it is desirable or needful for one to do, or for how things should be, if the course of one's life is to be good. Thus, already carried in the onset of passions there are conceptions of the importance of our lives being a certain way, however fleetingly possessed these conceptions may be, however little considered, and however little informed by awareness of any other considerations. We naturally and inevitably entertain such conceptions, which structure our apprehension of the significance of certain matters to the well living of our lives, as part and parcel of our being possessed by certain active passions.

But does it not follow from this, given my account of what it is to take oneself to have a reason for aiming at or doing something, that the person who runs away in fear 'sees reason' to run away; and one who, oppressed by jealousy, wishes to end his life 'sees reason' for doing so? Thus such men have the purposes they have, do what they do, on the basis of practical reasons, and there is therefore no difference between the mode of agency involved in the arousal of active passions and that involved in determination by practical reasons. This conclusion does not, however, follow. For, although it is true that one who is possessed by fear, for example, will take himself to have every reason to run away, it does not follow that he forms the purpose of running away on the basis of his judgement that he has reason to do this. It is rather that in consequence of or alongside the arousal of the desire to run away we are caused to think of this as something that we have a strong or overwhelming reason to do. It is not that, judging we have such reason, we form the intention of running.[9] The opinion as to what we have reason to do is, in this case at any rate, only an accompaniment to our desire, our impulse, to run and is not the basis or foundation for that desire. I shall return to this point below. For the present, the point of considering such cases as these is only to show that we do have conceptions of how we think it appropriate or imperative that our lives should be. And this is amply shown by the undeniable fact that we do acquire such ideas, if only for a short time, as an element in the onset of particular active passions. This, for the moment, is all that needs to be taken from these cases.

But, clearly, if we only possessed such conceptions so long as we were moved by a certain passion, we should have advanced the case very little. For there would be little or no stability in our pictures of what was significant to us; one moment something would be all-in-all to us, which at the next was a matter which seemed to us of negligible significance. I do not mean by this to imply that all our passions are fleeting. Some persist, remain with us as long-term dispositions in our concern, and establish a relatively stable sense of the import of something to us. But even in this case, that sense will not always be uppermost in the subject's mind; it will be apt to be overlaid by other preoccupations as they come upon him with insistence in particular situations. Now it is, I think, barely conceivable that someone of adult years should not have 'taken stock' of the variety of concerns he has felt from time to time and with varying intensity and permanence. These concerns will establish first this, then that, as being for a time of cardinal or substantial importance to him in his life. But he will come to some sense of which of these things have a more enduring significance to him, a sense of their significance which will survive the occasional disappearance or overlaying of any passionally engendered sense of their importance. One could say that he will come to an appreciation of their value. This need not, as I have said, involve arriving at any fully systematic, comprehensive, everywhere thought-out system of values, scale of priorities. (Such

9 Compare Anscombe 1963: sect. 35. She writes: '. . . not everything . . . coming in the range of "reasons for acting" can have a place as a premise in a practical syllogism'. See the surrounding examples which illustrate this point.

'systems' may indeed omit to register as important as many things as they do sufficiently register.) It is rather that his picture of what matters to him for the satisfactory content and direction of his life ceases to be the creature of his feelings of the time alone. It acquires instead a certain degree of independence of that, a certain consistency and fixity which provides the outline, at any rate, of some of the matters which have an abiding import to him, which carry weight for him. Cases where someone is subject to conflicting desires, discussed earlier, would seem to provide a central occasion for the gradual establishing of this more stable sense of significance. Particularly where someone was in feeling inclined to attribute equal and great importance to two exclusive courses of action, he could hardly not be caused to consider which was overall the more material to him. To allow the importance of the one relative to the other to be decided simply by how his feelings happened finally to settle would not be to do justice to his present sense of the importance of both of them. It is no matter to be so lightly decided. (Cf. Wisdom 1964a: 107–10 on 'ethical effort'; also Wisdom 1964b: 163.)

Through such consideration we can, in principle, come to have a view of our situation which incorporates an awareness, a mindfulness, of much that is not immediately concerning us through the arousal or present insistence of our passions. We can come to see our present attractions and aversions in the light of a more general awareness of the matters which hold significance for us in relation to the wider context and direction of our lives. We do not, or need not, simply move from circumstance to circumstance, being wholly absorbed in the influence each has upon us, living through a sequence of fragmented and unconnected experiences. We can come to see our present position, with the concerns it arouses in us, as one episode in a life which stretches before and after, to the well conducting of which matters other than those which presently exercise our feelings are significant and material.

It is not, then, at all implausible to suppose that we come, no doubt only slowly, falteringly and partially, to acquire some sense of what has importance for the satisfactory shape and order of our lives which goes beyond what seizes us as having such importance when affected by the arousal of passion. And in this way I maintain that someone can see reason to do something, in terms of this conception and the priorities and saliences it contains, even although what he now sees reason to do is not presently and immediately connected with a passionally aroused desire.

However, even if this line of thought is cogent, it establishes, as yet, only that we hold beliefs about what it would be needful, desirable or important for us to do beyond what we are in our present passions inclined to believe to be such. It says nothing about whether or how holding such beliefs will make any difference to how we act. It might be, for example, that such beliefs merely provide an idle accompaniment to a course of behaviour entirely determined by the intensity of present passion, and that they are not actually effective in contributing to the order and direction of conduct – at least so far as what has been argued for up to now goes. It is necessary, therefore, to consider how and why we are disposed to realise this conception we have, in the actual substantive content of our life. This is to turn to the second of the questions I raised earlier: is it at all plausible to suppose that we have a concern to realise these conceptions we have of a satisfactory shape and order for our lives to possess?

It is neither necessary, nor correct, to argue that if we do have such a concern – the character of which remains still to be specified – it is by virtue of that *alone* that we would translate our ideas of what we should best do into reality. As I shall explain in chapter 6, we can, so to speak, 'harness' the dispositions to act we have in our passions so that, through these, we may achieve that course of life we think appropriate. This we can do by duly informing and rectifying those valuations which occasion our passional responses, and those which we are disposed to make as a result of their arousal. But it is clear that, if this is to be done, there must be originally some determination to realise our considered conception of what is valuable and important which is over and above the determination to act we have through our passional desires. For, were this not so, we could of course do nothing different from what they inclined us to do since, *ex hypothesi*, this conception is not (or is not necessarily) operative in our passions; and if these are to be rectified, this must be through some other disposition to act than they provide. So whilst, in the end, it is not alone out of a specific distinctive concern to realise our conception of how we should best live that we realise that conception, there must be, in the beginning, some such distinctive concern if that conception is not to be merely idle and incapable of finding any place in

113

the actual direction of our conduct. The question then is: is there such a distinctive concern, and what is its nature?[10]

It should not be so hard to conceive of our being able to give our concern to something, to commit our interest to it, just because we think of it as something which is material to the well living of our lives and without it needing to evoke a passional response from us. It would be strange rather than natural if we had a capability of coming to a conception of how best to conduct our lives, which extended beyond the concerns which possess us in our present passions, but we had no capability of having regard to this in the actual direction of our conduct, in how we specifically choose and act. Just as we can, and do, come to recognise that certain ends or forms of conduct have significance to us, even although we do not presently 'feel' their significance in our passional responsiveness, so we can, and do, come to have a concern for them which makes us intent upon giving them that place in our lives which would duly answer to their significance, even although a present passional interest in them is lacking or, though present, is ineffective. I am not saying that we always are duly mindful of their significance to us and duly concerned to reckon in our decisions and actions with them, but this is not what is at issue. The issue is whether we can, *at all*, extend our interest to these matters when they do not presently excite an interest in us or do so insufficiently. And it is hard to see that this can reasonably be doubted. The awareness of ourselves as having a life which extends beyond the present moment, a life which involves matters of import to us beyond those presently exercising our feelings and engaging our passional desires and aversions, is an awareness which naturally involves a concern to shape the course of our lives to those matters.

We are not creatures who simply blunder from situation to situation wholly taken up in each of them, but we are interested in our life having a certain overall direction and shape, at least in respect of some of its features. We attribute such significance to certain factors or purposes that we cannot allow their effect upon our choices and actions to be dependent upon whether they simply *happen* to be uppermost in our minds or

---

10 I take this 'distinctive concern' to be what Aristotle intended in the notion of *boulesis*, and in the dependent notion of *prohaeresis*. See E.N. Book 3, chaps. 2, 4; also Dent 1976a: *passim*.

inclinations at some particular moment. Rather we govern and rule those passing inclinations with a view to making our life go (or not go) a certain way; we do not leave it to the adventitious economy of our present feelings to see whether or not we shall be prompted to act in this way or that. We *make* it our business to direct our lives so that they shall follow one path rather than another; the path of our activity is not merely the outcome of our uppermost aroused interest. It is as natural a propensity in human beings to have some concern to mould their lives to a certain image of how their lives should be spent, as it is for them to be worked upon, in feeling, by this or that as it happens to engage some desire or aversion.

Butler, discussing the 'authority' which attaches to conscience, writes thus:

And the conclusion is, that to allow no more to this superior principle or part of our nature, than to other parts; to let it govern and guide only occasionally in common with the rest, as its turn happens to come, from the temper and circumstances one happens to be in; this is not to act conformably to the constitution of man: neither can any human creature be said to act conformably to his constitution of nature, unless he allows to that superior principle the absolute authority which is due to it.[11]

Without intending to discuss all the implications Butler sees in his notion of a 'superior principle' (but see Midgley 1978: chap. 11 for a very interesting interpretation), we can take, none the less, some important points from this passage. First, that it is just as much a 'part of our nature' to possess a 'superior principle' – which, for present purposes we may say is a conception of how best that we should live our lives – as it is to possess what Butler would call 'particular passions'. Secondly, that it would entirely defeat the character of that principle as 'superior' if the governance it had over our lives was merely dependent upon whether or not it happened to catch our attention and engage our interest at any particular moment. That is, in my terms, it would entirely defeat the character of one's conception of how one should live one's life as a conception which could serve to rectify one's passion, or could serve to

11 Butler: *Sermons*, Preface, sect. 24; also Hampshire 1965: 44. Butler was clearly very anxious to distinguish the nature and rôle of 'principles' from that of 'particular passions', as not simply happening to be stronger or dominant at a time in their governance of a person's conduct. See also *Sermons*, Sermon 1, sect. 8; Sermon 2, sect. 3; sects. 8–11; and elsewhere.

cause one to act where no passion was excited, if the only hold that conception had over one's choice and action was 'as its turn happens to come, from the temper and circumstances one happens to be in'. That would reduce it to having the same status as objectives established by passions, perhaps dominant over or perhaps subordinated to these. Rather, one must 'allow' to it a measure of concern which will ensure that it has governance and control over occasional impulses; one must *give* it precedence and not simply hope it will take precedence.

In relation to one's stabilised sense of the significance to one of certain matters, one may recognise the importance that one's passional concerns give to some things is excessive or defective, deformed, distorted or illusory in some way and degree. Or it may, by a happy chance, be appropriate and fitting. Through one's intent to acknowledge this significance, one may over-ride the inclinations to action which come from one's passions, or the inertia which comes from the lack of them. It should not be so difficult to credit that we can and do so conduct ourselves; nor to acknowledge that our doing so cannot be the outcome of just a further, different, aroused passional concern. Were it such a thing, it could not have any distinctive place in relation to the effect of our other concerns; it would simply stand alongside them. But then our sense of the significance of certain matters would precisely 'govern and guide only occasionally in common with the rest'. It is a fundamental rôle of our resolved intent based upon our judgements of significance to enable us to give a place in our lives to matters which attract an inapposite or no passional concern. We *fix* or *lodge* our concern in them, and do not remain merely dependent upon their catching our interest for them to direct our conduct.

We could put the contrast between a passional elicitation of interest in something and the deliberate placing of interest in something in recognition of its import to us in the following way. When the passional elicitation of interest is at issue, it is in consequence of accidents of our temperament, upbringing, the circumstances of the time and so on that certain things exercise a hold over our feelings, engender a desirous or aversive responsiveness in us, and cause us to attribute importance to doing or avoiding something, after the fashion I have tried to characterise in chapter 3. When the deliberate placing of interest is at issue, it is in virtue of our assessment of the significance of something as contribut-

116

ing to the achievement of a satisfactorily lived life that we make it an object of concern to us, out of our overall determination that we should actualise that conception of a well-conducted life that we have. It is a concern grounded in our belief about the importance of the matter, and will survive as long as that belief does. It is not, as is the case with passions, a concern and a belief which are drawn out from us and survive only so long as we continue to be worked upon. When we place our deliberate interest in something we *make* it material to our lives; we do not remain reliant upon its having some impact upon us for it to enter into the directing of our affairs.

By this we can see the answer to the third question I raised earlier, concerning the differences between the nature and rôle of the concern with the well-conducting of one's life and the nature and rôle of sense and passional desires. When our desire of this or that is a rational one, it comes out of our recognition of the significance of some matter to the proper conducting of our lives as we conceive of that. We form a desire to undertake that purpose or this action upon the basis of its importance or claim to be acknowledged, as we assess it. Our having such a desire is not dependent upon the arousal of some active passion, does not depend upon 'the temper and circumstances one happens to be in'. One might put the contrast in terms of a difference between active desires and re-active desires; desires which embody our active intent to make our lives take a certain shape and order, and desires which embody our reaction and responsiveness to circumstances which impinge upon us.

None of this is, of course, to claim that we shall always be appropriately mindful of the considered significances that we place upon various matters for our lives, as I remarked earlier. One may become wholly absorbed in the concerns of the present, dominated by a certain passion, and be unable to retain clear awareness and heedfulness of those other considerations of which, in less trying times, one recognises the importance. I shall be discussing in later chapters what may contribute to or detract from the possibility of one's practically rational concerns having the proper governing place they should. But this has not been at issue in this discussion. The present purpose has been to try to clarify what it is to take oneself to have a reason for action and how and why it is that so taking oneself is a state which can direct one's conduct. That we do not always retain full awareness of what we have reason to do, as we believe, and that we do not always act as we have reason to act, as we believe, are familiar problems. Clearly, however, to have any clear account of them we must understand what it is to be aware of and act on practical reasons. And I have been trying to offer such understanding at this point.

On the other hand, we are not always presented with a conflict and antagonism between our rational and our passional and sense-desirous concerns. As I mentioned above, it can well be that what, through one's passional arousal, one is led to think of as important one also recognises, in reason, to be important. Indeed, one may seek to rectify and order one's passional concerns so that this is not by chance but by design so. Also, it is most likely that some, at any rate, of those matters to which one affords importance in one's conception of how best to live one's life will be ones which first assumed an importance to one because they engendered some passional concern. Benson (1976: 183–4) emphasises this. One's coming to apprehend them as truly important will comprise principally only a stabilisation and consolidation of an existing desirous interest, not something quite separate and distinct from this. Equally, however, it is not plausible to suppose that everything one comes to attach importance to is the object of a pre-existing concern. And even when it is, coming to be appreciative of the importance of this object of an initial concern changes the rôle that plays in one's choices and conduct. It ceases to be only something which happens to call out an interest, but becomes something to which one determinately gives one's concern.

I have been trying to explain the character of the state of taking oneself to have a practical reason for pursuing or doing something, the state of having a 'rational desire'. It is necessary to say a few further words on the relation between having a rational desire and acting upon that desire. In the case of passional desires, the onset of the desire is at one and the same time the onset of a prompting, an inclination, to act in a certain way (on 'inclination' see White 1964: 93). It is, already, an incipient movement. But one's having a rational desire to do something is not a spontaneous prompting which impels one into movement in the same way. It would be absurd to think of having to check or suppress an 'impulse' to action if one was disposed to acting on the basis of reasons. Rational desires are not states of excited readiness or propensity to move. A rational desire involves a belief that something has importance to the conduct of our lives and the determination to give place to that in our activity. This is not to be subject to the 'prick of desire', in Anscombe's words (1963: sect. 36); it is a form of self-determination by which we embody in our conduct our conception of what it is appropriate that we should do. The reasons upon which one acts, when one acts upon the basis of reasons, are identical with the reasons upon which one forms the desire of so acting, when one desires upon the basis of reasons. There is no question of one's finding in the fact that one has a rational desire to do something a further reason for doing it over and above the reasons one had for forming that desire in the first place.[12] Whereas the fact that one has a passional desire to do something may feature as a further reason for doing it (i.e. precisely in order to gratify that desire) over and above the reasons for doing that thing as such (i.e. without regard to the fact that it has engendered a desire in you). And this alone is sufficient to show that having a rational desire is not at all like a state of aroused interest. To say that someone has a rational desire to do something is to say that, providing the reasons to do it make a sufficient case in his eyes, he will do it; it is to say that he will act in view of those reasons. It is not to say that he is in a state of excited propensity which expresses itself in a certain kind of movement.

My purpose in this section has been fairly circumscribed. I have sought only to explain how and why believing oneself to have reasons for acting can direct one's conduct, by explaining something of the elements and structure comprised in that belief. I have not, however, intended to consider all that goes into the formation of a conception of how best to live one's life; in particular I have not sought to discuss the grounds on which such conceptions may fitly be judged adequate or inadequate, appropriate or misconceived and so on. My paramount concern has been to show how it is possible that we may be capable of directing our lives in ways which cannot be accounted for in terms of the arousal and effect of passions. (I have said nothing specifically about sense-desires in this context, since they display, in this connection, no

---

12 See Nagel 1970: 30; and Dent 1976a: 167–70. But see also Raz 1975: *passim*. The apparent counter-examples to the claim made in the text which come in Raz's argument are, I believe, only that. And, anyway, they are cases sufficiently abstruse as not to represent a serious challenge to the claim.

special features.) This I have done by reference to the emergence of estimates of the importance and significance to us of certain matters which survive changes in, or the disappearance of, a passionally induced sense of their importance; and by reference to a deliberate concern which attaches to things understood in this way, such that we give them a rôle in the direction of our lives. By this account I hope to have vindicated the integrity of the concept of a rational desire, and to have shown that our employment of that notion in, for instance, our interpretation of the resolution of conflicts of desire by practical deliberation is legitimate. There is no need to suppose that the interpretation is radically flawed or lacking in application. And, in particular, the attempted 'reduction' of practical deliberation to the oscillation of mind or will is now seen to be as needless as it is erroneous.

The possession by human beings of the power of rational desire has profound and far-reaching implications for the whole of their lives. Its relation to those other 'parts of our nature' which determine our action will be studied closely in the chapters to come. But I want now to discuss one very general implication of this power as it bears on the overall character of our activity. This has to do with the contrast between being moved and being a self-mover, one who is acted upon and one who acts, to which I have referred in many places already.

iv   AGENTS AND PATIENTS

The possession and exercise of the power to direct ourselves by practical reasons, according to the requirements of our conception of how fittingly to dispose our lives, enables us to be the agents of our own destiny, so far as circumstances allow, to originate our leading concerns for ourselves, or at least to regulate and direct already possessed concerns so that they shall influence our lives in due degree, as we see fit. We have the capability of controlling and ordering our conduct according to our judgement, and we are not merely creatures led and directed by the prompting of the engaged feelings we happen to be possessed of.

Contrary to Hobbes, one cannot ascribe to animals the power to deliberate in any serious sense. Their behaviour exhibits only the effect upon them of desires and aversions elicited by their perception of their environment. And just because they may be subject to conflicting inclinations which take some time to resolve themselves and for a dominant impulse to emerge, we cannot say that this displays deliberative reflection and choice. But with adult humans the case is, at least potentially, very different. One whose ends and actions are what they are only as his feelings determine is in thrall to those things which work upon his feelings, and in thrall to the desires which are thereby engendered. I am not denying that it is possible for people to live like this; or that this is most people's position in respect to at least some things. I am, rather, concerned to display what the resultant character of the case is, namely that we are, in these respects, acted upon and not agents, possessed by certain concerns and not in possession of them, subjects of influence and not masters of the direction of our interest and action (cf. Aquinas, *Summa Theologiae*, 1a 2ae, Q 1, Article 1).

This is not to say that we could, or should, originate all our concerns on the basis of a judgement that such would be merited by the nature of the case. By the time we come to possess and to be able to exercise the power to command the direction and magnitude of our concern we shall already have acquired any number of desires and aversions, be attracted or repulsed by any number of things. But a fundamental difference is made to how these concerns are related to us, and how they occupy a place in the governance of our lives, by our reflection upon the significance of what they concern us with. Through this reflection we cease wholly to be taken up by them and to live wholly through them; we cease to be wholly constituted by such concerns but can shape and order them to a different pattern from that they happen to make up. We can and do moderate and regulate these concerns, and by this they come to be embodiments of our considered judgement and to be expressive of our achieved conception of the proper mode of conducting our lives.

Thus there is this quite general transformation in the mode of our living made possible by the power of acting upon practical reasons. We come to be agents, those who can, if they will, shape and direct the purposes which their lives display. Where this concern is absent, our lives embody only the shaping of exterior influences and pressures, and that is to be, in a measure, enslaved by these and not the master of one's life.

It may be objected that I lay far too much stress upon having an understanding of the value of ends and activities and of directing one's interest and action by this. For are there not abiding passions the possession of which gives sense to many lives, which do not acquire their sense from our rational judgement? Is not one who is devoid of unchosen, deeply bedded, passional concerns only a 'hollow man', for there is, in his case, no full involvement of himself with anything?[13] This objection rests on a misunderstanding. For I have not said that our deepest abiding commitments could or would arise from deliberated rational judgement on the fitness of their objectives alone. I have, indeed, often suggested otherwise. My concern has been to emphasise the differences between being possessed of a dominant, central, concern which is understood to have significance and is endorsed and lived out ultimately because its significance is fully apprehended and appreciated; and being possessed by such a concern without such apprehension or appreciation or, at least, none that goes beyond what the passion of itself presents as having significance. Those who deny that there are any differences here, or who deny that they are material, always take cases where a man is absorbed by some purpose which we *can* see as important and worthwhile. But as commonly people are led by passion to give a misplaced and inappropriate importance to various purposes; and unless we suppose that these judgements can only be made by outsiders and not by the subject about himself, we are bound to concede that a person can know the difference between simply following a suggestion as to the value of something put by his feelings, and recognising the value of something and ordering his feelings and actions accordingly. And the acceptance of this difference as crucial is all that I have been insisting upon.

It is, I grant, important to remember that any individual's practical reflection will not be infallible. And some passional concern he has may betoken a truer appreciation of some value which he cannot properly acknowledge in his considered judgement.[14] But that it does so is something one is capable of learning, something that is there to be understood. Such cases do not show that practical reflection made in the

13 See Eliot, T.S., 'The Hollow Men'; and Dent 1976a: 172–3, with the included references to Williams and Lawrence.
14 A classic account of this is given by Tolstoy, *The Death of Ivan Ilyich*; and in the novel, *Resurrection*.

pursuit of true judgement is impossible or irrelevant. They show only that one is not always capable of reflecting very perceptively; and that is hardly news.

v THE GROWTH OF THE DELIBERATIVE POWER

I have concentrated in the preceding discussion on the character of the power of practical deliberation, and of the capacity of forming rational desires, in their most distinctive and obvious manifestations. This is clearly an essential thing to do, for one will only be able to clarify and interpret what is involved in them if one can identify and work from their most salient and characteristic features. However, it should not be supposed from this that the possession and exercise of practical rationality in the direction of conduct takes always such a substantial form. In this closing section I want to indicate how the possession of this power becomes apparent in many small and incidental details of the life of a growing child, and by this to suggest that we should not regard the exercise of practical rationality as inevitably involving a profound re-valuation of our entire lives. That is what it can involve. But that is not all there is to its place in shaping the conduct of human lives.

In infancy, a human child is possessed of a few, and these often very intense, natural urges – for food, sleep, comfort etc., which succeed one another according to the dictates of nature. The infant does not, of course, apprehend the objectives of these desires as food, sleep, etc.; rather, these are what, in fact, answer its need and procure relief. Equally, though these things are evidently good for the child, important for its well-being, it is not as being good that they are understood nor, even less, are they desired on the basis of being so understood. The child has, as yet, no such powers of comprehension, or of acting and desiring on reasons. In due time, a normal infant's intellectual and emotional capacities develop, and its range of interests widens. It begins to take more diverse kinds of interest in its environment, and new kinds of relationship with people and things emerge. And quite soon it comes to be possessed of quite a considerable number of concerns which it acts out throughout its waking life just as one or another happens to surface. But also some of these concerns come into conflict; they cannot be simultaneously satisfied at a particular moment. At first these conflicts will resolve themselves in a way which merely reflects the preponderance at the moment of one impulse over another, as when a child wanting to join in play is held back by anxiety and we observe the characteristic oscillation toward and away from the other children as each desire makes its presence felt. A child's face and bearing will display the conflict it feels, until one or the other desire dominates, or both dissipate in another spontaneous change in interest. We have looked at such cases already, and seen that as yet no deliberation is present in making an ordering of the child's interests or conduct.

At some point, however, the child's powers develop in such a way as to carry him beyond this level of behaviour, and a new structure in his conduct begins to appear. What begins to happen is that instead of these conflicts resolving themselves by the contingent preponderance at a moment of one or the other desire, the child begins to take stock of the possibilities and to order them into some very rough and ready, and by no means necessarily stable, order of priority. For example, instead of playing with his train and not his cars as the desire to do so exerts the stronger pull, he will plan to play first with his train and then his cars (cf. Mabbott 1953: *passim*). It occurs to him that he can satisfy both of his desires by ordering their importance to be satisfied, and taking one after the other. In such-like small occasions we see the beginnings of the emergence of deliberate choice-making and enacting.

This emergence is specifically dependent upon the child's increasing awareness of the passage of time, and the consequent appreciation that activities can be ordered in time, and that a purpose can extend into the future such that what is done now can aid or impede the realisation of it (see Hampshire 1965: 44; also Aristotle, *De Anima*, 533b 5–10; Book 3, chap. 10). This latter also involves the mastery of causal relations. The child is no longer wholly absorbed in the present moment, with no memory or expectation. He recognises, little by little, that he is situated in an environment which is predictably structured and manageable (within limits) and extends before and after the present. Going along with this is the child's gradual understanding of hypothetical propositions, particularly those that make it clear that the occurrence of certain things is conditional upon the prior occurrence of others. From this he gets the idea that there may be reason to do or secure the latter if he is to do or secure the former. For example, a child may be told: if you eat

124

your dinner, you can go and play; but if you do not, you must stay at the table. Trading upon the child's given desire to go and play, he is given reason to eat his dinner, even although he may not find doing so at all pleasurable or an attractive prospect as such. And he may be impressed and given an incentive to act by his recognition of this reason.

The coming of this power to recognise and act on reasons – of even this very restricted and simplistic sort – constitutes, as every parent knows, a great step forward into humanity on the part of the developing child. Before it emerges (and, of course, it does not come all at once, but piecemeal and intermittently with many regressions) a child will not 'listen to reason' but acts at the imperative dictates of pleasure and pain, demanding instant gratification or relief. If he wants to play but dislikes the sight of his dinner there will be rage, tears, insane resistance to the acceptance of the requirements of getting what he wants. The child who is beginning to be able to recognise and heed reason can over-ride his resistance to eating his dinner for the sake of achieving his objective of going to play, seeing reason to do this even although it is no pleasure to him at all to do so in itself.

It is in such-like trivialities that a child begins to enter a whole new 'world', the world of practical reasoning giving grounds for and against doing and wanting to do various things – a world which fully understood and possessed comprises the entire life of practical reason in the conduct of man. The child is now able to give to his desires a pre-ferential weighting or importance, to assign one priority over another, in however unsystematic, unsteady and uncomprehensive a way. He is in effect judging that his aversion to eating his dinner is less important to him, for now at any rate, than his liking for playing; were it more, he would refuse, and forego the chance of play. It is not that being so totally taken up in the latter purpose he swallows anything necessary to getting it, though that can happen. Rather, he asks himself what it mat-ters to have to eat one's dinner in relation to what it matters to him to play, and concludes, for this occasion if for no other, that it matters not so much. It is these small seeds which fully grown comprise the achieve-ment and living out of a comprehensive, steady and consistent picture of what is most material to one's life, of what is to be held dear and what may be forgone. The child is taken out of the life of mere successive impulses which move him to this or that and begins to determine for himself what he shall best do or forsake, and deliberately to seek to realise that. At first this change in the character of his action is small and insignificant in its scope and effects, but it is far-reaching in its final implications.

As I have stressed, the child's preferential ranking of goods is not typically at all fully thought through, does not take in much of a range of possibilities, is not very stable from occasion to occasion and so on. But it is just more of the same sort of deliberation and deliberative election of what to do that results in this larger and more consistent pattern. The essential transformation has occurred, from his being merely a 'moved mover', into his being, in some degree and in some respects, a self-directed seeker after a critically appreciated good; and it is the carrying through of what is implicit in this basic transformation that can eventually lead to possessing and enacting a more complete conception of how one should live one's life, in which the power of practical reason in the directing of one's life has achieved its full scope. So, although there is a distinctive, and uniquely human, form of understanding and action involved when acting on reasons, it is a form which takes its occasion from more elementary forms of activity and does not appear, like a *deus ex machina*, as a fully formed and complete instrument for the immediate re-shaping and re-directing of one's life. There is both continuity and change here, as the child comes to develop and express more completely the full range of its active powers in their full scope. We should not picture the situation to ourselves as being a matter of modes of interest simply agglomerated in one soul; but of modes of interest which are mutually dependent and related in many complex ways.

Finally, I want to examine one possible complaint about the preceding remarks. The bulk of this chapter has concerned what gets called 'deliberation about ends', namely, reflective consideration and weighing of the merits of objectives which could be undertaken, and undertaking these on the basis of the outcome of that deliberation. Whereas in the case of the child just discussed, deliberating about whether or not to eat his meal, the topic of deliberation appears to be one concerning means to an end. It may be said, therefore, that the case fails to illustrate the emergence of a power to deliberate of a kind relevant to the main theme of the previous discussion. Furthermore, while the claim that we can deliberate about ends is widely doubted or challenged, it is equally

126

widely allowed that we can and do deliberate about means to ends. Thus I appear to have adduced the easy (or at least the widely accepted) possibility in support of the difficult (or at least widely questioned) possibility, lending the latter a false colour of plausibility.

These objections are misplaced. First, it is *extremely* rare in actual practice for the meritorious or demeritorious feature of some means to an end to be solely and exclusively its efficacy or inefficacy in producing, leading to, that end. The taking of means to ends almost always involves other benefits or costs over and above the matter of efficacy. For instance, time, money, effort to be expended – let alone 'moral considerations' – all normally enter into the matter. In which case the merit or demerit of such and such an expenditure, for instance, incurred in taking a certain means, even the most efficacious means, will have to be considered and weighed against the value the agent sees in achieving the end. So doing may, indeed, lead to his abandoning that. So, I suggest, in all but the most artificial cases, so-called 'deliberation about means' necessarily extends to take in 'deliberation about ends'; and the cogency of the former cannot be admitted whilst disallowing the cogency of the latter. This is why I have said very little explicitly about deliberation over means as a distinctive topic for deliberation, and why the illustrative case I took is entirely relevant. It would, further, be nothing but a verbal manoeuvre, changing nothing of substance, to say that considerations of expenditure – or whatever – were all 'aspects' of the efficacy of some possible means. (For some relevant remarks on this, see Williams 1979: 20.)

Aristotle may appear to give his authority to making the contrast between deliberation over means and over ends an important one. (E.N. Book 3, chapter 3; especially 1112b 20ff.) However, a satisfactory interpretation of these passages is given by Wiggins (1976a: *passim*), and it is one perfectly consonant with the overall view I have been trying to present. I shall say a little more about Aristotle, below.

The second major point to be made is this. Even were the remarks I have just made mistaken, we should still need to allow the cogency of a notion of a deliberatively formed desire which is essentially different in character from any passionally induced desire. The outcome of a piece of, as we may say, 'pure' deliberation over means will be, for example, the judgement that such and such a course of action recommends itself as

127

the most efficacious, and hence the most (instrumentally) rational one to undertake. Now, this course of action may very well be one which, on its own account – that is without reference to its here meritorious instrumentality – excites no passional interest in me; or, indeed, it may be one which excites repugnance in me (consider, for instance, lancing one's septic wound oneself'). Nor, despite Hume (*Treatise*, 414) is it at all plausible to say that we have a general 'passion' for taking what are (as we judge) instrumentally the most effective means to our ends; or that, in some quasi-hydraulic or quasi-capillary way, our passional interest in our ends 'flows back' down to the discovered means to those ends and infuses them with borrowed passional interest for us. So how then are we brought to undertaking this course of action; what actually gets us to perform it? What we have here is a choice of pure practical rationality that sets me upon doing the thing which is, as I judge, the most efficacious. This is an act I (very often) undertake solely and precisely on the ground of its recommending itself as the (instrumentally) rational thing for me to do, with no other 'spur' to its accomplishment. Here, then, we must allow that there is a distinctive form of 'motivation' which accounts for the action done. And once the necessity for such a thing has been recognised in this sort of case, I do not see that it should be so difficult to recognise its presence and effects elsewhere also. The instrumental effectiveness of some course of action in relation to our goals is just one kind of merit such a course of action may possess (and not always the most important merit in it). There is no reason to suppose this kind of merit in an action is capable of giving us cause to undertake it in a way distinctively different from the way in which other merits or demerits in actions may do so. There is nothing obviously *un*problematic about this case in contrast to the others.

The final point concerns Aristotle again. He says (E.N. 1112b 12): 'We deliberate not about ends but about means'; and similar remarks are made elsewhere. But these claims permit, indeed require, an interpretation which is consistent with the views I have been putting forward about the nature and scope of deliberation. First, it is now generally understood that the Aristotelian notion of *ta pros to telos* (what is towards the end) covers not only instrumental means but also component or constitutive means, those things (e.g. human activities) which comprise (some element in) living well and doing well. We need, that is to say, to deliberate over what 'living well and doing well' might actually consist in, involve us in doing, wishing etc. And this is to consider the merits and demerits of objectives, actions etc. as proposed components to be incorporated in a satisfactory life, which is surely the significance of deliberation about *ends* as this is usually taken. Secondly, there is one end which, for Aristotle, we do not and cannot deliberate about, that end of living well and doing well. Having that as an end is presupposed as the background to all non- (or not merely) technical deliberation. But this does not exclude, it rather requires, deliberation about the merits of the pursuit of wisdom, honour, pleasure etc. as things to be sought. And this is, once more, surely what it is to be deliberating over what ends one might take as one's own ends. (For relevant interpretative literature, see p. 107; also Dent 1976a: *passim*.)

What I want to do in the following chapters is to consider some of the ways in which the possession and exercise of practical rationality, as manifest in practical deliberation and in the formation and enacting of rational desires, can modify the nature and expression of sense and passional desires. I have already indicated, in outline, the character of some of these modifications. I shall now try to explain what is involved in them in a more complete and systematic way.

5

Deliberation and sense-desire: the virtue of temperance

i INTRODUCTION

I hope to have given, in the preceding chapters, sufficiently clear and convincing accounts of those kinds of desire which may actuate a man which are of relevance to determining the structure and elements of the virtues. The accounts have been of these forms of desire, and related action, as if they were more or less wholly discrete and self-contained structures in the human psyche and its expression in behaviour. Some reference has, however, already been made to ways in which these may be related and interconnected. It is now imperative that their possible modes of interconnection be made the central topic of concern, for two principal reasons. First, doing so will serve to correct any impression that may remain, despite prior warnings, that the normal and natural way in which a man possesses and enacts these modes of concern is as three independent, but concurrently had, lines of active interest in pursuing certain objectives, each severally prompting him to act, perhaps pointing him in the same direction, perhaps in different directions. It is true that, from time to time, this may be a proper enough characterisation of a person's state; and I shall discuss some such cases in due course. It would, however, be a fundamental mistake to suppose that this is the only possible character that the concurrent possession of these different modes of concern should have. Rather these modes of concern may become so interconnected and inter-dependent that we find only a single bent of interest possessed by a man and expressed in his activity, one to which these modes contribute as comprising elements in a complex but subtly integrated, unified, structure of desire. These differing modes of concern exist as sub-structures within one overall, complex, structure; not as self-contained psychological powers merely agglomerated in one soul. For purposes of analysis only, we isolate these sub-structures and examine them separately. But they are normally present in the life and activity of the human agent only as facets of the expression of a single self in action.

The second reason for now concentrating on the character of the inter-relation of these modes of concern follows immediately from the first. For an account of the fully and properly integrated condition of these concerns is an account of the structure of that psychological state which comprises a man's possession and exercise of a virtue. This has, of course, been my claim all along; and the wish to show this provided the reason for the prior discussion of these modes of concern. But this claim must now be made good, and can only be so by following through the consequences of the accounts given to see whether what results is, indeed, an account clearly and properly recognisable as an account of that state which comprises the possession of a virtue.

However, although I have just been stressing the importance of the possibility of a thorough-going integration and unification of these modes of concern, it will soon emerge that the first case I want to consider, that of the relations that may obtain between sense-desire and rational desire, fails to provide the possibility of this kind of integration. The reasons for this will be fully discussed. It should not be concluded from this case, though, that the idea of achieving full integration represents an unattainable ideal, or is merely confused. To think this would be to neglect what are, I believe, the most central and significant possibilities which are crucial to understanding the character of very many virtues. These will, however, be the principal topic of the next chapter, not of this one.

Let us then first examine how sense- and rational desires may stand in relation to each other, and see what possible forms of integration of them exist, and why.

ii   SENSE-DESIRE AND REGULATION BY REASON

I have presented a conception of sense-desire as being desire for the enjoyment of sense-pleasure, pleasure which comes from the gratification of the five senses, but particularly of the sense of touch. (On the centrality of touch, see Aristotle, E.N. 1118a 25, 1118b 7.) That we are apt to desire such pleasure is, I maintained, a natural fact of our psychological constitution; it is something to which human nature is naturally heir. Having once tasted such pleasures, we just do, as a matter of fact, very often wish to taste them again. The persistence and intensity of such desires are, originally, dependent only on such factors as, for example, how recently such pleasures have been enjoyed, how naturally susceptible to them the subject is, his general level of vitality, whether he be young or old, sleepy or fully awake and so on. There are significant variations between people, and in one person at different times, in how much such pleasures are desired and sought after.

Given a mode of concern with the enjoyment of sense-pleasure of this general character, what scope, if any, exists for the moderation and regulation of it by practically rational judgement and desire? Through his power of practical reason a man is capable of assessing what it would be good for him to want and to do, and of desiring and pursuing things on his judgement as to the merit or fitness in so doing, on the ground that this would be the best thing for him to employ himself about. Now it could be that a man comes to recognise that it is appropriate to want to enjoy, and to enjoy, a certain measure of sense-pleasure as an element in his life. This recognition would show him that he had reason to seek such pleasures; and he could deliberately determine himself to seek to secure such pleasures for himself on the ground of the appropriateness of this. However, we are to suppose that he already has, in his sense-desire, an interest in procuring the enjoyment of such pleasures for himself. And the question then is, how these differing kinds of interest in procuring such enjoyment might come together and be co-ordinated in his pursuit of pleasure.

Let it first be supposed that a man finds that he has, on a particular occasion, naturally aroused in himself a degree of desire for the enjoyment of a certain sense-pleasure which he judges is entirely appropriate, after a consideration of the desirability of enjoying that pleasure. He could then, quite properly, allow his sense-desire 'its head', allow it to influence his conduct and secure its gratification. In this case we could say that deliberative judgement 'endorses' the prompting of sense-desire; and the fact that he would have reason deliberatively to resolve upon procuring the enjoyment of that sense-pleasure for himself, which might lead him to procure it, drops out of the case as irrelevant. He already has a sufficient prompting to do this; it is already what he would like to be doing, and all he has done is ascertain that it would be appropriate to do what he would like to be doing, that is enjoying this pleasure.

It may be noted that there are two rather different kinds of basis upon which the sense-desirous interest may be endorsed. It may be that what the man is desirous of is judged good, or at least innocent, and thus his interest in it endorsed. Or it may be that although what he is desirous of is not particularly good, it is judged that it would be better to gratify his desire for it, given that that has been aroused and does exist, than to suppress it, perhaps with some such guiding thought as that it is by and large harmless to indulge one's desires once one has them, better than it is to suffer the frustration and dissatisfaction their denial would cause, other things being equal.[1] This second kind of basis is, I dare say, less common than the first, though it is occasionally employed. No theoretical importance attaches to this distinction, however, so once it is clear that these differing kinds of source for endorsement are possible, nothing more need be made of this.

This kind of co-ordination of sense-desire and rational judgement appears to be of an extremely minimal kind. However, once we introduce the phenomenon of the 'endorsement' of desire into the case, the behaviour of the agent possesses a complexity of structure far beyond any present in the simple, original, enactment of the prompting of sense-desire. For now the agent's pursuit of the sense-pleasure expresses not only the impulse of excited desire but also his choice, his rational election or acceptance of the pursuit and enjoyment of this pleasure as a fit object of pursuit and enjoyment. He no longer acts heedlessly and headlong at the beck of pleasure; he acts deliberately and intentionally for the sake of enjoying that pleasure, even although the proximate source of his conduct still remains his state of aroused desire. One very obvious token of the far-reaching change in the structure of agency produced by this 'endorsement' is that, whereas it would be absurd to blame a small child for acting at the beck of pleasure, we might well blame an adult for doing so. For we suppose an adult to have the capacity to regulate the effect upon his conduct of aroused desire; and if

---

1 Compare Blake: 'He who desires but acts not, breeds pestilence'; and other 'Proverbs of Hell'. See also Blake, *Complete Poetry*, 99, 100, 182.

that desire does direct his behaviour, and that behaviour is improper in some way, we take him either culpably to have failed to regulate the effect of his desire or culpably to have endorsed its prompting. Just because the capability of giving or withholding endorsement to desire, and of regulating its effects, is (normally) possessed by adults, we properly interpret their conduct, even that which is the enactment of aroused sense-desire, as having significance and implications about their general attitudes and judgements which we do not ever think of discerning in the case of a small child (or an animal). Behaviour of an adult human motivated by sense-desire is still the behaviour of a 'rational animal', and attracts the assessments proper to the conduct of an animal possessed of rationality, even if that rationality was signally unexercised on a particular occasion. The 'endorsement' of desire by rational judgement displays one way in which conduct may be proper to a rational animal even when the primary incentive to that conduct reposes in a mode of concern shared with animals and small children.

Another way of presenting the kind of difference to the structure of the agency of one prompted by sense-desire made by his endorsement of this desire, would be to say that his desire ceases to be only a stimulus to action and becomes also understood and enacted as a reason or ground for acting. The recognition of the objective of the desire as one fit for pursuit and enjoyment gives to that desire the status of an appropriate and legitimate basis upon which to act, incorporates it as a proper occasion for bringing into existence that plan of life which we think it best to try to actualise. Thus we no longer are simply moved as and when our desires happen to be caught; we order the effect of our desires so that we shall, through them, do only what we think it fit we should be doing. Thus we possess them, and direct them for our purposes; they do not possess us, take us over, and we are not led by their calling. So even although this is not a self-originated desire dependent upon our deliberation, but one that comes upon us we can, so to speak, 'use' it or 'harness' it to achieve that course of life which it is our determined intent to accomplish.

Between the arousal of desire and its enactment we often do, often should and often can, interpose reflection. And the possibility of doing so enables us to incorporate the purposes such desires incite us to undertake into a deliberatively understood and sought plan of life, and enables us to make the actions we undertake on desire embody our deliberate intentions. Such actions thus can express at least one element of our guiding conception of how we should live our lives, and are not bound to be unrelated and unconnected interludes when we are assailed by non-rational impulses, which we can do nothing about.

None of this is, I would expect, particularly controversial. The case becomes more complex when we are unable to endorse the prompting of our sense-desire. For then we must deny it gratification if we are to do as we think fit. And we need to consider how, if at all, this divergence of sense-desire and rational judgement may be reckoned with and rectified, if possible. To this matter I now turn.

iii THE INHIBITION OF SENSE-DESIRE

It is as often as not the case that one does not think it fit to enjoy that pleasure which one's aroused sense-desire incites one towards the enjoyment of. This may be for a considerable variety of reasons. Perhaps it may be that one is, as one thinks, spending altogether too much of one's concern and time upon the enjoyment of such pleasures when other things are more important or more rewarding. Perhaps it is that although the enjoyment of the pleasure would be, as such, perfectly satisfactory, the occasion is not an apt one for the indulgence of desire. And so on in other cases.

The case I want to concentrate upon is that where someone has become so susceptible to the pleasures of sense that he is desirous of their enjoyment to an extent that is, in his reflective judgement, inappropriate. He may, for example, be almost wholly taken up by the quest for sensual gratification, his energies almost entirely bent upon securing further and more intense delights for himself, his mind preoccupied with fantasies of future indulgence and so on. It could also happen that someone finds himself less desirous of such pleasures than he thinks natural and appropriate;[2] but such cases are the exception rather than

---

2 This is what George Eliot says about Casaubon: 'Hence he determined to abandon himself to the stream of feeling, and perhaps was surprised to find what an exceedingly shallow rill it was . . . Mr. Casaubon found that sprinkling was the utmost approach to a plunge which his stream would afford him; and he concluded that the poets had much exaggerated the force of masculine passion.' *Middlemarch*, Book 1, chap. VII.

the rule and I shall not discuss them further, but only that of excessive desire.

What, if anything, can be done in such a case to make it that the frequency, intensity and persistence of sense-desire becomes congruent to the judgement of practical reason about the appropriate degree of importance to be placed upon the enjoyment of sense-pleasure? It seems to me that the basic mode of regulation and ordering to which sense-desire is susceptible is through 'inhibition' of its expression, as the title of this section indicates; and I want to try to explain the nature, scope and limits of such inhibition.

A crucial first aspect of this process is achieving some degree of 'detachment' from the claims of sense-desire. Such desires may be so intense and insistent that a man's mind and attention and concern become entirely absorbed in the purpose of securing this or that pleasure; he is capable of thinking of nothing else, is aware of only those aspects of himself or the world which bear upon the success or failure of his attaining to it – his whole being is constituted by this desire. It seems clear that for so long as the hold over him of his desire is of this utterly dominating kind there is no possibility of his ruling it; it entirely rules him. (Cf. Plato's account of the nemesis of the tyrant: *Republic*, 573a–574a.) There must be some natural relaxation in its hold upon him, some freedom of mind from its persistent demands must occur, before any reckoning with it could become possible, before what he is interested in securing can become, for him, something the importance of which can itself be assessed rather than its remaining the point of view from which, implicitly, the importance or unimportance of everything else is assessed. There can be, I think, no self-applied procedure whereby this detachment can be procured in such a case; it can only occur by natural changes. At best one can hope to regulate one's desires so that they never do come to be so entirely dominant over one.

Clearly people may dispute the need to or value of regulating desire in this, and in other, ways. It is not my purpose here to argue that this is (or is not) necessary or desirable. My argument is only that *if* one is going to be able, should one want to, to introduce some deliberate order into one's desires, then one must hope . . . etc. My purpose in this, as throughout, is to try to understand and explain the preconditions for, the structure and elements of, such an ordering, and not to approve or disapprove of making any ordering, let alone this rather than that order. I have not defended any norm of what may be appropriate in this, or in other, cases. Rather, my concern has been to show where, and how, normative considerations can come to bear in these matters, to display their position in the structure of the various cases.[3]

This said, we may now consider a case where some degree of detachment from the demands of sense-desire has come to be possessed. We may, then, judge it inappropriate to satisfy one such desire and deliberatively resolve upon not doing so. We have then both an impulse to act in a certain way and a deliberative determination not to act thus. Of course it may be, for one reason or another, that this determination is insufficient to prevent our enacting our impulse; for one reason or another our sense-desire may evade or subvert this determination and we proceed to the enjoyment of that pleasure which is its objective. But I wish to defer a discussion of such failures in the rational regulation of action, commonly referred to under the general head of 'weakness of will' (see chap. 7, sect. ii). At this point I am more concerned to determine what may be the result of the successful checking of the impulse to act contained in the sense-desire. The mere stifling of the expression of that impulse in action through deliberatively ordered denial would seem, of itself, to take us only a very little way towards moderating the frequency or intensity of such-like desires. It may still be that the pleasure holds one's concern and attention for all that one does nothing about securing the enjoyment of it for oneself. Or it may be that one achieves a certain partial gratification of the desire through imaginary or fantasy enjoyment of the pleasure. And in either case either the particular desire, or one's tendency to feel desires of such and such intensity for such and such pleasures, would seem to remain present very much as they are.

It would appear, then, that the prospects are dim for securing any real moderation of sense-desires, either in their intensity or in their frequency of occurrence. Perhaps all we can do is to check the promptings of such desires as and when they occur. But it seems to me that there is more room for change here than may seem obvious at first sight. Aristotle

---

3 If, however, it is thought that no normative issues do arise here, a reading of Shakespeare's Sonnet 129 ('The expense of spirit . . .' etc.) may suggest otherwise.

mentions that 'the exercise of appetite increases its innate force' (E.N. 1119b 10); and that seems to be true to experience. Sense-desires wax upon their gratification; desires for similar pleasures return more frequently and become more pressing. And it is reasonable to conjecture also that, in contrast, sense-desires do eventually wane upon their denial; appetite unexercised decreases in its innate force. But the denial must be thorough-going; if one allows one's attention to dwell on the desired object, if one conjures up in imagination the pleasures to be got from it, then appetite is still receiving at least a partial 'exercise'. But if one completely puts aside any thought of enjoying the pleasure, refuses to allow the prompting of desire to engross one's mind at all, one not only denies it expression but also, in effect, deletes it, expunges the desire, at least on that occasion. And it is possible that consistently and thoroughly 'expunging' the desire as and when it occurs, refusing it any lodgement in the direction of thought and intent, would lead to a decrease in the frequency and intensity with which such desires tended to occur, tended to be aroused. To have a sense-desire at all is to have a certain direction in one's attention, a certain focus in one's thoughts, a certain pleasurable expectation of certain states of affairs which might be brought about or occur, amongst other things. And one is not so passive and unable to direct one's attention, thoughts and expectations, that one cannot substitute for these some different concerns and preoccupations. In doing so one is ridding oneself of the desire, at least to the extent that it persists only as a tendency to revert to the prior pattern of thoughts, expectations etc. A desire which is no sooner felt than it is thus expunged might well be less and less likely to recur.

In due time it could be that one achieves just that liability to experience desires for the pleasure in question, or desire for the enjoyment of sense-pleasure generally, which seems, in one's practically rational judgement, to be appropriate. And then one has secured a congruence between the dictates of such judgement and one's tendency to be possessed of such desires, so that one is able to endorse the promptings of such desires when they occur, as discussed previously. It is likely to remain an unstable congruence, for the reason that even the endorsed desires, when gratified, will tend to 'increase in innate force' once more, and perhaps require restraint once more. A state of securely equable and moderate desire for the pleasures of sense, such as is fully and firmly in accord with one's judgement on the importance that the enjoyment of such pleasures should have, is not easily secured or retained.

It may be worth saying a little more about how it can come to be that we 'expunge' or 'delete' particular sense-desires. In an interesting paper[4] Pears mentions two ways in which 'the pleasures attached by nature to the gratification of basic desires are . . . alterable by rational desires'. The first is where a 'virtuous person would be revolted by certain indulgences . . . and this revulsion would be something more than the rational pain of doing what he believed to be wrong'. This produces a 'reduction of basic pleasure' and hence 'an instant diminution in a basic desire'. Pears does not unfortunately amplify his suggestion, so any interpretation of it must be conjectural as to his meaning. But it seems certainly true that one's capacity to find something pleasurable in such a way that one can continue to desire it may be restricted by the thought (correct or incorrect) that it is a morally objectionable or offensive pleasure. The disgust one feels at the thought of thus finding pleasure may effectively reduce or remove any possibility of finding any pleasure, or of thinking there could be any pleasure in having or doing whatever it is. Knowing how *pâté de foie gras* is made one may cease to be able to think of eating it as pleasurable and cease, then, to feel any desire to eat it, if one's knowledge 'colours' one's appreciation of it. But I cannot think of any general rule whereby one's knowledge of the character of an object may restrict one's capacity to think of it as pleasurable to the senses, rather than only creating a 'rational pain' which might dispose one against choosing it.

Pears's second suggestion, also not further amplified, is that a virtuous person might refuse 'to identify with' a 'deviant desire', and this might weaken it. It may be that this has already been taken into account of in my discussion of the ways in which we could refuse to entertain the thoughts and expectations which the arousal of a sense-desire brings with it. If we continue to give to these 'mind room', so to speak, this betokens a certain degree of willingness to go along with the prospects

---

4 Pears 1978: 276. Though Pears is principally concerned with the nature of courage, he begins with a very subtle discussion of temperance. Pears's notion of a 'basic desire' is not quite the same as my notion of a 'sense-desire', since it does not differentiate between e.g. hunger and desire of gustatory pleasure. This does not affect the points from his paper I consider here.

opened up by the desire, a willingness to think of doing what one's desire inclines one to do. A 'refusal to identify' would, presumably, involve at least treating such thoughts and expectations, if they continue to recur, as alien irruptions into one's mind which one gives no real assent to; and, more strongly, as I have suggested, trying to give one's mind to concerns other than those incorporated in one's sense-desire. There are many points at which the 'movement' from idle wish to desire, from desire to formation of an intention, from intention to decision and action, may cease. At each step other concerns can come in, or can be introduced, which can modify the eventually emergent interest and action. At least tacit endorsement of sense-desire is involved when a rational agent enacts such a desire. The hold of sense-desire will be weakened by strengthening other interests more effectively than by waiting for such desires to return, even if one 'refuses to identify' with them (on this, see Spinoza, *Ethics*, Pt 4, Proposition 7; and Plato, *Republic*, 485 d–e).

It is often said that too extreme a curb on the desire of sense-pleasure can lead to that desire finding other 'outlets'. This view displays the idea that the desire of sense-pleasure is an unalterable persistently recurrent interest, on analogy with hunger or thirst, which must be gratified on pain of psychological harm. But there is no reason to think that this analogy is correct. I argued, in chapter 2, for a distinction between hunger, as indeed a recurrent unalterable physiologically based motivating state, and the desire for gustatory pleasure which does not appear to have anything like that kind of physiological grounding. Some people seem to have little or no interest in the pleasures of the palate, for instance, without thereby suffering from anything more than indifference to something which can be enjoyable. Of course, if someone has frequent and intense desires for sense-pleasure which he is never able to gratify then this may be distressing. But this is true of *any* permanently frustrated strong desire, and gives no case for thinking that sense-desires are bound to be frequent and intense. Perhaps also if someone never desired sense-pleasure he would be missing out on something which would make his life more rewarding and satisfying than he possibly finds it to be. But that is again true of someone who never desired other things which are rewarding and satisfying; it gives no reason for thinking sense-desire is in a special place here. In any event, it has not been argued that the rationally appropriate response to the possession of sense-desires is their complete removal. There is reason to think that the enjoyment of such pleasures is good, and hence due concern for such pleasures is perfectly legitimate; thus feeling and acting on sense-desires is also perfectly appropriate.

I have been trying to indicate ways in which one may moderate the frequency and intensity of the sense-desires to which one may be liable, to such an extent that one is moved by such desires only as and when it seems, in one's reflective judgement, fit that this should be so. I have suggested that real moderation of such desires is possible, and not simply the suppression of their behavioural promptings. If and when that is achieved, one has achieved a state of congruence between one's rational judgement and sense-desire, and not by chance only, but as a deliberately sought and sustained congruence. In it, one gives to the enjoyment of sense-pleasure just that weight and centrality in one's life overall which seems to one appropriate. The pattern in one's liability to sense-desirous arousal will then as much carry the 'imprint' of this assessment as one's rational judgement and determination immediately express it, so that in both these modes of concern with the enjoyment of sense-pleasure there is carried, though in different ways, a single common estimate of the good and importance of that enjoyment. It will be useful, now, to explain more clearly how the pattern of the arousal of sense-desire does bear this 'imprint', does carry and express this estimate. For this will bring out what kind of limits there are to the rational ordering of sense-desire.

iv   THE CONGRUENCE OF SENSE-DESIRE AND RATIONAL JUDGEMENT

I have said that, by one's practically rational judgement, one may judge that the enjoyment of this or that sense-pleasure would be appropriate or inappropriate; or that, more generally, such and such an importance being attached to the enjoyment of sense-pleasure as an element in one's life is proper or improper. But sense-desire is for pleasure *tout simple*; the arousal of sense-desire is not naturally and originally governed by the belief that enjoying such a pleasure would be good, but simply by the belief that it would be pleasurable (cf. Plato, *Republic*, 437d–438b). It is

141

therefore impossible that rational judgement on the good or bad of enjoying a certain sense-pleasure, or sense-pleasures generally, should directly and immediately modify the principles of origination of sense-desire, since the originating principle of sense-desire is not any belief about what it would be good or bad to enjoy, but only a belief that a certain experience would be pleasant. It follows that the moderation of sense-desire by practically rational judgement must take place by an indirect route, by the gradual modification of one's liability to have such desires through the effort to inhibit or dissipate them when they occur, in the way I have tried to explain. The moderation achieved may be stable and secure to a very large extent; but it is still a moderation which takes the form of bringing an 'external' check upon the arousal and expression of sense-desire, and relies upon natural factors which influence the 'waxing' and 'waning' of one's tendency to have such desires. Nothing other than this is, in the nature of the case, possible. For there is no possibility of correcting the occasioning beliefs of sense-desire by rational judgement. That judgement speaks of what is good or bad; it does not claim that something which is believed to be pleasing to the senses is not so (though, as we have seen, in some cases a reduction of the pleasure may be produced).[5]

We do not, and cannot, have in this case, therefore, any more complete unification of right judgement with desire than this. The conception of there being separate modes of concern with the enjoyment of pleasure concurrently possessed, which I said earlier I wanted to claim was very misleading in general, is to a certain extent justified here. But only to a certain extent, for two reasons. First, it does not merely just so happen that the intensity and direction of sense-desire is coincident with the judgements and determinations of rational judgement about what should be enjoyed; this co-incidence is deliberately sought and sustained by one who seeks to control his desire by his judgement, and succeeds in doing so. So, although the respective characters of these modes of concern are radically different, the common purpose they direct a man to is,

---

5 Plato does, however, suggest that 'reason' may go further than I have here allowed; *Republic*, 586d–587a. I think there is a good deal to be said in favour of Plato's view on this. But fully to consider the question would take me further into an 'analysis' of pleasure than I have wished to be taken.

so to say, an 'agreed' purpose, and not one which merely happens to be identical. So there is a real unity in disposition here.

Secondly, as I have explained in my discussion of the 'endorsement' of sense-desire by rational judgement, it would be a mistake to suppose that whenever I act upon a sense-desire I judge to be appropriate, I act both from aroused sense-desire and from a deliberative resolve to act, as quite discrete motivations. I act as my sense-desire prompts me, on that desire; that alone is sufficient to direct my behaviour. Only it is a desire which I enact because I recognise in it an appropriate expression for my deliberatively resolved intent. That intent is concretely embodied and articulated in my thus acting on that desire; it does not have to actuate me aside and apart from the incentive to act contained in the desire. Thus we see that my rational endeavour may, on a particular occasion, be wholly and fully carried in my having and acting upon a certain sense-desire; and hence the conception of there being here quite separate modes of concern is again seen as significant distortion. The endorsement of desire by rational judgement does not and need not take the form of explicit ratiocinative and deliberative resolve on every occasion, over and above the impulse to act provided by the desire.

What concrete form does it then take? I suggest that it is contained in a range of possible actions which would be taken, and reactions which would occur, if the desire were to be deviant, that is, not such as receives the assent of rational judgement as appropriate. I shall not spell out what this range of actions and reactions includes here, for in respect to this there are, I believe, no significant differences between endorsed sense-desires and endorsed passional desires, whatever other contrasts exist between these cases. I shall be examining this matter fully in the next chapter. But to give an indication of my meaning, one instance of such a hypothetical tendency, a tendency to act or react which would be shown if the desire were deviant, may briefly be mentioned. (This is discussed in Dent 1974.)

If there is someone whose liability to sense-desire is in no way shaped or moderated by rational judgement, then if such desires should come to occur with any differing frequency, intensity and persistence, this change will not be of any material significance to him. One whose desire is, on the other hand, shaped and moderated by his rational assessment and direction will be apt to respond to such changes with distress and with an effort to reorder the pattern of his desires since, for him, such changes will constitute an inappropriate deviation from the structure he thinks should obtain. That there is this likelihood of a differential response to such changes does not mean that on any occasion when the desire is non-deviant, the behaviour of the person who is mindful that the frequency, intensity etc. of his desires should be appropriate will be any different from the other person's. Both men may act with equal immediacy at the prompting of their desire. The fact that one man is thus mindful and the other is not may consist wholly in a differential responsiveness to circumstances which simply are not involved in the present case. Such 'mindfulness' need not comprise something that the one has always 'in mind' which the other does not; it may be only a matter of what each would respectively feel or do if . . . But that there are hypothetical differences of this kind changes the interpretation that we make of the significance of the action each undertakes on his non-deviant desire; in the one case we see this as endorsed, in the other as neither endorsed nor unendorsed.

That he who is mindful of the appropriateness of his sense-desire is liable to distress, to 'rational pain' in Pears's phrase, should these become deviant enables us to see a connection between the points I have been making and a remark of Aristotle's quoted before. Aristotle writes (E.N. 1104b 4ff): 'We must take as a sign of states of character the pleasure or pain that ensues on acts; for the man who abstains from bodily pleasures and delights in this very fact is temperate, while the man who is annoyed at it is self-indulgent . . .' The exact interpretation of this passage presents some difficulty (this passage is discussed by Pears 1978: 284; see also chap. 1, sect. i, above). For it would seem that one who abstains from bodily pleasure, even if he finds denying gratification to his desire painful, is self-controlled rather than self-indulgent. Or, if Aristotle is not thinking of the pain of frustrated desire, but the annoyance *at* having to deny a certain desire (perhaps yielding to the pressure of public opinion about the undesirability of gratifying it, as Pears (1978: 284) suggests) then he should analogously be thinking of the pleasure the temperate man feels at succeeding in making a certain appropriate abstinence. But presumably the temperate man feels appropriate desires, and does not (any longer at any rate) have to struggle to make any abstinence; he would not anyway want any pleasure inappropriately. There must, I think, be five kinds of case here when we are faced with a pleasure which it would be inappropriate to desire to enjoy. First, where no desire is felt for that pleasure and one is pleased at having no desire for it, at not wanting or seeking it. This would be temperance. Secondly, where a deviant desire is felt for the pleasure, but one is pleased to be able to stop oneself acting on it, to make the abstinence because it seems appropriate. This would be rational self-control exercised in the name of what one thinks fit. Thirdly, where a deviant desire is felt for the pleasure, one embraces that pleasure but is distressed at having done so. This would be rational regret at one's lack of self-control. Fourthly, where a deviant desire is felt, one abstains from gratifying it and feels the pain of frustration, and one is also pained at abstaining from it because one is yielding to the pressure of public opinion about the evil of something one does not oneself think to be evil. This case has no convenient name, but it is very close to the fifth case, where one feels a deviant desire, has the pleasure of gratifying it and is pleased at having gratified it since, in one's (mistaken) view, the desire is not deviant. This would be self-indulgence. This is very like the fourth case in that, in that case, what stops the man from taking the pleasure and being pleased at having done so is not any rule of right desire and action he takes for his own guidance, but only the fear of shame or disgrace. (Cf. Aristotle on the 'courage' of the 'citizen–soldier': E.N. 1116a 15–21, and following.)

But whatever the precise construction to be placed on Aristotle's meaning it is clear that the 'delight' or 'annoyance' at having and acting or not acting upon certain desires is crucial to determining someone's state of character. One who is not even tempted by an improper pleasure and is glad that he feels no temptation shows that he has a settled and endorsed disposition with regard to the enjoyment of such pleasures. Without the gladness at this state of his desire and action we cannot say that he has a settled and endorsed disposition. For either he feels annoyance at his abstinence, or the pain of frustrated desire, or both; in which case it is clear that his rational approval and sense-desires are divergent. Or else he feels neither approval nor disapproval of his action or abstinence, in which case he neither endorses nor does not endorse his desire; thus has not employed his rational judgement in

145

relation to it at all. But then his having and acting upon such desires displays nothing whatever of his deliberative purposes and designs; it is a merely accidental feature of his nature quite unconnected with the intended governance and direction of his life. As such it cannot, it seems to me, be understood as part of his character.

If to this picture of a pattern in sense-desire endorsed and sustained by rational judgement and determination we add one further point, it seems to me we have an account of the psychological structure of the virtue of temperance, of which, of course, I have already begun to speak. This further point concerns the agent's ultimate reasons for seeking and sustaining the appropriate pattern in the frequency, intensity and persistence of his sense-desires, his ultimate motive for wanting this pattern to be as it is.

We can readily think of cases where someone might seek to moderate his sense-desires, and not merely refrain from acting upon them, only because he thought that were he not to do so this might lead to some undesirable consequences for him. Thus a spy might seek to cultivate indifference to the 'desires of the flesh', or more thoroughly to mute such desires, for fear that he might otherwise be subject to temptation in situations where he might be discovered. Would it then be appropriate to say that it is part of the spy's character that he has a temperate desire for sense-pleasures? I think not, for the following reason. If for instance he leaves his profession, or there is now no longer any threat of discovery, any cause to continue in the regulation of his sense-desires is removed for him. This means that that regulation was only ever present and sustained in response to an external necessity, a requirement imposed by the contingencies of his circumstances. Thus the ultimate source for the regulation lies in considerations dependent on factors independent of the intrinsic character of a moderated or immoderate state of sense-desire itself and only accidentally related to it. For a state of moderated desire to be an element in the agent's character the reason for its existence and maintenance must lie in the agent's own recognition of its excellence as a state to possess and enact.

But why is this so? Because by its being so someone has in himself, from himself, the reason why his state is so and not otherwise, and his state is not as it is in relation either to adventitious circumstances attaching to that state; nor further, is it as it is because someone other than he

146

himself prescribes this as the appropriate state to be in.[6] He himself possesses and sustains the state out of his own judgement of the character of that state itself, as something good and desirable; it is that state in which he desires and is moved to seek the enjoyment of sense-pleasure just to the extent to which it is appropriate, in relation to the importance of this enjoyment as an element in the course of his life. The cause of his state being as it is lies in him and in his appreciation of the intrinsic character of the state itself. And that seems to make it a part of the man's own proper nature, what constitutes him as the man he is. He is not at all the embodiment of external pressures or accidents working upon him in relation to his possession and exercise of this state. Thus we see this state of temperate desire as an element or aspect of his own self.

I suggest, then, that in the possession of a state of moderated desire for the pleasures of sense, a state moderated by its possessor's own judgement of its inherent appropriateness as comprising that degree of concern for such pleasures as is fitting, we have that state which is someone's possession of the virtue of temperance. In tracing the relations between sense-desire and rational judgement, and in showing how the former may be shaped by and carry the 'imprint' of the latter, we have uncovered the elements and structure of temperance as a trait of character, the character of one who possesses a moderate, equable and ordered desire of the pleasures of sense in recognition of the appropriate significance of the enjoyment of such pleasures.

Aristotle specifies three conditions which an action must satisfy, over and above its being an action typical of a certain character, if we are to be able to see it as the *expression* of that state of character actually being determinative of the act. He says (E.N. 1105a 30ff) that the agent of the act must (i) have knowledge; (ii) choose the act for its own sake; and (iii) that the action must proceed from 'a firm and unchangeable' character. As with the claim of Aristotle's discussed above, the exact interpretation of this one presents difficulties. But it is plausible to suppose that in arguing, first, that the temperate man seeks a certain sense-pleasure in

---

6 See Aristotle, E.N. Book 6, chap. 12, 1143b 32. This is a further point in addition to that already made about dependence upon 'adventitious circumstances'. Aristotle explains, at 1144a 14ff, that the importance of these points is related to the very basic distinction between doing, e.g., a just act and doing a just act justly (as a just man would do it) – i.e. in one's act displaying or enacting one's just character.

the belief that it is one it is appropriate to enjoy; secondly, that he seeks the appropriate enjoyment of sense-pleasures because he recognises this to be something which is in itself good as an element in his life; and thirdly, that he deliberately sustains the degree of concern he has for the enjoyment of such pleasures, we have given a reasonable articulation to these three conditions. Of course, that my account should, as I believe, match Aristotle's in certain respects is hardly accidental, for I have been at many points guided by what I take to be his ideas. But I hope the account can be seen to have cogency in its own right.

v   SENSE-DESIRE AND THE LOVE OF SENSE-PLEASURES

I have been very careful in the preceding discussion to speak only of the regulation of sense-desire, that is of the desire of pleasures aroused in the belief that they are pleasant to the senses and not for any other reason. I argued in chapter 2 that sense-desire was a 'good-independent' desire of the pleasures of the senses; and it is as having that character that I have been discussing how it might be related to and ordered by deliberative judgement.

However, it would be quite wrong to suppose, as I have neither supposed nor implied, that we do not often, and perhaps characteristically, acquire some 'love' of the enjoyment of sense-pleasure, some passional desire for such enjoyment, over and above any sense, or even rational, desire we may have of such enjoyment. Independent of, and very probably prior to, any deliberative election to pursue such pleasures as comprising some good worth possessing, and differently also from our desiring them simply as pleasant, we may come to possess a passional concern to enjoy such pleasures in response to the belief that doing so would be, in some way and to some degree, good. No doubt after having tasted such pleasures we come not only to desire to taste them again but to feel that they are so delightful, so enjoyable, that a life without such pleasure would be seriously deficient. And thus we may come to have a passional love of such pleasures thinking that the enjoyment of them will make our lives the better.

If this be so, then the rational regulation of our concern for the enjoyment of sense-pleasure will have to bear not only upon the frequency and intensity of our sense-desires but also upon the magnitude and persistence of our passional love of them. I have yet to consider how a man's passional love of something as good may be regulated by rational judgement; this is the topic of the next chapter. But it would clearly be insufficient to the achievement of a full and stable temperate state if no ordering were made of our passional love of the enjoyment of sense-pleasure, but only of our sense-desire of this. And I have not meant to deny this. Rather I have concentrated here upon the ordering of sense-desire, since that exhibits special and distinctive features different from a passional love of them. This latter has the same general character as the passional love of anything. I shall discuss the regulation of concerns of this sort in chapter 6.

It may be objected that I am presenting here an impossibly complex and incredible picture of these differing strands of concern with the enjoyment of sense-pleasure. But the complexity is not invented; it is the necessary consequence of the fact that we can and do have both a good-independent sense-desire of such pleasures and a good-dependent passional desire of them. If a simpler account is to be possible then that distinction must be denied. I hope, however, to have shown that it is correctly made.

It does follow, however, from the fact that a passional love of sense-pleasure does often exist that the given characterisation of the state of rightly tempered desire stands in need of supplementation. To it we must add that such pleasures must be also rightly loved, that our passion for them be purposely ordered by the judgement of their importance; or else we shall still possess some deviant concern for them. But the character of this deliberate right ordering will not become clear until we go through the argument of the next chapter. For the present the need for this supplementation need only be acknowledged; giving the precise nature of what goes into avoiding this deviant passional concern can wait.

Whether one says that temperance is 'essentially' a matter of deliberatively ordered right love of the enjoyment of sense-pleasure, or of deliberatively ordered right sense-desire of such pleasure, seems to me not to matter. All I have been anxious to insist upon is that there is more to the achievement of temperance than the regulation of good-dependent desires, and that this regulation presents special problems and features. And if I have succeeded in making it clear how, in spite of these problems, such regulation is possible, then I will have succeeded in my main task in this chapter.

As was noted in chapter 2 (pp. 37 and 63) Fortenbaugh commends Aristotle for the presentation of a bi-partite moral psychology, in which a distinction is made between the 'part' which 'originates a rational principle' (a principle about what it would be good or appropriate to aim for and do) and the part which 'obeys' such a principle (see Ross's note to Aristotle: E.N. 1102b 34). In contrast to this I have argued that there is an appetitive power which neither originates nor obeys 'a rational principle' in the relevant sense in its inherent operation, but is governed by pleasure; and I have tried to show how, in spite of this, guidance of it by a rational principle is possible. And it may be worth noting that Aristotle himself, when he discusses the moderation of the desire of bodily pleasure, speaks of the need to 'chasten' the appetite for such pleasure (E.N. 1119b 1ff). And this suggests something very different from the kind of reasoning and argument which might convince a man that he has misestimated the importance of some good. It rather suggests the infliction of some chastisement (verbal or physical) or some corrective deprivation as a curb to check succumbing to the incitement of a certain pleasure, bringing about a moderation of desire after long 'training' (cf. Pears 1978: 275). So it would seem that however theoretically convenient and economical it might be to suppose that the moral psychology of human beings was only bi-partite, close attention to the facts precludes this view. Impulses which are not in the relevant way amenable to rational argumentation and modification are present in the life of man. And we must account for the possibility of their ordering and regulation despite this lack of an opening for rational argumentation directly to re-shape them.

But having tried to give that account, it is now necessary to look at the way in which desires which *are* 'amenable to rational argumentation' may be modified and moderated. Such desires are those we have from passion. And I want to show how these can come to be informed, inwardly shaped, by right judgement, in a way which goes beyond anything that is, in the nature of the case, possible for sense-desire.

A final point regarding sense-desire is this. It is no part of my view that, in adults, we find sense-desire of pleasure unconnected with any passional love of such pleasures (as a good we wish to enjoy). My claim has only been that our 'interest' in the enjoyment of sense-pleasures does not have its rise in a passional love of them alone, but has another (more primitive) source with a distinctively different character. For purposes of analysis I have separated out this distinctive source because specially problematic issues arise about the possibility and nature of the regulation of it. It may further be noted that the desire of sense-pleasure can acquire extremely complex affective and cognitive accretions. One of the most typical roots of greed is the desire (not normally recognised by its subject as being of this character) to compensate oneself for the lack or deprivation of other pleasures or goods. (I have heard it said that cigarettes and television are the two great love substitutes.) One thinks as it were: I must fill myself with gratification and then my life will be good. Oral gratification plausibly relates to very basic rewards and deprivations. By ignoring these complications I have, of course, produced a much over-simplified account. I am not oblivious of these highly interesting and highly important further considerations. But I have preferred to concentrate on the primitive phenomena before they become encrusted.

6

Deliberation and passional desire: the virtues of passion

I have argued that having a sense-desire is not dependent upon holding that the enjoyment of any particular sense-pleasure would be good, or upon holding that such and such a degree and extent of enjoyment of sense-pleasure in general is good. These views may be held; but the occurrence of sense-desire does not depend upon this. Since this is so, deliberative rectification of the pattern of our sense-desires, of their frequency of occurrence, intensity, persistence, objectives, can only be indirect. Deliberative judgement concerns what it would be good or bad to enjoy, to do, to seek. But sense-desire does not depend for its occurrence upon such judgements; therefore changes in such judgements after deliberation cannot affect, modify, the very occasioning beliefs of such desires, the very principles of their occurrence.

Passional desires are, I think, crucially different from sense-desires in this respect. Their occurrence *is* essentially dependent upon their subject's holding something to be of value, importance. And from this difference stem the differences I want to lay stress on over the nature and scope of the way reflection upon values, and the determination based upon this, can moderate and order passional desire in contrast with sense-desire. It is easy to see, in general terms, why there should be differences and what these are. For to the extent to which we may change our estimate of the value of something upon deliberative reflection, to that extent our passional responsiveness, dependent as it is upon the estimates we make of the value of things, is liable to modification, not now indirectly, via some process of inhibition, but directly via a change in the inherent occasioning beliefs for the passion and of its attendant desires. What makes it possible that we should feel these passions, have these desires, at all is that we think of some things as good (fine, valuable – whatever quite be the appropriate kind of good) and of others as bad

152

(base, loathsome – whatever quite be the appropriate kind of badness). If, therefore, we modify our estimates of good and evil then the very beliefs upon which these responses depend are changed, and these responses are, therefore, liable to a co-ordinate change.

It is not, of course the sole purpose, nor the sole effect, of deliberative reflection upon the real importance of some good to us, on a particular occasion or in general, to moderate, specifically to reduce or remove, our passional responsiveness. Such reflection can as well 'endorse' the response we feel as appropriate, and reinforce and sustain our liability to such responsiveness if this is seen to incorporate a just and sound recognition of the importance of something. We saw earlier, too, that deliberate judgement could endorse the prompting of sense-desire. But it is when and where a reflective estimate of the importance of some good (or evil), and that estimate which is implicitly embodied in the intensity and persistence of our passional responsiveness to it, do not coincide that we come across the most interesting and difficult issues in the regulation of passion by deliberative judgement. It is for this reason, rather than for the reason that passional desire and deliberative intent are bound to be divergent, that I shall concentrate on such cases. As I remarked earlier, this divergence is better represented as a conflict within practical judgement itself, between considered and unconsidered, reflective and prejudiced, assessment, than as a conflict between practical judgement and something wholly different in nature. Reflection takes the implicit claim of the importance of something carried in a person's passional involvement, and examines that critically and consciously. This is an extended activity of practical judgement, not consideration of something which is of an altogether alien character bearing none of the marks of practically rational judgement (as was true in the case of sense-desire).

It is not, and I am not supposing otherwise, always easy to dispossess ourselves of estimates of the importance of certain goods of which we are deeply enamoured, and to modify our responsiveness accordingly. I shall look at some of the reasons for this below. In some such cases we may have to resort to that kind of control of passion which was central to the control of sense-desire on my account, if we cannot rectify the passion itself. But I would insist that there is a way, and it is the most important way, of rectifying passions which does not proceed by inhibiting them and their effects, but proceeds by in-forming them, ordering their occasions and direction, by perceptive and intelligent judgement of the real importance of various goods and evils.

What I want to try to do in the rest of this chapter is to fill out this outline by giving a more detailed examination of what goes into the modification of the opinions carried in passions and the attendant regulation of the passional responsiveness itself. I shall also explain some of the ways in which the reflective modification of passions is concretely embodied and enacted in the stream of our lives. For, as I already have indicated in relation to my discussion of sense-desire, it would be extremely misleading to represent the actuality of a reflective moderation of passion as the existence of a completely discrete and separate line, structure, of concern alongside our passional concern. What we have here is, rather, a complex but tightly integrated and ordered structure of concern which expresses a blending of diverse forms of interest into a single intent.

ii   THE REGULATION OF PASSIONAL DESIRE

I have suggested that the centrally significant form that the regulation of passions and passional desire takes is the achievement of a modification of that estimate of the importance of the goods and evils which is incorporated in our passional responsiveness. If this can be achieved, the very ordering principle of passions and passional desires may be reshaped and given a more appropriate character, providing that the informing deliberation be sound.

The way this rectification proceeds may be illustrated through a discussion of the moderation of anger, of one's liability to be angered over this or that, with such and such an intensity and persistence. Roughly, anger is evoked in response to suffering an unwarranted injury or slight, or, at least, what one takes to be such. Being angered, one is moved to desire to avenge this injury or slight, to return evil for evil, this being now thought of as something it would be desirable to achieve. And when the angry fit is upon one, this desire prompts one immediately to act for the realisation of its objective, typically by hitting out at one's antagonist, this being behaviour naturally expressive of anger which has a primitive aptness to achieving the desired end. The subject of anger is moved to desire to rectify his situation in the respect in which it is, as he believes, undesirable, as I explained in chapter 3. The subject of anger does not reason out that this rectification is an appropriate response to the injury he has suffered, as he believes. That is indeed possible, but not what takes place when we are angered. Rather the idea of avenging ourselves seizes us as desirable, even as imperatively necessary – we are caused to want to do this and do not decide upon wanting to after deliberation.

Deliberative reflection may, however, bear upon the organising principles of this pattern of occasion, engendered purpose and evoked impulse in three basic ways, the first two of which are the most important. First, a man may come to review, and to alter, the estimate of the importance of the evil which he thinks himself to have suffered. As an aspect of this, he may review the estimate he places upon the importance of certain goods, upon which estimate his perception of a certain act or omission as unwarrantably injurious depends. For at the root of anger is the wish to be in receipt of esteem and recognition from others, which the immediately occasioning injury or insult is seen as revealing the absence or denial of. It is by being attached to such esteem and recognition, taking it as a thing of such and such importance and significance, that a man is liable to be angered to this extent, for this long, over this or that which happens to him. One who is angered by much, often and long, may possibly be one who is in truth the victim of a great deal of undue disrespect. But it could instead be that he attaches an overly great importance to the receipt of esteem and regard, and is thus unduly angered when this is not shown, and also wishes it to be shown in ways and on occasions beyond what is reasonable. Irascible people are often so sensitive on this matter that they imagine improper indifference to themselves where none was intended, find fault where none can reasonably be claimed. In all of this a certain sense of the importance that he should have to others is embodied in the expectations and responses of the irascible man, a certain picture of the priority of himself and his dignity as a matter for concern. Practical deliberation can concern itself with the justness of this picture, the appropriateness of this sense, by considering whether, in truth, this extent of claim upon the regard of others is legitimate, in regard to whom, over what and so on. Most important, by a deliberate intent based upon this consideration, this modified assessment could be kept firmly before the agent's mind so that he can correct the immediate, improper, appraisals he is liable to make until such time these no longer govern his responsiveness but, instead, these are occasioned in reference to his corrected judgement. In due time his former conception of himself and his importance may have no longer any hold upon him, and thus feelings and desires, the frequency and intensity of whose occurrence depended upon his having that conception, will no longer occur, but instead feelings and desires related to his revised and rectified conception.

I do not propose to discuss here the issue of what might actually be a proper estimate of importance to be placed upon enjoying the respect and regard of others. That would, of course, be the central issue were I concerned to show what value states of moderated passion had and why; but, as I have said before, that is not my topic in this discussion. Three points about the rectification of the sense one may have of the importance of this do deserve note, however.

First, it is by no means a straightforward matter to come to an awareness that the occasions by which one is angered, the intensity and duration of one's anger, etc. all together constitute a pattern in which is embodied the fact that such and such a weight or significance is being attached by one to the enjoyment of the esteem of others. Typically one is absorbed in a conception of oneself and others which is structured by this estimation; it constitutes (part of) the perspective one has on oneself in one's dealings with others,[1] the form of one's relations with them, and one is not aware of possessing that perspective – that one has it is not an *object* of attention. It may need, for example, the shock of another's criticism to bring any realisation of the fact that one is placing this estimate upon one's self-importance and any possibility of questioning that. But, of course, such criticism is easily forgotten, discounted, or made an object for anger itself, by which the continuing hold over one of the criticised conception is reaffirmed, and the same habits of expectation and demand continue to persist. It is, however, often by particular shocks of this kind, rather than by any general overall effort of self-

---

1 On the notion of one's 'perspective' see Winch 1972: 178ff. The sense I give to this notion does not exactly correspond to that Winch gives it.

awareness and self-appraisal,[2] that one achieves a piecemeal apprehension of what one is setting store by and of how much store one is setting by it. It is by a slow and gradual process that one's estimates of value become the object of one's consideration, rather than remaining the framework of one's attention to other things. One may then attempt to work out a different order of emphasis and priority. Whether it is through a generalised endeavour after self-awareness, or through a multiplicity of particular efforts to correct one's response on particular occasions, that one comes to moderate one's tendency to anger, there are characteristic difficulties which may occur. If we simply try to come to terms in a more balanced way with each situation as it arises, there may remain areas of distorted and exaggerated emphasis which persist because, for one reason or another, they have not been involved in our life experience for some while. On the other hand, generalised self-assessment can result in what are merely fancies about what sort of person one is which have no actual hold upon, no substantive direction of, the responses we make upon particular occasions. For there to be an overall and stable rectification in the pattern of our responsiveness there would normally be a need to move between the general and the particular, a need to correct our sense of the individual situation and to try to form an overall more sound weighting of the values we lay store by.

Secondly, even should someone come to some clear awareness that he does, by his passion, show that he attributes an excessive importance to enjoying the esteem of others, it is not always going to be easy to know, or to reckon with, whatever factors might have established this as so important for him. Such attributions may be answerable to practical reason for their legitimacy; but they are not originally made on the basis of reasoning about their legitimacy – but as influenced by various vicissitudes of one kind or another which contribute to the hold of this assessment over feelings. Thus reasoning about their legitimacy may only 'scratch the surface' in relation to what actually holds them in place in a man's scheme of life. It is a familiar thought, for example, that

2   Compare Eliot, T.S., 'East Coker', sect. 2: 'The knowledge imposes a pattern, and falsifies,/For the pattern is new in every moment/And every moment is a new and shocking/Valuation of all we have been.'

157

overestimation of the importance of others' esteem is the obverse of an underestimation of one's personal worth. Unless this further conception is, in its turn, understood and reappraised, the emphasis upon receipt of the recognition of others will be apt to remain, sustained by this further need, however much a man tells himself that it is absurd and improper to require the acclaim of others as much as his anger at its absence shows that he does. Perhaps one may not be faced with difficulties of this kind in the effort after correcting one's passion. But it is clear that, if they are present, the correction of feeling can only be partial and faltering unless they are in their turn recognised and responded to.

This point is connected with the third one I wish to note. It is clear that one will be unable to come to any just and appropriate estimate of the importance to be assigned to enjoying the esteem of others if one does not possess some reasonable and appropriate sense of what else should matter to one, in what ways and to what degree. This means that one cannot rectify one passion without at least beginning to endeavour to correct all one's passions, comprehensively. For if this were not done, one would modify the weight one attached to one good in the name of a false and distorted weighting placed upon another or others, and one could not then, except by a happy accident, arrive at what is in truth an appropriate weighting for the first concern. This is part of what is involved in the idea that the virtues form a unity, in that one cannot possess one without possessing all. For if one lacks one virtue, this will mean that, with regard to its relevant passional concern, an improper importance is placed upon a certain good, its significance is being over- or underestimated or appreciated. From this it follows that, unless one's concerns happen to be fragmented and compartmentalised – and this may be a saving fortune here – this over- or underestimation of value will lead to a distortion of the value placed upon other concerns, since those valuations will reflect the over- or underestimation.

This point should not be exaggerated, however. For precisely that capacity of deliberative judgement upon the real import of some concern, which enables us to perceive, and perhaps eventually to correct, the erroneous emphasis carried in our passion, should enable us to discount this error on particular occasions and to be mindful only of the right weighting when we are concerned with forming a true estimate of the goods with which we are concerned in our other passions. It is only that this may be rendered a particularly hard thing to do if our passional responsiveness continually reaffirms our adherence to the erroneous weighting. I would suggest this is one reason why Aristotle maintains that one cannot have practical wisdom – a true and reasoned state of capacity to act with regard to the things which are good or bad for man (E.N. 1140b 5) – without moral virtue (E.N. 1144b 31). (There are other reasons for holding this view, some of which I shall consider in chapter 7.) For one who lacks any particular virtue, or virtues, will, in his wrong passion, attach a mistaken importance to some good and thus find it more difficult to appraise the true weight to place upon that. One who has, on the other hand, somehow acquired roughly appropriate passions will have already a roughly appropriate appreciation of what matters and to what extent. And it will thus be much easier for him to arrive at a true and reasoned assessment of the relative import and significance of these concerns. He has only the task of, so to speak, smoothing off the rough edges in his conception of the central concerns of his life and is not obliged to reconstruct that conception in radical ways. It is plausible to think that the former task is easier than the latter.[3] We should also note that habits draw secondary rewards to themselves. Even if they are the token of a misestimate of some goods, habits of feeling have served their possessor in 'coping' with the circumstances of his life and to do without them in the course of trying to change them can be very threatening or unsettling. Normally, too, as I indicated previously, estimates and misestimates of value do not occur discretely or atomistically – a deformation at one place may be as successful a way as the subject has available to him of dealing with what are severer, but more elusive, distortions elsewhere. Habits are often (self-) defensive.

Given the sorts of difficulty I have identified as lying in the way of deliberative rectification of passion, through a correction of the conception of the importance of certain goods to us which is embodied in our passional responsiveness, it is not to be wondered that we often find it extremely hard to leave our familiar habits of feeling behind, and to achieve any enduring redirection in our concerns. But I hope at least it

3 See Aristotle, E.N. 1152a 30; 1103b 25, on the permanence of habits. He also emphasises the distorting effects of enjoying wrong pleasures (or of wrongly enjoying pleasures), due to misplaced passion; E.N. 1113b 1; 1140b 16ff; 1144a 30–35, for example. See further chapter 7, section i, below.

can be seen where such efforts after rectification can find their point of lodgement and why such rectification occurs, if indeed it does.

My remarks have so far been confined to the question of modifying that valuation which governs the occasions upon which our anger, or other passions, may be aroused. It is now necessary to consider the ways in which we may deliberatively regulate the desire to avenge ourselves which is evoked in the evocation of anger, or whatever other desire may be engendered in the onset of any other active passion. This is the second point at which deliberative shaping of passional concern may be undertaken, the second place at which it may gain a foothold.

It may be argued that if and when we have achieved a secure and stable sense of the importance that should be attached to the receipt of the esteem of others, which now decisively orders our liability to being rendered angry, there is no further need of or place for deliberative correction of the vengeful impulse engendered in anger. For, as I argued in chapter 3, what we are in anger caused to desire as good is precisely the removal of that evil that we suffer, as we think. So if we now have achieved a proper sense of the importance of receiving others' esteem, we shall now, when we apprehend some injury or slight as an evil, be making a proper assessment of it. And thus, it would seem, our desire of avenging ourselves will be appropriate, since it will be a desire to remove what is in truth an evil we suffer. Our desire is then a justified and legitimate one; what we seek as desirable is indeed a fit object for our concern and action.

I do not think this argument is wholly misplaced. However, there is a distinct difference of focus between the questions, on the one hand, 'How important is it to receive the regard of others?', which concerns the appropriate occasions for anger; and, on the other hand, 'How important is it to return harm for harm?', which concerns what it is appropriate to aim for and do if we have been improperly treated. Evidently a proper answer to the first question is very material indeed to arriving at a proper answer to the second; for one who thought his dignity so important as to admit of no disregard will be apt to think it imperative that any disregard of it be summarily avenged. But it seems to me that there is more that can properly come into consideration in relation to the second question than this.

For example, one who comes to think that it is better to ignore or to be tolerant of injuries to his self-esteem, even quite improper injuries to it, and ceases finally to have any spontaneous, let alone deliberated, desire to revenge these has not necessarily come to think that improper injuries to his self-esteem are of no importance. He may rather think that 'two wrongs don't make a right', or that retaliation just prolongs or emphasises the harm done. (I don't say that it is right, or wrong, to think these things.) It might, indeed, be said that this is really just a further consideration which bears on arriving at a due sense of the importance of regard being paid to oneself – that it is, or is not, something which matters enough to merit inflicting injuries upon those from whom it is not forthcoming. However, I think it is more perspicuous to identify two points at which deliberative correction of anger may be made, at the point of its occasioning circumstances and at the point of its engendered purposes. And just because one *can* represent these as two aspects of the same concern does not mean that it is particularly helpful to do so.[4]

Whatever the rights and wrongs of this, the main point that calls for emphasis is that someone, when angered, places an importance upon avenging the injury he has suffered, as he believes. He does not, of course, deliberately and consideringly place that importance upon harming his antagonist; rather he is caused to feel this as a matter of possibly very urgent or paramount concern, depending on the intensity of his aroused impulse. To feel such an impulse is not simply to feel impelled to move in certain ways, though that may be involved; it is to apprehend, to assess, achieving a certain state of affairs as something which has to be done, is importantly to be achieved, to some degree at any rate. And this assessment is clearly open to reflective scrutiny, to consideration of its soundness in the particular case, or more generally as being the sort of thing it is worth trying to bring about. And it can, in due time, become habitual to a man that he sees this or that importance in avenging himself such that his inclination to do so is firmly and consistently shaped by this considered assessment; he no longer has any sense of it as more or less imperative of achievement than he reflectively assesses it as being, so that his desires are no longer 'deviant'.

Similar issues to those I discussed above in connection with the

---

4 Compare Aristotle, E.N. 1149a 30–35; anger reasons 'as it were that anything like this must be fought against . . . Therefore anger obeys the argument in a sense . . .'

awareness of the occasioning estimates of value in anger also arise here. But there is no reason to go through these points again. I am not supposing that it is only one minute's reflective thought that is needed to change the conceptions one has had, which have structured one's desire and action for years. My concern is principally with the matter of theory rather than practice; to show where one's passional desires admit of correction by judgement, given their inherent character as incorporating estimates of weight and importance, and the scope of practical judgement for assessing and moderating such estimates. I do not pretend to providing a manual of techniques for self-improvement (cf. Mill, *Essay on Bentham*, 266ff).

As I remarked in section i of this chapter, it must not be supposed that the only function of deliberative judgement will be to correct, to modify, those estimates of value that we come to be aware are carried in the pattern of our passional responsiveness. I have looked at such cases only because they serve to make peculiarly clear what kind of relation and interconnection there can be between passion and practical reason. If, however, we come to think that our passional concern embodies an appropriate valuation, then we may 'endorse' it in a way similar to the endorsement of sense-desire, save that, in that case, no estimate of importance occasions that desire, only the belief that something would be pleasant. But in this case, as in that, when the desire is endorsed it ceases to be a 'mere' desire, simply an inclination to which we are subject, and becomes instead a desire in which is embodied and articulated our deliberative intent to have our lives take a certain shape, our concern to incorporate these or those values into our living. Such desires carry, now, our conscious and deliberately sought scheme of values for our living and action; they serve as partial enactments of that scheme and are not just accidental interests which happen to possess us. Our resolved intent is realised through such patterns of desire; it does not, or not necessarily, exist aside and apart from them. I shall return to this matter later on.

The third point of application of deliberative regulation to our passions and passional desires is of the least theoretical significance, since it does not concern the reshaping of those estimates of significance which order our passions, achieving which is, as I have tried to show, centrally important in their case. This third mode of regulation is by the inhibition of action and the 'dissipation' of desire in a way identical to that I discussed in the case of sense-desire, and which was in that case the centrally important mode. There is no cause to repeat all the considerations adduced already in this connection, but two points merit notice.

First, it is at the point of translating desire into action that many values which may enter into the particular circumstances of undertaking the present act may be brought to bear upon it, upon whether to take action or to forgo it, and upon how precisely to take it, if it is decided to proceed. What I have in mind in making this point is that the kind of assessment of relative values which can go into ordering one's general liability to, say, anger can, it seems to me, be only fairly indeterminate and deal alone with what is for the most part so (see Aristotle, E.N. 1094b 18–27; 1109b 23; 1126b 4). It would be practically, and I think theoretically, impossible to prevision every conceivable range of considerations which might be involved in all the individual situations where one might be angered and caused to desire to revenge oneself. *Eo ipso*, it would be impossible to have, in advance, so ordered one's judgement that one could have regulated one's desire appropriately for every situation when it might arise. Such precision of prior judgement is a fantasy. Rather one has an approximately just concern which is appropriate by and large to most of the generally relevant other considerations that may bear, but one stands ready to appreciate that there may be particular exigencies in certain situations which would go counter to one's generally appropriate concern. Thus if someone with malice aforethought deliberately betrays one's confidence in order to procure one's humiliation it is entirely appropriate for one to be angered by this. And it would seem also that one was justified in returning some sort of hurt for this one has suffered. But we can suppose that one's antagonist is someone extremely dependent upon your good opinion, to whom it would be shattering to be rejected by you (perhaps it is some resentment at this dependency that made him do what he did). In this case one might decide to forswear one's revenge, but not because one has, or should have, so moderated one's proneness to anger that one should never have been angered by this, for so special a case does not lend itself to the formulation of a general rule which one might be mindful of. Rather, on the particular occasion, one checks the vengeful impulse in awareness of this particularly weighty desideratum. It is not through some overall

163

modification of the importance one attaches to the receipt of regard, or to the importance of not letting disregard go unremarked, that one does not take revenge here; one instead acknowledges a specific constraint operative in the particular situation. And it is, as I have said, at the point of translation of desire into action that the rôle of such-like constraints in regulating conduct is found.

Secondly, I want to suggest that the inhibition of action upon passional desire, and even the 'dissipation' of such desires, in a way analogous to the inhibition and dissipation of sense-desire, is less likely to result in a decrease in the frequency of occurrence, intensity and persistence of such desires than it is in the case of sense-desire. In the case of sense-desire, our desire is not related to, emergent from, a general attitude to the significance to us of doing, enjoying, having something. It is a specific mode of interest evoked by a specific kind of quality in objects (their pleasurableness to sense), which grows upon its gratification and withers upon its denial. However, passional desires are related to a conception we have of the importance, significance, that certain goods have for us, and there is correspondingly less reason to suppose that the inhibition of action or the dissipation of desire will have a very profound or lasting effect. For there is little reason to think that this would do much to modify that conception, to shift or weaken the hold it has over us. Its appeal is likely to have several sources; it is likely to command our assent (however uncritically and improperly) for a variety of reasons, and to extend itself over many aspects of our lives. And merely denying gratification to the desires engendered in relation to that conception will not, I think, achieve much overall effect. It will continue to shape our view of ourselves and our lives until we take some stock of it and of why it has such a command over us. Concentration upon *one* manifestation of it is likely to carry us only a little distance in coming fully to grips with the issue. Whereas, in the case of sense-desire, its entire nature is to direct us to the enjoyment of sense-pleasure, and denied its proper objective, denied a place in our thoughts and expectations, it is denied its very life as an element in the mind.

Of course, where there is a love of sense-pleasures over and above the sense-desire of them, that love will not, if what I have been saying is right, be likely much to wane just by the denial to oneself of the gratifications of sense. Such a love is a passional desire and thus what I have just said of passional desires generally applies equally to it. If that love is to be rectified, the conception of the importance of enjoying sense-pleasures embodied in it must be rectified, and nothing short of that will have much lasting effect.

The point just discussed must be carefully distinguished from the claim that, by performing the actions characteristic of the possession of, and of being moved by, a certain desire, although not actually moved by that desire but, say, acting under orders, we may in time come to possess that desire. This is the claim that by 'going through the motions' appropriate to a certain desire we may acquire the desire to go through those motions, rather than the claim that by not going through the motions appropriate to a desire we do have we may in time lose that desire. This idea is often ascribed to Aristotle, and with some justice (see Aristotle, E.N. 1103b 5–25; 1104a 20–25). But it is surely mistaken, and arises from a regression to modelling virtues on skills in a Socratic fashion. By going through the motions appropriate to skilled bricklaying, not guided by my knowledge of what is required but under instruction, I may indeed acquire the skill of bricklaying. But there is no reason at all to suppose I shall acquire any desire to lay bricks, any personal incentive to exercise my skill.

A much more plausible interpretation has been offered by Wallace (1978: chap. 2, esp. sects. 6–7) that what was intended was that if I act on my occasional, fleeting, desires I shall tend to consolidate and stabilise my tendency to have those desires. And this habituation of desire, by acting upon such occasional desires as I may from time to time happen to feel, is essential to the acquisition of a consistent disposition of desire which is requisite to virtue. And that may well be right, or at least a part of the truth. I think, however, it is quite as unlikely that I shall acquire a consistent habit of desire if what these are desires for is something I think of very little importance indeed, even if I act upon them, as it is unlikely that I shall lose a habit of desire if what these are desires for is something I continue to think of very great importance indeed, even if I don't act on them.

Perhaps Aristotle's thought was that if I act on them I shall learn how enjoyable and rewarding doing whatever it is can be, and this will be likely to lead me to feel it is a more valuable and important kind of activity than I thought previously that it was. This could, in fact, also be true if I did something only under instruction or duress and without even a fleeting spontaneous interest in doing it. This is perhaps the way in which someone may, after years of sitting at piano practice under duress, come to want to play for its own sake. When a certain proficiency is eventually acquired this is something which typically comes to be valued. But I do not know how plausible this line of thought would be as applied to undertaking the activities characteristic of a virtuous disposition of desire in the absence of such desires, whether occasional or settled.

Whether or not one's *desires* be appropriately ordered, it is the general rule that one should, if one can, *act* appropriately. And in the vast majority of cases, except where desire is truly overwhelming, one can do so upon a deliberative decision so to do. This is an obvious contribution that the possibility of deliberative control of our conduct can make to its fitness. I have not laboured this point, not because it is unimportant, but because it does not relate to the moulding of desire by practical judgement, which has been my paramount concern. But I should not be taken to be implying that it is only by right ordering of one's desire that one can effectively direct one's conduct by right judgement. Of course this is not true; the virtue of self-control is, if nothing else, that virtue by which we do what we should even although our desires incline us otherwise. My interest has been here, however, to see how our desires might be 'taught' not to incline us otherwise.

I have sought to characterise three ways in which we may, by deliberative judgement and purpose, seek to achieve a rectification of our passions and passional desires. Most distinctively, this can be done by the modification of the implicit estimates of importance and significance which are embodied in the patterns of our passional responsiveness. The presence of these estimates makes these patterns in principle amenable to rational ordering, for it is the character of deliberative reflection to appraise and assess the soundness of such estimates. There is a character possessed by passions, the fact that they incorporate a 'rational principle', which makes it possible for right reasoning about practical principles to order them in their very nature. And I have tried to explicate the details of this. I want now to consider how the fact that the ordering valuation of a passion is endorsed by our rational judgement will be comprised, substantively realised, in the pattern and elements of the stream of life of a man. I want to make it as clear as I can that we have here one complex but unified structure of judgement and desire, not separate, quite discrete, but fortunately parallel lines of concern. What is achieved here is a genuine unity of the mind and heart, a singleness in spirit expressing itself in the activity.

iii   RATIONALLY ORDERED PASSIONS

How will the concrete detail of a man's life display that he has or has not ordered his passions by his deliberative judgement? Potentially, the range and variety of manifestations of this will be enormous; there is practically no area of man's thought, feeling and activity which cannot display something of the deliberative ordering he makes of his passions.[5] So it is necessary to be selective of points which will help to show what is at issue here. In doing so, I shall return briefly to some of the examples I discussed in chapter 1. It will now be seen, I hope, that we are in a position to understand more clearly and fully what those examples showed.

The most illuminating case to examine is that where we have a contrast between someone's possession of a mere customary habit of desire, and the possession by someone of a habit of desire which displays, in part, his deliberative recognition and endorsement of the objective of his desire as significant and important. (This was my strategy in Dent 1974: *passim.*) I looked at one aspect of this contrast in connection with sense-desire, and now I want to explore it more fully, supplementing that discussion. In what ways would this difference be shown; how would it manifest itself in features of the reactions and actions of a person? That there is a contrast to be made here is, I hope, undeniable. For, to take an extreme case, it can be that there is a customary pattern in someone's passional responsiveness which he deeply regrets, is trying to rid himself of, but is at present unable to, so that he remains still possessed of it, or possessed by it. For example, it may be that whenever things start going wrong for me I begin to be overcome by feelings of

5 See White 1964: 100, on the multiple aspects of 'desire', all of which will be modified by deliberative correction.

self-pity; I think of myself as ill-used, as suffering unmerited misfortune, and I am moved to seek the sympathy and support of others. But it may be that I loathe this habit of response in myself, that I repudiate this tender self-regard which moves me, for all that I lapse into being governed by it time and again.

Here, clearly, there is a pattern in a man's desires, a pattern which indeed incorporates an estimate of the importance of his not being caused pain or distress. But it is not one which he endorses, and it is not present in his life, neither does it exert a hold upon his responses, because he endorses it. In what, then, would his having endorsed it be displayed? How would this be apparent in his life? What we must consider here is not two quite separate paths of concern, but two different configurations or structures of concern. The endorsement of passion by practical reason does not comprise merely an additional kind of concern alongside passional concern; it forms a new order in that pattern of the agent's desires and actions, as well as introducing new elements into it.

Some of the concrete modifications which will result from the endorsement of a habit of desire are these. First, a mere habit in desire may come and go, as the hold over one of a certain conception of the value of something changes, is replaced by other concerns or simply ceases any longer to have any influence upon one. If this is a mere habit, these alterations will not much concern the agent; so far as he appreciates that they have occurred at all, they will be for him simply matters of the 'natural history' of his interests. In this respect a mere habit of desire to help others in need, for instance, will be no different from a general liking for drinking beer, to use the analogy I employed in chapter 1. Mostly that is what one will like to do; but sometimes one will have another preference, and since one's possession of this liking for beer was a mere matter of how one happened to feel, one will act differently if one has a different preference at a time or if one's preference gradually changes overall.

It is, of course, more valuable for a man to have a liking for helping others, for this to be something which catches his concern, than it is for him to have a liking for drinking beer, even if both are, to him, no more than things he happens to like doing. And we may well praise a man who has this sort of concern for others. But I think it will be clear that such a concern, even if pretty consistently possessed, which is regarded by its possessor in this way, as one he just happens to have and one he acts upon just as it happens to be uppermost in his concerns at a time, is nowhere near to what is involved in the possession of the virtue of generosity or kindness. For there is no operative belief in the man that the possession and exercise of this concern is important or desirable because it is important and desirable that the needs of others be answered. Such a man is merely acting 'as the mood takes him'; and despite the fact that his moods are often good and beneficial, he is not concerned beyond how he feels at the moment. He does not concern himself and act in recognition of this as something that *befits* concern, whether or not it happens to arouse his concern at any particular moment.

We look for, in the virtue of kindness, a committed intent to answer the claim of the needs of others which goes beyond the occasional effect of quickened feeling (cf. MacLagan 1960: 206, 216 and *passim*). That committed intent will include seeking to make the liability to a passional response to the needs of others more than merely occasional. One who takes the claim of others to receive help when in need as a matter which merits concern will try to resist any alteration in or disappearance of his tendency to be moved by their plight. He will endeavour to suppress the growth of inclinations which may obstruct or remove his tendency to this responsiveness; he will so order his other thoughts, expectations, hopes and fears as to procure and to secure a steady constancy of regard to the needs of others, a steady disposition to have his concern awakened by their plight. He will not, if his feelings are in a particular case left untouched, or more generally he finds his concern is less and less liable to being caught, simply be unmoved by this. He will regret this, perhaps blame himself or feel remorse for allowing his heart to become hardened. And furthermore, if he is not on an occasion moved by the plight of another, he will not simply let the moment pass because he felt no spontaneous movement of pity or care. In this case he will, directly out of his deliberative intent to procure this good for others of relieving their need, undertake to do what is required, perhaps, as I have said, feeling remorseful at the fact that it is, for him, something he has to do only as a matter of deliberate intent and cannot be doing out of involved care and sympathy.

That someone will be ready to undertake an 'endorsed' purpose even when his passional responsiveness to it deserts him, fails him, deserves further comment. It would be easy to think that, because this constitutes a quite decisive difference between one who endorses a certain purpose and one for whom that is his purpose only when his feelings are aroused, this is the single most important element in deliberative endorsement of and adherence to some end. But this would be a mistake, for it would represent that endorsement as consisting only in the deliberate, principled, undertaking of the action quite aside and apart from any passional concern for it (cf. Kant, *Groundwork*, 398–9; also Williams 1971: 22–4). Whereas we have seen that that endorsement manifests itself in many more ways than this, ways which directly concern the agent's continued possession of, and prompting to action by, his passional concern. That intent we have in recognition of the merit of some objective as a matter for our concern can be and is expressed in the way we order and direct our liability to passional responsiveness. And, if it is, we can and will act as we are moved by this responsiveness, reasonably trusting that it constitutes a due and proper measure of concern on our part.

I have identified four aspects of the relationship between a committed intent to answer the claim of the need of others and our liability to respond in feeling to this need, our liability to be moved in response to the plight of others. It will include (*a*) an endeavour to suppress contrary concerns and inclinations to this one; (*b*) an endeavour to stabilise and consolidate the liability to such responsiveness; (*c*) a liability to react with regret and self-blame if one is left unmoved on a particular occasion or if, more pervasively, one's heart becomes hardened; and (*d*) a capacity and readiness to do what is appropriate should any spontaneous inclination to act be absent. I should perhaps say here, to avoid misunderstanding, that I am not suggesting that it is necessary to act to relieve the needs of others on every imaginable occasion. There are other activities which it is proper for someone to engage in even if there are still some people whose need one could answer. But the fact that the claim of the need of others is only one claim among many which a person may properly take account of does not mean that there will never be occasions upon which one is giving it less than its due, occasions upon which one has less of a concern than one should. And it will be in relation to those that it will be essential to cultivate and sustain a proper measure of responsiveness. Not every occasion in which we do not help those in need is a case of an improper failure to do so. But still there will be cases where not feeling moved to help and helping will be such a failure.

In these four aspects of this relationship we have the substance of what may be called a meta-, or second-level, desire directed on to a basic, first-level, pattern of desirous interest, concerned with the sustaining and consolidation of that. (On second-level desires, see Dent 1974: 566–7; Frankfurt 1971; Körner 1973; Monro 1967: chap. 17; Neely 1974; *et al.* See also chap. 1, p. 18, above.) As will be seen, a major part of the manifestations of this second-level concern will be in surrounding the first-level concern with a range of additional 'supports' to its existence and expression in action. When everything proceeds smoothly, when, that is, the agent is appropriately moved and acts accordingly, these surrounding supports of his concern and action will not be 'visible', will not be present as elements in what is actually going on at the time; they will be present only as readiness, potentialities for certain sorts of additional feelings and actions. If the flow of natural interest and action is impeded, then these potentialities will be actualised in order to compensate for the absent concern, to ensure appropriate action and to take steps to guard against comparable failures in the future. It may be because the manifestations of this second-level concern are not apparent on every occasion of action that its presence and importance can be overlooked. But I hope I have made it clear how it is crucial to the transformation of a mere habit of desire into a habit of desire which embodies, and is meant to embody, its possessor's due and considered apprehension of the claim upon him of the objective of the desire as something which befits, demands, his active concern.

The existence of this 'hierarchy' of desire permits us to say that what the agent does represents his choice, his deliberate intent, without our having to say that whenever he acts he there and then engages in prior deliberation and makes the choice of doing this rather than that. It could be in the agent's general unwillingness to allow his habit of desire to lapse, or in his tendency to self-blame if he is left unmoved on a certain occasion, that the fact that some desire or action of his constitutes his deliberate choice consists. Thus someone may act immediately and

171

spontaneously out of a loving regard for someone in a particular situation whilst yet also thinking that this is something he ought to do, and he be doing what he does mindful of that thought. His mindfulness does not have to consist in what he has 'in mind' at the time of action, as I have remarked before.

It may be noted, in passing, that these points enable one to resolve what appears to be some inconsistency in Aristotle. He says:

> it is thought the mark of a braver man to be fearless and undisturbed in sudden alarms than to be so in those that are foreseen; for it must have proceeded more from a state of character, because less from preparation; acts that are foreseen may be chosen by calculation and rule, but sudden actions must be in accordance with one's state of character. (E.N. 1117a 18)

But bravery is a virtue, and in virtue we choose how we shall act – that is, decide upon acting after previous deliberation (cf. E.N. 1112a 15). What Aristotle does not, perhaps, always make wholly clear is how precedent deliberation may relate to a whole pattern in action, feeling etc. over a long period. The remarks I have made have tried to make this clearer (see also Sorabji 1973: 111–12).

It is crucial to this account that the second-level desire I have spoken of should be one which the agent has formed or ratified on the basis of a judgement of importance of its objective, that it should be a deliberatively rational desire. For it is certainly possible, though perhaps not all that common, that a man should have a desire directed upon sustaining the pattern in his first-order desires even although he does not really hold the objectives of those desires to merit concern. Thus, just as I considered earlier a case where we explicitly did not endorse some value to which we were yet in our feelings attached and responsive, so it could be that we reject a certain assessment of the importance of something which orders a second-level desire. For example, someone may have been brought up to be very ambitious, such that he not only has a frequent inclination to seize opportunities for advancement, but is perhaps also liable to feelings of guilt and inadequacy if he is too lazy, anxious or indecisive on various occasions to create or embrace such opportunities. His liability to guilt or self-reproach would indicate that he did not merely seek advancement as it happened that an interest in it was uppermost for a time, at other times reposing in quiet contentment with his lot untroubled about getting ahead. It would indicate that he thought that securing advancement was something more important than that, something about which he should be exercised, for he feels various kinds of self-dissatisfaction when he is not. But it surely can come to be that he thinks anxiety on this score is quite unnecessary or improper, yet for all that he is still prone to guilty and self-reproachful feelings about his lack of ambitious drive on this or that occasion.

How can we take account of this? Must we have recourse to a third level of desire here? And perhaps other levels beyond, for why could it not happen that the same lack of endorsement of a third-level concern also occurred? I think we need have no worries on this head. What gives rise to the problem is treating the person's second-level desire as constituting an assessment of the importance of something which was quite as unconsidered and unregulated as was the assessment embodied in the pattern of his first-level desires. That is, the second-level desire was, in this way of looking at the case, just as much a matter merely of the hold over a person's feelings that a certain conception of the importance of something happened to exercise as was the pattern of his first-level desires. If our desires were only ever such *de facto* attachments we happen to be possessed of, then I do not think this progressive elaboration of levels of desire could be avoided. But if we can, and do, order the nature and degree of our concern with something on the basis of a considered judgement of its importance and significance, then there is no question of coming to reject the conception of the importance of something implicitly ordering our desire in the way indicated. The ordering of our desire by this conception would not then be something which just happened to be true of us, and we could not feel estranged from it. We should have made that conception order our desires and activities as it does; it would be the very source of our considered and deliberate intent. This is what it would be decisively to 'identify ourselves' with our desire, in Frankfurt's phrase (1971: 16–17; see chap. 4, sect. ii, pp. 102–4) – for that desire not to be one which possessed us, but for it to be one we possess, either because we have deliberatively conceived it or because, given that we already possessed it, we endorsed it as fit and appropriate. In his own account, Frankfurt does not, I believe, give due place to the formation or regulation of desires by practically rational judgement. And it is in consequence of his failure to do this that he can-

173

not provide an adequate account of an agent's 'decisive identification' with his desires. On his account there remains always the possibility of 'alienation' from one's desire at whatever level.

I am not, of course, denying that one may change one's mind about the estimate of importance one places upon something. But this is an altogether different thing from finding oneself possessed of first- or second-level desires which embody a conception of the importance of something that one cannot, on reflection, accept as appropriate. In the case of a change of mind, one revises one's deliberatively achieved estimate of significance. Where one is 'alienated' from one's desire, that estimate is one which happened to have a hold over one's feelings, and one did not arrive at it or moderate it out of one's own judgement.

My concern has been to try to show what some of the manifestations are of the fact that one's passions and passional desires embody a conception of the importance of something which one endorses as appropriate, and one which is embodied by them because one believes it to be appropriate. I have argued that the thought of the pattern in one's passion being appropriate will not necessarily consist in anything one has in mind at the time when one feels a particular inclination and acts upon it. Rather it may consist in various surrounding 'supports' of that inclination and action of the kind I have tried to describe, potentialities for action and reaction which may be actualised in various exigencies but need not be present features of every occasion of action. It is proper to add to these points that one who does endorse the promptings of his passions will, most likely, be able to say, if asked, a certain amount about the significance there is to him in doing whatever it is that he does, beyond saying simply that it was just something that he felt like doing at the time. He will be able to say something about why it is that this seemed to him the thing for him to be doing, about the kind of significance so acting holds for him. Here again, though, it will not be a matter of having his reasons before his mind every time he acts. Rather, the kind of import his concern and activity have for him is something he will be ready to articulate, so far as he is capable, if the question is raised. No such elaborated structure of significance is present in the case of a mere habit of desire. This is a mere regularity in the man's concern, not the expression of a rule he makes for and in his life.

In these several points we see, I believe, something of what goes into

174

the distinction Aristotle makes between those who are 'living, and pursuing each successive object, as passion directs', and those who 'desire and act in accordance with a rational principle' (E.N. 1095a 5–11).

iv   THE MOTIVES FOR THE REGULATION OF PASSION

The issue here is in essence identical to that concerning the motive for the moderation of sense-desire, which I considered in the last chapter. It can, therefore, be given a brief discussion.

There are three cases here which need to be distinguished. First, a man may modify the estimate he makes of the importance of some good, and seek to moderate his passional attachment to that accordingly, only because it seems to him that his being so concerned with it stands in the way of other things which he feels to be more important. If there were some way in which he could secure these other things without giving up or qualifying his other interest, he would do so. He accepts the need to moderate his concern only as an unwelcome necessity. Thus if this incompatibility were removed, his prior degree of concern would return, and he would see no unfitness in this.

For example, someone may seek to moderate his temper because he finds that his irritability and outbursts estrange his friends and those upon whose support he relies. But if these unwelcome consequences did not result, he would be likely to return to his previous state, for it was not with the idea that he attached any wrong estimate as such to the importance of receiving the esteem of others that he had undertaken this moderation. Were these consequences no longer to result he would see no point in keeping a curb on his temper; and his former demandingness on others for respect would be likely to return.

A second case would be where someone seeks to moderate his temper in compliance with the demands or instructions of another, either because he is fearful of that other's disapproval, or because he accords that other some authority over him. In this case, also, the agent modifies his sense of the importance of enjoying the esteem of others in consequence of features which attach only accidentally to his making that estimate and reacting and acting accordingly, namely that it is disapproved of or required otherwise by another. And were this disapproval or demand withdrawn, there would again be, for the agent, no further

175

point in continuing to conduct himself as he had previously done, and his former pattern of assessment, response and action would be likely to re-establish itself. In both these cases, in fact, it would be more natural to suppose that no real modification of the estimate made of the importance of receiving the esteem of others takes place, but only that the manifestations of this in behaviour are checked. But even should we suppose that some such modification is made, it is only made, as I said, as an unwelcome necessity, as something the agent feels required of himself in response to features of his situation which he wishes were not present in it. He undertakes such modification only because he feels he has to, in a way under duress.

In contrast to both these cases is that where a man, out of his own assessment of the importance of the good in question as such, endeavours so to order his responsiveness and action that he gives to that good an appropriate place in the scheme of his living. In this case, since it is both his own interpretation of the significance of the good in question that results in its having that place in his life that it has; and since it is an interpretation of the significance to him of that good as such, in itself, and not by virtue of its adventitious concomitants, that results in its having that place in his life that it has; since both of these things are true, the reason for his possession and exercise of that estimate lies in himself and his understanding of its rightness, the reason for its existence comes from his own nature. And I think we can in this case say that this moderation of, for example, his proneness to anger is part of the man's 'essence', part of what makes him the man he is, because it is made and sustained out of the agent's own understanding of its fitness as an element in himself and his life. It borrows none of its hold over him from anything outside of, only accidentally connected with, the agent's attitude to, interpretation and appreciation of, the significance of this state and outside of the character of the state itself.

In this third case the agent's motive for possessing and retaining the estimate of the importance of a certain good is his sense of the value of that good as such and in itself. And in this case also we can attribute that estimate, and its hold over his life, to him as part of his own character. So it follows that, for example, even-temperedness is only properly seen as an element of a person's character when that state is present and sustained because it is believed to be good as such, because it is understood that, in possessing that state, one attributes to the relevant good, the enjoyment of the esteem of others, just the appropriate importance that should be attributed to it. In the other cases, although a man's temper may be moderate and moderated by him, its being so depends upon accidental features of the case, and so does not constitute a firm and permanently established element in his character. His so esteeming the good in question does not constitute his own choice in regard to it as it is in itself.

This is only to say, in effect, that virtues are good in themselves and must be valued by their possessor as good in themselves, and that any ulterior motive for acting in accordance with the requirements of virtue or, indeed, for moderating the passional concern relevant to the virtue, denies to the agent the real possession of that virtue. All I have tried to do is to explain why this familiar saying is a justified one.

However, if one says that in order to be, for example, a generous man, for generosity to be a part of one's character, one must believe generosity to be a good state in itself and be motivated to possess and exercise it on the basis of this belief, this may give rise to certain misunderstandings which should be guarded against. It may, for example,[6] suggest that one who acts generously does so with the thought that it is good to be generous, that his intent in acting is to see that he behaves generously, this being what he thinks he should do. This would be a misunderstanding. The intent one who is generous has in his acting as he does is to try to bring good to another; this is what a generous man is of a mind and heart to do. The specification of his motive in being generous, that this is as he thinks something good in itself, provides a specification of the respect in which his objective appears good and desirable to him, specifies this in this case as something he thinks it valuable as such to bring about. It is not as if the generous man thinks of what he is doing as being generous, even if that is something he wholeheartedly wants to be. Rather he thinks of the good of another, and wants wholeheartedly to enhance that. To say that generosity is his motive will be to say that there is nothing else he wants from his act (no return, no praise or whatever); to say that this is no merely casual or fleeting desire he had;

6 Compare Weston 1975: chap. 2, e.g. at p. 34; Wiggins 1976b: 374 n. 1: Harrison 1975: chap. 2. See also chap. 5, sect. iv, p. 147.

to say that he will not later regret having or acting upon his desire; and so on. Having such a motive in acting generously is having a steady and consistent disposition to seek the good of others, is finding in the possibility of enriching their good complete and sufficient reason for wanting to do so and for doing so, and so on. It would be an altogether different thing to think of being generous as something which was important because it enabled one to think well of oneself, or brought the praise of others. But none of this is implied by, rather it is denied by, the idea of being generous as good in itself.

One who is not yet of a consistently generous bent of heart may indeed ask himself from time to time what generosity would require from a man in a particular situation, that is, what one who was generously disposed would be apt to do. And this, providing that it is not coloured by the wish for a flattering conception of oneself or other possibly dubious concerns, is perfectly appropriate. But one who has a full and consistent generous disposition does not ask himself that question; he askes himself: 'How can I benefit this or that man?', this being the question which naturally occurs to him, and by the answer to which he is given what is, for him, a sufficient reason for doing something, an answer which is sufficient to command his assent as a reason for proceeding (cf. Scruton 1975: 154).

So, to value generosity as good in itself is not to take 'being a generous man' as one's objective in action; one does not act in order to make this description true of one, even if one's desire to make it true of one would be reason enough for one to act. It is to have as one's objective bringing good to another, but for this objective to be one's in a certain way, after a certain fashion, namely consistently, without reservation, and with an understanding of the good of this. That is what it is to have 'being generous' as one's end; it is to have what a generous disposition is a disposition to care about, that is the good of others, as one's end. Concern to possess the virtue is not a concern which interposes itself, creates a 'screen', between concern for that end with which one is concerned in one's passion, of which the virtue is a right regulation. It is to be duly and appropriately concerned with that end, for it to have a place in the structure of one's care and activity which is appropriate, known to be such, and for it to be present because it is so known.

I have already fallen to speaking of what the possession and exercise of virtues involves when I have spoken of the motive in action and for possessing certain states, of consistency of concern, of liability to regret for wanting and acting in certain ways and so on. It is, I hope, reasonable to say that the characterisation I have tried to provide of the structure and elements of a condition of passional concern, informed and ordered by right practically rational judgement, is the characterisation of that state which comprises the possession of those virtues which involve the ordering of a passional concern with or attachment to some good, such virtues as, for instance, generosity, even temper, compassion, courage and so on. In all of these there is involved a certain estimate being made of the importance of some good; in relation to generosity, the good of benefiting others; in relation to even temper, the good of receiving the esteem and regard of others; in relation to compassion, the good of relieving the suffering of others; in relation to courage, the good of avoiding danger to oneself. And these estimates govern our responsiveness to certain situations and our liability to being moved to act in certain ways. If that estimate be just then our responsiveness may be appropriate, and what we are prompted to do may be just what it would be good that we should do. In which case we may be said to possess these virtues, providing that the conditions I have explained concerning, for example, the motives for the possession and enactment of this estimate be appropriate, our responsiveness be consistent, it not occasion regret and so on.

In order to see the adequacy of the account I have presented as an account of what the possession and exercise of such virtues as these comprises, it may be useful if I summarise the salient aspects of the account so that its cogency, or lack of it, may be more plainly visible. And I shall supplement the account in two respects in which the preceding discussion has been incomplete or may have occasioned a doubt. I have laid emphasis upon the following points, many of which are closely related and interdependent:

1. One whose passions are informed by right practical judgement has a sound understanding of the true significance and importance of the ends he sets himself and of the activities he engages in.

2. This understanding forms the ultimate basis for his having the concerns he has, for his living and acting as he does; the conduct of his life embodies and enacts this understanding in its overall shape and direction and in its particularities.

3. The estimates of value which occasion the passions of such a man, and those which he makes of the purposes he is by his passion induced to pursue, are steadily and consistently informed and ordered by his understanding of the true import, significance, of these values as objects for concern.

4. He whose passions are informed by right practical judgement still acts upon his aroused desires, these forming the proximate sources of his interest and activity.

5. Such 'consented to' (see Anscombe 1968: 192) passions, and passionally prompted acts, are ways in which the agent's elected upon and chosen purposes are expressed, and do not comprise merely aspects of his passivity, aspects of his life wherein he happens to be worked upon, aroused by, features of his situation.

6. Such a man 'acts well', in that he does what he does not alone in recognition of its fitness as a thing to be done, but also with full-hearted assent to this, wholly committed in mind and feeling to his action as one consonant both to his judgement and to his desirous interest.

I hope, as I have said, that these points can be seen as adding up to an account of the structure and elements that comprise the possession and exercise of the 'virtues of passion'. There are, however, two points which may be further commented upon; the first concerning the nature of 'acting well'; the second concerning the overall rôle given in the account to the need for the understanding of the importance of ends and activities, which may seem to be exaggerated.

Concerning 'acting well', the following points may be noted. Aristotle constantly emphasises that *eupraxia*, well-doing, is the end of the virtuous man, and that this involves not just doing what one should but doing it as one should. (See Aristotle, E.N. 1139b 3; 1144a 15; and Book 2, chap. 4.) The differences between merely doing what one should, and doing what one should as one should, are not adequately captured by speaking of doing the right thing for the wrong or for the right reasons.

For it would be true to say of a self-restrained man, who curbs the prompting of some deviant desire, and is explicitly guided to do what is fit by his deliberative judgement and resolve, that he acts for the right reasons. He acts as he does precisely because he recognises this to be the right thing for him to be doing. But he does not 'act well', for his conduct does not express his passional commitment to the goodness of what he is doing, but is undertaken against a desire for something else. What the notion of acting 'for the right reasons' omits is that the 'right spirit' must also be expressed in the act if it is to be well done; the act must express a passional attachment to the good achieved in or sought through the action. The assent to the good of what he is doing comes, in the self-restrained man, only from his deliberative judgement, his passional concern being otherwise engaged. But in the virtuous man there is co-ordinate assent of judgement and passional involvement, and not fortuitous coincidence either, but deliberately sought and sustained unity in assent. In the action of the virtuous agent his self, whole and entire, finds expression; his rationality and his feelings are not divided, nor only accidentally do they carry him to the same end.

Why does well-doing matter? Why should it be of importance that a man's activity is expressive of the right spirit? It matters both to the agent himself and to those who are recipients of his activity (if it is other directed). To the agent himself in that action which is well done gives a full and unimpeded expression to all aspects of his nature, to his understanding and to his feeling concern, and he is not obliged to stifle or deny parts of his personality or nature. It matters to the recipients of his activity in that, if any passional involvement is absent, they are denied his loving concern in one respect or another, and that is to be denied a great good. To be an object of the heartfelt concern of another matters a great deal to people, contributes a great deal to their sense that they matter, have any importance, even if, for one reason or another, that concern finds little or no concrete expression in action. It adds a great deal to the sense of oneself as having any significance, making any difference, that one is an object of real care and attention to another, that one makes an impression on them, has some importance as an individual to them. If we are only the recipients of deliberatively undertaken conduct, which is possibly curbing hostility or indifference towards us, we are apt to find this in some degree hateful and unwelcome, even in spite of whatever material benefit that conduct may procure for us. The importance of enjoying someone's 'loving concern' will, of course, vary somewhat from case to case. Where one's relation to someone remains exclusively formal or 'institutional' then due conduct from them is perhaps all that one reasonably expects. In closer and more intimate relations, however, it is very often the 'meaning' of the conduct – that is, what it displays of the agent's regard and care for one – that matters very much more than what is actually done. Even here there are differences depending on the significance of the act in relation to the salient components of the relation. Merely dutiful tidying up, in a household, is (normally) less of a denial of caring than would be the merely dutiful giving of a gift. The very sense of the latter is largely subverted if the principal motive is consciousness of duty alone, the thought that this is the sort of thing one should do (particularly if this is a disagreeable thought) (see chap. 1, p. 7, above). I shall not, however, amplify these remarks here, since they concern the value of the possession and exercise of virtues, which is not my topic in this book. My concern is only to try to explain the elements and structure of the virtuous state and its expression in action, and my concern in this place with 'well-doing' is only to show how it is connected with that.

The second point I want to amplify here concerns the question of whether or not I have over-emphasised the significance of the rôle of right practical understanding in relation to the virtues of passion. I have maintained that such understanding must be possessed by the virtuous agent and that it must serve him as his ultimate reason for his concerns and activities, by ordering and regulating his passions as proximate sources of such concern and activity, as well as in many other ways. And it may be felt that such understanding serving in such a rôle really is not necessary to the possession of virtue. For if it were, would this not result in having to deny virtue of many who we would ordinarily think do possess it, for it really would not be plausible to ascribe to them 'a true and reasoned state of capacity to act with regard to the things that are good or bad for man' (E.N. 1140b 5; see also 1140b 20; 1141b 13). Such a 'true and reasoned state' may be possessed by some, a practically wise élite, but appears not to be essential to virtue.

We may see the justice, or otherwise, in this objection by looking at some of the contrasts there are between what Aristotle calls 'natural' virtue and virtue 'in the strict sense' (E.N. 1144b 8; and Book 6, chap. 13 *passim*, esp. 1144b 26–30. See also chap. 1, sect. i, and p. 11, above). It is not, of course, absolutely clear what we should understand by 'natural' virtue, either in Aristotle or in general. It is a term of art without a firmly established sense. I propose to understand by it the following. Someone possesses natural virtue, or possesses a virtue 'naturally', if the direction, frequency, intensity, persistence and occasions of his passional responsiveness embody his giving to a certain good just that degree of concern which is *in fact* appropriate to its importance. He does not, however, have any views as to its appropriateness; and, perforce, he does not have the responsiveness that he has on the ground that it would be the appropriate kind and degree of concern to have.

Now, it seems to me that someone may indeed possess natural virtue in this sense (see Dent 1974: 568; Winch 1972). And that he should is something we value. However, it should equally be clear why I do not think that we can, in this case, say of him that he is truly or fully virtuous, or virtuous 'in the strict sense'. For his state is precisely that discussed in section iii above, wherein someone acts merely 'as the mood takes him', without any recognition of the claim upon him of so acting as something that requires his concern and has an importance beyond how he happens to feel disposed at the moment. And I have discussed the reasons for finding such a state wanting as a state supposed to constitute what it is to possess and enact a virtuous state of character.

It is true that when such a man is possessed of a certain passional concern at a particular moment he will think it is important to do something or achieve something. And, *ex hypothesi*, such a thought of his will be the correct one. So, it may be said, he acts in recognition of the importance of so doing, he is mindful of the claim upon him of so acting. But this is to distort the character of the case. His attributing this importance to what he does is in consequence of, part of the expression of, his passional response; it is a 'product' of that, and not a determinant of it. His sense of the importance of the end is nothing more than a manifestation of the degree and extent of his passional involvement with it; and if that changes or goes so will his sense of the importance of the end change or go. That sense has no hold upon him over and above how it happens that his concern is elicited at a particular time. It plays no rôle in ordering his response; it is just a partial expression of that response. So it

183

would be quite wrong to say that here, too, we have an understanding of the value of something being recognised and acknowledged. A judgement of the importance of doing something is being made; but its being made is the result of the passional response, and it remains only so long as the response remains, and it is not a foundation for that. This point came up earlier, also.

On the other hand, the sense that the requirement that understanding be possessed and ground the response made is over-stringent may be allayed if it is properly appreciated what this requirement really involves. It does not necessarily involve a fully articulate, worked out and rationally impregnable 'scheme of values', though it does not preclude that (if such a thing be completely possessable). It need involve little more by way of understanding than that there is something here of material concern which calls for more of a response than the accidental elicitation of interest would afford to it. And it need involve little more by way of ordering one's conduct than the readiness to do something more than one would do if one simply acted at the prompting of aroused interest, and less than total indifference to the fact that sometimes one's concern may fail to be caught and prompt one to act. Such a degree of understanding, and self-regulation in the light of such understanding, is hardly uncommon nor the preserve of an élite; on the contrary, its complete absence would be the rarer thing. Few are so little mindful of the shape their lives should take that this degree of self-direction is not to be found. Of course, more than this can be found; and, if it is, one could expect the shape of a person's life to be more fully and completely responsive to a greater range of things that matter, and in due measure responsive to these, more fully and completely appropriately to bear the mark of, and to embody concern with, these. I made similar points to these in chapter 4. I hope that their relevance to the understanding of the nature of the virtuous state can now be appreciated.

In the effort to bring out the importance of the possession and ordering rôle of practical understanding it is, perhaps, inevitable that one should seem to present that as a more fully conscious and explicit matter than it is. But this is an impression given by the necessities of the account; and I hope these necessities are now seen not to be necessities in the actual facts of the case (cf. Anscombe 1965: 144, 148–50. See chap. 4, sect. iii, and p. 109, above).

In chapter 1 section ii, I emphasised that there were differences between, for example, a conscientious concern to benefit others and the virtues of, for example, generosity or kindness. And I adverted again to such differences in the previous section here when contrasting acting 'for the right reasons' and 'in the right spirit'. In this concluding section I want to consider the virtue of conscientiousness more fully (for virtue it is) to see just how it is like, and how different, from the virtues of passion just considered, and to see what scope and significance it has in relation to these other virtues.

Conscientiousness is a steady and consistent willingness to do one's duty just because it is one's duty, to do what is required of one for no other reason than that it is required of one. If my prior arguments have been correct, then the virtues of passion, and of sense-desire, must all include an aspect of conscientiousness in them. For, I have claimed, they all involve their possessor in recognising that something is required of his concern and activity, and in ordering his concern and activity ultimately by reference to this recognition. If that is absent then someone will, for instance, simply not help those in need when he is not moved by their plight, not feel any compunction at his lack of concern, and so on. I do not think we can say he has the virtue of kindness even when he does respond, if this is the overall nature, context, of his response. To have that virtue, one's response must be regulated by the appreciation that, in the needs of others, there is something that befits one's concern, in the way I have examined at length. One who possesses the virtue of kindness sees the need of others as something that rightly commands his interest and action (cf. MacLagan 1960: 206, 216, and *passim*. See p. 169, above).

However we do not, and rightly do not, equate kindness with conscientiousness; nor generosity, even-temperedness, courage etc. with conscientiousness, even although there is also in these cases the recognition and answering of something seen as being required of one. In these cases, there is a passional concern, a spontaneity of involved responsiveness, which is quite central to the agent's activity. And we think of conscientiousness as being what someone's conduct exhibits when it is the thought that he would be doing something required of him which is what alone, or principally, provides him with the incentive to undertake that. This is not the case when someone is moved by pity or generous feelings to his action even although there is, in the background of his feelings and action, the conception of what he is doing as right and requisite. The primary incentive to action in these cases still comes from the agent's aroused and committed feelings. There is also a further contrast here. As I remarked above, conscientiousness is principally a disposition to do one's *duty*; and one's duties are only a sub-class of those actions which it is fitting that one should perform. One's duties comprise those actions which can rightly be asked or demanded of one by another, for one reason or another. Whereas even if it be true that one should perform generous acts, and indeed that one should be generous, we do not normally think of these as things a particular other, or others, can properly demand of one as due to them. In generosity one gives 'over and above the call of duty', does more than one owes it to others that one should do, in the sense of fulfilling a requirement they can fitly enforce. Of course, the distinction is not a hard and fast one, and the scope of 'duty', even in this 'stringent' sense, is capable of expansion. But that there is a distinction of this general kind is clear enough, and conscientiousness is typically associated only with one side of it. (On 'wide' and 'narrow' senses of 'duty', see Whiteley 1952; MacIntyre 1971; Mill, *Utilitarianism*, chap. 5.)

So, for these two reasons at least, conscientiousness is not identical with, nor co-extensive with, the whole of virtue, even if there is an aspect of the conscientious in every virtue. Now, the fact that conscientiousness is a disposition to act grounded solely, or principally, in the recognition that something is required of one, displays it as a quality that someone can only possess when he has come to be able to appreciate the importance of various ends and activities, and it constitutes a form of direct and explicit governance of oneself by such appreciation. Conscientiousness, one might say, is *the* virtue of practical rationality in conduct, that disposition of oneself which explicitly declares one's rational and deliberate adherence to some purpose. And that is why one neither looks for, nor finds, conscientiousness in children; for they have as yet little understanding of, let alone capacity to govern themselves by, the reasons for or against certain undertakings, but act only as they are moved. With the growth of the capacity for rational self-determination

186

comes the growth of the capacity for conscientious concern and conduct; these are two descriptions of the same facts.

It should not be inferred from this that we need to be primarily conscientious only when we have some deviant passional concern we need to check. We shall, indeed, need to be conscientious in our conduct in such cases if we are to act rightly. But in such cases we are exhibiting self-restraint; and although the capacity and disposition to self-restraint is a signal exhibition of our conscientious mindfulness and intent, it would be a mistake to suppose that all cases of conscientiousness in conduct are cases of self-restraint over our feelings. We can be conscientious, and shall importantly need to be, when there are objectives which properly befit our recognition but which do not elicit a passional concern from us, either when they should or, most crucially, when they are such that there are no passional concerns of a relevant nature to concern us with these matters in the ordinary course of things. I shall return to this latter point when I discuss justice, below.

Thus, the relation of conscientiousness to the other virtues is that it is the expression of practical rationality *alone* directing our concern and action; whereas, in their case, that rationality is embodied and expressed through the order and direction of our passional desires and interests. And even when it takes into consideration various desiderata which are not connected with any passional concern, this is not necessarily to restrict or curb the concerns proper to our passions. For, as I have argued, it is requisite to the possession of any virtue of passion that a just estimate of the good that passion interests us in be made, and our passional concern be ordered by this. Arriving at such a just estimate will involve taking into account not merely those other goods which *are* objects of passional concern to us, but others which are not, to which we can give weight only through our conscientious attention to them. But when this is done, the weight attached to that good which is the objective of any particular passion will reflect one's conscientious weighting of other goods; thus one will not attribute an importance to the objective which is discordant with one's solely conscientious concerns but one which 'meshes' with them, fits in consistently with them. So there will be no inbuilt tendency for conscientiousness to check or regulate one's other virtuous inclinations as if these were dispositions which are apt to direct one in conflicting directions. It is true that this account perhaps overweights the idea of the virtues forming a unity, is overly sanguine that there can be a single, consistent, ordering in our concerns overall which no contingencies will severely strain.[7] But, equally, the idea that conscientiousness always serves to check the generous or kindly impulse, in the name of some other value not already recognised in relation to the importance we attach to generosity or kindness, is a caricature. Some real compatibility and integration of relevant valuations is possible here.

The most important element of our conduct which depends fundamentally upon our conscientious disposition is our just action, that is our rendering to others what is their due, what is owed in natural or conventional justice to them by us. It is perfectly true that other virtuous dispositions than justice will make us more ready to render to each his due, and other vicious dispositions much less ready. Out of benevolence, friendship or generosity we would never render to someone who was the object of these concerns less than his due. But it is not incompatible with the possession of any of these virtues that one is benevolent, friendly and generous towards only a few men, not all, and these as accidents of relationship and circumstance dictate. One does not cease to count as benevolent if one's benevolence is not universal and equal for all. But justice requires the rendering of what is due to each and every man alike, whether he be friend or stranger, fellow countryman or foreigner, and so on. It is not simply a matter of the requirement to render to each his due not being conditional upon our feeling a certain way towards this or that man. For this is also true of the requirement to be mindful of the good of others which we acknowledge in our benevolence or generosity; this is not seen as something which has no importance if we fail to be moved to benefit others. It is rather that, in justice, we are required to have a kind of concern for all other men; whereas in benevolence or generosity, though these may perhaps be of wide scope, this is not essential. They can be, quite properly, confined to a few, but justice cannot be thus confined. One's concern with the improvement of the lot of others is not deviant just because one is not concerned alike to

7 See Mill, *Utilitarianism*, 320–1; Hampshire 1977: sect. 10; Sorabji 1973: 114–15; Lovelace: 'To Lucasta – Going to the Warres': 'Yet this Inconstancy is such,/As you too shall adore;/I could not love thee (Deare) so much,/Lov'd I not Honour more.'

188

improve the lot of all others to the same extent. But one's acknowledgement of the due of others would be deviant if one were not concerned with that due as it is owed to each and every man in whatever measure it is owed. (I discuss this issue further, in the context of a treatment of Plato's views on justice, in Dent 1983.)

There is no one particular passional concern of which the virtue of justice constitutes the due regulation and moderation. It rather requires the regulation of all those dispositions which would render us liable to fail duly to acknowledge what we owe to others in such a way that they do not obstruct our just intent, at least to the extent to which it is important that we should not fail to act justly. (The requirement that one act justly may, or may not, always be an over-riding requirement; I am not concerned to consider this matter here.) We may fail to act justly not only because we are mean or malicious, but also because of our benevolence or generosity which, as we have just seen, may be partial as between men and unless 'supplemented', so to say, by a concern to render to every man his due, could lead to the well-being of some being procured at the cost of others (cf. Butler, *Dissertation*, Paras. 8, 10).

That 'supplementary' concern comes from a deliberate willingness to acknowledge this due and is not a matter of assigning the right importance to one good that we may be concerned with in our passions in relation to others.

There is another way of bringing out the fact that justice is a right disposition in deliberative intent as such, by contrast with the other virtues which are the right ordering of particular passions. This emerges if we consider, on the one hand, the relationship between the possession of the virtue of justice and the performance or omission of certain specific actions, and, on the other hand, the relationship between such virtues as temperance or generosity and the performance or omission of certain specific actions (I discuss this fully in Dent: 1975. See also chap. 1, sect. iv, above). It is true that certain kinds of behaviour are typical of temperance or intemperance, generosity or meanness. But we know what these are because they are the sort of actions which would be apt to be done by one who had a right (or wrong) desire of sense-pleasure, or one who had a right (or wrong) degree of concern for the well-being of others. And the knowing and deliberate performance of an act typical of excessive desire of sense-pleasure, for example getting drunk, does not automatically show that the agent had, there and then, an immoderate desire upon which he acted, let alone show that he is overall of an intemperate character. For he may have got drunk to keep a friend company, and not at all out of an excessive desire of the delights of intoxication. So the omission of such acts is not necessary to temperance; nor is their knowing and deliberate performance sufficient to show even the occasional intemperate desire. There are no exact performances or omissions in action prescribed by the requirement to be temperate. What that requirement demands is that we do not desire the pleasures of sense to excess, and what we do may be typical of such excessive desire, may be just the sort of thing one who had excessive desire would do, but yet not, in this case, have been thus motivated. And what is true of temperance and intemperance in relation to action and omission is true equally of all virtues which require essentially the right ordering of our concerns, the right directing of our desire and interest. In all these cases, what is done is at most 'symptomatic' or, in Hume's words, is 'signs or indications', of the state of our desires and does not decisively establish, let alone constitute, their being rightly or wrongly disposed (*Treatise*, Book 3, pt 2, sect. 1, 477; also Book 3, pt 2, sect. 6, 530).

In the case of justice, by contrast, the deliberate and knowing performance or omission of certain activities does decisively establish at least the *in*justice of the agent. (It may not establish the justice of the agent, because he may have acted for the wrong reasons; but the contrast over injustice is sufficient for the case.) This is because doing certain acts is *constitutive* of injustice, and we need inquire no further into the operative motivation of the agent on the occasion to establish that he is unjust (see Anscombe 1968: 204–6). If we do inquire further we may discover other vices, or even (partly) good dispositions. But no such inquiry is needed to determine the agent's injustice, to determine that he is, in some respects at any rate, an unjust man. For instance, one who knowingly and deliberately bears false witness against another has, by that act alone, shown himself to be unjust, for he has failed to render another what was due to them from him precisely by doing that. His injustice is comprised in his knowingly and deliberately doing what he did. He cannot plead in his defence that he really does have proper concern to render what is due to others, and that his action, though typical of one who lacks such

190

concern, was not demonstrative of that on his part in this case. It *is* demonstrative of that, because to lack proper concern to render what is due to others is partly constituted by doing just what he did, along with many other things. We have the notion of 'committing an injustice', but no notion of 'committing an intemperance' or an ill-temperedness or whatever. And this shows that 'injustice' can consist solely in committing a certain deed, doing something specific, whereas committing a certain deed never as such constitutes being intemperate or ill-tempered but is only ever symptomatic of that. For these states are essentially comprised in the nature of the agent's desire; whereas to establish that a man has committed an injustice, and is, in one respect at any rate, unjust we do not need to inquire into the character of his desires.

That to be unjust need involve no more than certain acts or failures to act is very obvious when to render another his due requires acknowledging the particular terms of a contract or the requirements of a particular position. In these cases it is often quite determinately specified what we must do to fulfil the demands upon us, and any knowing and deliberate failure in performance is a failure to render what is due, hence a failure to be heedful of what is due and hence a failure in justice. In these cases also it would be absurd to suppose that any moderation in direction and intensity of desire could lead us to do just these or those highly determinate acts like, for example, paying a bill on a certain day or writing a reference (if we have promised to do so). To undertake these we must understand, and act upon the basis of, the fact that they are particularly required of us. To act thus requires the exercise of our deliberate intent as such (cf. Laird 1946: 118).

It is in recognition of this sort of point that Aquinas calls justice a virtue of the 'will', of deliberative practical purposing as such, in contrast with the virtues of our 'concupiscible' or 'irascible' powers.[8] Other philosophers also have recognised that justice stands in a special position in relation to the other virtues. It is, I think, plausible to suppose that it was because he saw that no regulation of desire alone could be sufficient for rendering to each and every man what was his due in (natural) justice that Kant located true moral worth in the exercise of pure practical

8 See, for example, *Summa Theologiae*, 1a 2ae, Q 59, Article 5; Q 60, Articles 2, 3; and elsewhere.

reason in accordance with universal law.[9] Respect for others, which Kant reckoned the highest practible good, cannot be dependent upon the regulation of desirous concerns for others alone, as we have seen, but requires deliberate acknowledgement of what is due to them. Also, the special place Hume gives to justice, at least in the *Treatise*, is in response to the point that there is no 'natural motive' adequate to doing those things required of one by justice (*Treatise*, Book 3, pt 2, sect. 1, esp. 483).

None of the points I have made about justice being an expression of pure conscientiousness implies either that justice is, or is not, the most important virtue. This is a matter which falls outside the scope of this discussion. All I have tried to explain is how such a solely conscientious concern is like and different from the concerns we have in the other virtues and how it relates to those. Whether that conscientiousness displayed in justice should always and everywhere be paramount is a different matter.

This completes my discussion of the ways in which our passional concerns may be ordered by our practically rational judgement. In the next chapter, I want to consider how the possession of passional concerns, and of sense-desire, affects the employment of our practical rationality. I want, that is, to look at the way these affect our practical rationality, rather than vice versa as I have been doing in the last two chapters.

9 See Kant, *Groundwork*, 393–4, contrasting 'the good will' with talents, qualities of temperament etc. Also Baier 1970: 29.

7

Desire and practical reason

i MORAL VIRTUE AND PRACTICAL WISDOM

In the last two chapters I have been concentrating upon how our sense- and passional desires may be moderated and ordered by our practically rational judgement and intent. And that is, indeed, their proper order or priority;[1] by our practically rational judgement and determination we endeavour to give to our life that shape and direction we think it best it should possess, one which it would not, save by chance, assume if we simply acted as and when we were prompted to do by our aroused desires. However, as I have tried to show, the endeavour to give our lives this shape and direction is not an endeavour which proceeds entirely separately from, nor necessarily in opposition to, the purposes which engage us out of our sense- and passional desires. It is an endeavour which can be, in good part, carried through the motivation that such desires provide; they can come to embody and enact our deliberatively adopted concerns precisely because we have so ordered them that they direct us to what is appropriate, in the appropriate way, with the appropriate degree of concern, and so on. Further to this, many of those purposes we come to accept as important constituents of a satis- factorily conducted life are purposes which originally held an import- ance for us as being the objectives of our aroused desires. It is, so to speak, from the teaching of such desires that we can learn how signifi- cant and material such matters are. And, perhaps, in some cases had we not had any such original concern for them we should never have come at all fully to appreciate their significance out of our reflective con- sideration alone.

So this priority of rational self-determination over direction by sense-

---

1 Compare Aristotle, *Politics*, 1254b 5ff. He writes: '. . . intellect governs the appetites as a states- man or a king . . . the . . . dominion . . . of the intellect or rational element over the passionate, (is) evidently natural and expedient, whereas the equality of the two or a reversal of their roles is always harmful'.

desire and passional desire does not amount to any kind of total or complete denial or extinction of such desires. On occasions, however, this priority is in various ways subverted, and the attempted governance of ourselves by our rational judgement is unsuccessful. In this chapter I want to consider some of the ways in which this can occur, as the result of our sense- and passional desires coming to occupy a place in the ordering of our lives which obstructs or deforms the ordering of our conduct by our practical rationality.

I shall begin with a consideration of Aristotle's repeated contention that a man cannot possess practical wisdom – excellence in deliberative understanding and action ('a true and reasoned state of capacity to act with regard to the things that are good or bad for man' (E.N. 1140b 5)), without possessing moral virtue – rightness of desire for the things that befit a man's pursuit (see also E.N. 1140b 17–20; 1144a 30–36; 1144b 30–1145a 5). This claim is often misunderstood, even to the extent of its being said that reasoned understanding makes no contribution to determining the ends of a virtuous man's life nor to the nature of his concern for them, and that these ends are simply established by his desires (this is discussed by Allan 1953; 1955; Sorabji 1973; Wiggins 1976a). But we can, I think, make better sense of the view than this.

Why then might it be that one could not have a reasoned and true state of capacity to act with regard to human goods without a right measure in one's desire for such goods?[2] There are many reasons for saying this, which we may take in order of increasing complexity. First, if a man's desires are altogether disorderly, such that he is subject to intense, dominant, cravings or aversions, he may lose the capacity for deliberative assessment of the appropriateness of his desire and action altogether, and hence, perforce, have no scope to guide himself by his deliberations (see Aristotle, E.N. 1119b 7–11; 1149b 35). He is so totally absorbed by, taken over by, his present desire that he can think of nothing else but that which is its objective. In this case, quite obviously, a man cannot possess practical wisdom; at least this extremity in desire must be absent. This has been discussed before.

Secondly, if a man's desires are disorderly, but not so extremely, he

2 It is perhaps odd that Aristotle should speak of a 'capacity', rather than of a 'disposition', to act here. But his sense is perfectly clear from the remarks that follow E.N. 1140b 21.

may be capable of deliberating, and correctly, about what he should best do, but he may not be able to carry out his deliberatively decided upon purpose. But practical wisdom is a capacity to *act* upon our reasoned and true understanding, so it is absent if this is the situation. This sort of case is usually described as one where the agent exhibits weakness of will, or acts incontinently; and I shall consider it further in section ii, below.

Thirdly, it may be that the agent deliberates, deliberates correctly and carries out his deliberatively decided upon purpose. But if in order to do so he has had to suppress some contrary inclination which makes him resistant or reluctant to do this thing, then no passional desire is expressed in his action and he has not acted well. For although he has done the right thing he has not done it in the right spirit, with full-hearted consent to the action. But practical wisdom has acting well as its end, so in this case, also, it cannot be possessed. In this case we have self-restrained or continent action, which again has been discussed before. For practical wisdom to be possessed the concurrence of practical judgement and passional concern in the action must be exhibited. And thus again the need for rightness in desire to having practical wisdom is seen.

Fourthly, and most important, we must look at the point that Aristotle makes that disorderly desire 'causes us to be deceived about the starting-points of action', that is about 'the end, i.e. what is best (being) of such and such a nature' (E.N. 1144a 32–36). The thought here seems to be that if, in desire, we are concerned with what is no good, or overly concerned with something that is good, we shall be unable to arrive at a reasoned and true understanding of what are the best ends of action, let alone be unable to enact this understanding in our lives in the proper way. Often, Aristotle says that the error is due to 'pleasure', and I shall return to that claim (E.N. 1113a 35; 1140b 17). This is the subtlest of deformations to which practical reason is subject owing to the effects of inappropriate desire, for in this case it is the actual deliberative assessment that is distorted and not only the translation of the deliberative purpose into action. How, then, is the case to be made out?

I have argued, in chapter 4, that a major element of our practical rationality consists in formulating a conception of what would be the best shape and direction our life should take, into which conception we shall incorporate many goods with some sense of their relative priority or importance to us as components of our lives. Now, if it is to be possible to do this, we must enjoy some degree of detachment from the purposes which our passions at the time suggest or demand we undertake. For, while we are subject to those passions, we shall be seized with the idea that their objectives have this or that importance to us, and be unable to come to a stable or secure sense of their overall significance relative to our other concerns in the shape of our lives in general. If we are subject to a disorderly, a misplaced, passion, it can be that we are for a time so firmly possessed of the idea that some state of affairs is crucially and decisively important to us that we cannot bear the idea of not trying to bring it about. Thus any picture we might try to formulate of the relative importance of this purpose to any others we might have would be out of true, since this idea claims an overly large place in our 'scheme of things'. So long as we continue to be under the influence of the passion, that long will the idea that something is importantly to be done continue to return and occupy our attention. And if the passion be a misplaced one, that idea will be a mistaken one. So when, in deliberation, we are faced with trying to reach a just assessment of the importance of these matters we shall find ourselves faced with an entrenched, constantly reiterated, but mistaken opinion on the value of one or some of them. And it will be extremely difficult in such a case to come to appreciate that this opinion is mistaken, to give it no place or weight, or a reduced weight, in one's deliberative reflections. Instead, one is likely to assign to other things a lesser importance in relation to it. But when this happens practical rationality is corrupted in that we have given our assent to the value of something not after a duly balanced appreciation of its importance in relation to other matters which have a significance to us, but just because it exerts such an insistent hold upon us through the effect of our passions. Reason thus becomes the slave of the passions, not because it is inevitably always so, but because, in this case, the importance that something has to us is settled by our passional attachment to it and not by our reflective appraisal of it.

Thus to be able to possess a true and reasoned understanding of what we should best do, we need to be (at least relatively) free of distorted emphases on the importance of various matters which come out of wrong passions. If we are not, we shall simply 'capitulate' before the suggestions of value our desires put to us and we shall fail in our endeavour to assess the true soundness of these suggestions. Our conception of what we should best do would then be only 'propaganda' for the valuations our passions present to us and would no longer represent a rule for their ordering. Our ideas about how best to live our lives would simply echo our dominant or uppermost feelings, and if these were misplaced so then would our ideas be misconceived.

I remarked earlier that Aristotle suggests at various places that this kind of error in rational judgement is often due to wrong pleasure, finding pleasure in the wrong things, to the wrong extent, etc. There are two strands to this thought, which need to be separated. If Aristotle has in mind what I called, in chapter 3, the 'celebratory' pleasure or delight we feel at securing what we desire in passion, then that pleasure will be wrong if what we desire is wrong. Wrong pleasure, in this case, would just be a token of a wrong valuation being made, and thus to have practical reason corrupted by wrong pleasure and to have it corrupted by wrong desire would come to the same thing.

If, however, we think of the desire of sense, or bodily, pleasure this need not, as I argued, depend upon any valuation being made of the good to us of enjoying that pleasure. Sense-desire, I maintained, is good-independent. In this case 'wrong pleasure' would, presumably, be excessive (or, less likely, defective) enjoyment of bodily pleasure, which argues to an excessive desire for such pleasure. But since the excess of such desire does not involve making a misplaced valuation, how can excessive sense-desire lead to a distortion of practically rational judgement of the kind we have just been looking at? It seems not to involve being caused to make the kinds of judgement which could result in a deformation occurring.

What I conjecture may happen in this case is this. Just because we are creatures who wish to make our lives take a certain shape and direction, we shall be inclined to rationalise an act – to invent an adequate pretext for having undertaken it and to pretend that we undertook it for good reasons – in cases where, in actual fact, there was no such pretext and we did not act for good reasons or upon reasons at all, but simply as prompted by desire. By this we shall be able, so to say, to reconcile ourselves to our behaviour, to present it to ourselves (and to others) as behaviour which was as we intended it should be, which embodied our preferred conception of how our lives should be led. We incorporate it into our designed scheme of life. But, of course, if a man does so rationalise an act in which he pursues a wrong sense-pleasure, he deforms his practical judgement by making it, after the event, produce a case for doing something, a case which had nothing actually to do with bringing it about that he did what he did. Practical judgement is made to fit the demands of appetite, instead of vice versa.

Thus, I suggest, if we are possessed of a strong and persistent desire of sense-pleasure, if we desire such pleasure wrongly, we shall be apt to persuade ourselves that that degree of desire is appropriate just so that we can make a satisfactory picture to ourselves of our life having the shape and order we would wish it to have. So in this case also, though for rather different reasons, wrong pleasure can give rise to a deformation in our understanding of how best to live our lives, even although it is not a case of being dominated by a misplaced valuation. I am not suggesting that Aristotle had anything like this in mind; it is by no means certain that he would distinguish the two kinds of 'wrong pleasure' that I have. But we have seen how, on both accounts of what this involves, a distortion of judgement about what the best ends for action are can take place.

We may understand the actions of an agent who has the power to deliberate and act on reasons as, in effect, being an answer to a question he has put to himself, the question 'What shall I do?', which invites consideration of what there is reason to do and the determination to carry that out (see Plato's introduction of this idea, *Republic*, 437c). However, not every act we perform is performed after such consideration either on the particular occasion or at some earlier time. When this is so, there will be an inducement to reconstruct the history of the origin of the action so that it can be seen by the agent as being a satisfactory answer to the question. By so doing the agent preserves the sense of himself as rational agent, heedful of and governed by good reason. But when the act is undertaken on the impulse of wrong desire the price of preserving this sense is a deformation and degradation of his practical rationality, amounting even to self-deception. It becomes the tool of desire, accommodating itself to its demands, rather than that which commands and directs the occurrence and effects of such desire. And one of whom this is true is evidently without practical wisdom.

Thus I think we can make real sense of the idea of practical rationality being deformed by wrong desire without having to say that the wrongness in judgement is nothing other than a wrongness in desire, without having to say that these just come to the same thing. It is because, on the one hand, passions incorporate valuations, estimates of the importance of things; and because, on the other hand, practical reason is concerned to reach a true and considered assessment of these matters, that there is a real inter-relation between these, whether of an appropriate or inappropriate kind. Once we leave behind once for all the idea of these as 'faculties' altogether different in kind, sharing no common features, we are enabled to see properly how they can and do interact.

We may briefly look now at the converse claim, which Aristotle also makes, that there can be no moral virtue without practical wisdom. We have, in fact, considered aspects of this before, so there is no cause to linger on the point.[3] In Book 2 of the *Ethics*, when Aristotle sets out to discuss the general character of moral virtues, he makes clear that he is discussing them without reference to the 'right rule' of virtuous action (E.N. 1103b 32; see 1138b 20). When he takes up this matter again in Book 6 (E.N. 1138b 20ff), he makes a number of points about its relation to moral virtue. First, he distinguishes 'natural' virtue from virtue 'in the strict sense', the former not implying the possession and employment of practical wisdom in the direction of desire and action (E.N. Book 6, chaps. 12–13). By the possession of natural virtue we do, indeed, desire what we should, in the degree we should, but not in consequence of our having and using a reasoned and true understanding of the importance of what we desire. Further, he considers the possibility of a man who acts rightly, but only under the direction of another (E.N. 1143b 31). Such a man lacks moral virtue since he does not understand for himself the rightness of the principle of action and, because he sees it to be right, so acts upon it. To have virtue 'in the strict sense' one must recognise oneself what befits one's doing and why it does, and out of this recognition set upon the doing of it. One must be a carrier of moral understanding and not just one who follows the path marked out for one by others, though this will be in its way good.

3 This was discussed in chapter 6 when treating of the likenesses and differences between 'natural virtue', which does not involve practical wisdom, and 'strict virtue', which does. See chap. 6, sect. v, and p. 183.

We see that Aristotle is not here involved in a vicious circularity in the claims that practical wisdom requires moral virtue and that moral virtue requires practical wisdom. The 'moral virtue' requisite to come to possess practical wisdom is a rightness of desire that accords to the requirements of the right rule, which may be present either as 'natural virtue' or because one lives under the rule of another who has wisdom. My earlier statement about what we were to understand by moral virtue in that case deliberately implied no more than this. If the 'moral virtue' Aristotle had had in mind were virtue 'in the strict sense', that is a state which 'implies the *presence* of the right rule' (E.N. 1144b 26) informing and ordering desire and action, then clearly his claim would be circular. For to say one could not possess practical wisdom without moral virtue would be to say that one could not possess practical wisdom without possessing a state to have which requires practical wisdom. And this would be empty. It might just be possible that the thought is that moral virtue, in the strict sense, and practical wisdom grow up together, so that at no time will the latter be improperly presupposed in the characterisation of the former. Rather the progressive acquisition of moral virtue would be at one and the same time the progressive acquisition of greater practical wisdom. And then the insistence that practical wisdom required moral virtue would only be the insistence that there was more to being practically wise than right understanding of good and evil alone; there is also the need for this to be embodied in the right control and direction of desires which are not solely 'creatures of the understanding'. This is the point Aristotle makes against Socrates (E.N. 1144b 16ff), and is perfectly just. But whether or not this view could be worked out, it seems to me that Aristotle had something more in mind, which I have tried to explain.

On the other hand when Aristotle says that moral virtue requires practical wisdom, he is no longer thinking of 'natural virtue' or action undertaken under wise instruction, but now of virtue 'in the strict sense'. Thus I think his claims are perfectly consistent and, indeed, they can be seen to be correct.

I want now to return to some points made earlier when I spoke of the way wrong desire did not impede or deform the process of right practical judgement, but impeded or deformed the issuing of that judgement in deliberate action. This is where we exercise, or fail in our exercise of, self-restraint; and it is to aspects of the nature of these states I want now to look, under their philosophically accepted names of continence and incontinence.

ii   CONTINENCE AND INCONTINENCE

I have said a good deal already in various places about the nature of continent and incontinent states and actions, so I shall not here give any general restatement of their salient characteristics. I shall devote the bulk of my discussion to the question of how incontinent action is possible, how it is possible to fail in the exercise of one's self-restraint. And I shall move on from that issue to consider two further issues to which this forms a good preliminary, namely the issue of the kinds and degrees of freedom men enjoy in the various states of character I have been discussing; and the issue of what comprises a man's 'true self'. Although these topics seem, at first sight, quite unconnected, I shall hope to show that there is a natural continuity between them.

Aristotle contends that, strictly speaking, the sphere of continence and incontinence is principally the control of desire for bodily pleasure, and secondarily the control of anger, particularly angry impetuosity (E.N. 1147b 24ff; 1150b 20ff). He allows an extended use for the terms, where we speak of continence, or more usually of incontinence, 'in respect of . . .' for example, (love of) honour (E.N. 1147b 33; 1148a 29ff); but 'continence' and 'incontinence' used unqualifiedly have for their province of application a man's control of or failure in controlling his appetite for bodily pleasure and angry hastiness. I shall make no such restriction of use. I shall be concerned quite generally with cases where a man does not enact his considered judgement of what he should best be doing, whatever the nature of the temptation or impulse that results in this. Also I shall consider only cases where the judgement which is not acted upon is a just or sound one. Cases where this is unsound and then incontinence leads, by a happy chance, to the right thing being done (though not, of course, to its being 'done well' because, in this case, it does not receive the assent of understanding) raise no special problems (E.N. 1146a 19; 1151b 17–22). Now, in classical and modern times, it has been deemed that incontinent action is impossible, that there cannot be anything which fits the specification of that notion. And I want to look at some of the things that might be involved here, particularly with a view to uncovering more of the ways in which there may be faults in the relations between our desiring and practically rational powers. I intend no exhaustive discussion, which would have to cover a very wide range of cases and considerations; I shall rather focus on only a few possibilities and examine some of their implications.

What are we to understand as being a case, at least a *prima facie* case, of incontinent action? We must determine this first of all before discussing the possibility of such action; for it would be to no avail to prove the possibility (or impossibility) of something that was not even *prima facie* incontinent action. It is, I dare say, true to contend that there is a wide variety of cases which fall under the general heads of 'moral weakness', 'weakness of will', 'being unfaithful to your convictions', 'backsliding' etc; and that no one account will do for all of these (see, e.g., Matthews 1966). It is important to remember the range of possibilities here. But it is the possibility of one state of affairs which is fairly specific that produces the greatest dispute, which may be described thus: a man voluntarily, and in full present knowledge of what he is doing, does not do that which he sincerely believes, and with full present consciousness of that belief, to be the best thing all in all for him to be doing at that particular time. Can this situation obtain? Or does the description of it include an inconsistency (or several), a contradiction in terms? Will a man's failure to enact his considered judgement of what he should best be doing be bound to be a case of one or some of: an involuntary act; of his doing something he didn't fully realise that he was doing; of a case of this not being a sincere judgement; of his having secret reservations; of his making a general judgement but excepting the present case; and so on?

Of course, many of the terms used in the specification of the case are vague; and some threaten collapse of its description into obvious contradiction. For example: if a man does not act according to his considered judgement it may be said that that fact *alone* proves that his knowledge of what he was doing wasn't 'full'; or said that that fact alone proves that his judgement wasn't 'really' sincere. But the case cannot be decided that easily. It is, indeed, a logical issue we are concerned with, not the empirical question of how good men are at carrying through their deliberated intentions in the face of contrary inducements. But the

202

contradiction in the terms of this description – if there is one – must have a deeper basis than this, be dependent upon deep-going conceptual links and not be derived from the special use of qualifying adjectives ('full', 'real' etc.) if there is to be anything serious to debate here (cf. Bennett 1966: 42).

With at least apparently the same case in view people differ radically in the response they make to it. Some contend it is not only possible for a man so to behave but that it frequently happens; others that the case as described is inconsistently described so logically impossible, and something other than what it seeks to specify must, necessarily, be taking place. Whatever the initial response, the *explanation* of what is going on in the situation is not thereby determined; and without an explanatory framework one's original intuition on the case, if any, is bound only to be a provisional one, and may well have to be revised.

Taking this as the central case then, what response to it *should* be made? That a man makes it his considered choice to be doing something at a particular time does not entail that this provides the only active interest he has in doing anything at that time. In particular, when the question of incontinence arises at all, there will be some contrary interest the agent has, contrary to what he has by choice determined upon doing. And it is somehow out of the 'tension' between these divided active concerns that incontinent action, if it occurs or can occur at all, ensues. Neither the virtuous (nor the vicious) man suffers any division in their active concerns; their active powers 'speak with the same voice' and, in their case, the possibility of desertion of their choice does not arise. It is only where a man's practically rational intent and, for example, his passionally evoked desires are at odds that we can come to entertain this possibility.

It is worth noticing that the question of incontinence does not come into the case where a man suffers what is merely a conflict in his desires – for example, between his desire to go on the swings and on the round-abouts, when doing both is not possible. In this case the perplexity is resolved just by the preponderance of one desire over the other, and the giving up of one does not involve any issue of incontinence. It is only where it is thought better, more important or desirable in some way, to fulfil one purpose rather than another, and when this purpose is not pursued, that incontinence becomes a possibility. It is only forsaking *better* judgement, and not just different judgement, that introduces the occasion for the question of whether we have incontinent action. But we can, I believe, take a clue from the case of a 'simple' conflict in desire, with no priority being given to one desire over the other, being resolved by the occasional preponderance of one over the other, in the examination of the possibility of incontinent action. For I believe that a conflict between an objective preferred as good and an objective merely desired is not resolved upon the basis of the respective merits, as the agent believes, of these objectives, but simply resolves itself upon the respective 'strengths' of the agent's present interest in them, in one kind of case of incontinent action. That this should occur is a culpable failure on the agent's part, for he has the power to resolve conflicts of interest between objectives upon the merits of the objectives in question. If he does not do this, but this conflict resolves itself without his 'intervention', that is his responsibility. (I do not say: he *lets* this conflict resolve itself by occasional preponderance of interest – that would be a considered judgement, indeed one inconsistent with his considered preference for one objective over the other.) His not deciding the case on its merits is voluntary; he is not overwhelmed by his passional interest. The desire is of normal, controllable, intensity; only it is not ordered in its expression by rational judgement but, instead, disorders rational judgement in its direction of a man's action, and finds outlet by making the issue one resolved by the present hold of each respective interest and not by the merits of the case.

Let me try to spell this out more carefully. My contention is that in some cases where we have incontinent action, the incontinently acting man, although he has a rationally preferred purpose and a merely desired purpose, does not resolve the conflict between them as he should, on their respective merits or claims for fulfilment. He fails to carry through his deliberative preference into action across this conflict, and it resolves itself for him simply in terms of the present influence that each purpose, in its different way, exerts upon him. Incontinence is often called by the name 'weakness of will' or 'weakness in willing'; and if we equate 'will' with deliberately conceived purpose, then we can with some plausibility say that when a man acts incontinently his will is too weak; too weak, that is, to cope with the contrary desire he is susceptible to and to determine his conduct by the merits of the case. Instead, as I have suggested, he comes to treat both his deliberately conceived purpose and his evoked desire as if they were just interests to which he was susceptible. He no longer acknowledges the claim or demand in the end for which he formed his deliberate purpose. Instead he behaves as if the matter were simply one to be settled by how he chances to feel at the moment.

Possibly the term 'weakness' is not quite apt to the character of the case as I am suggesting it to be. More exactly there is an incompleteness in carrying through the commitment we undertake in forming our will. Instead of appraising the merits of every alternative to our original project that we come across, and either reaffirming that project or deliberately altering it if we find fit cause, we come no longer to fulfil the commitment to guidance by reasons and according action implicit in our original will. The continent man determinedly follows through the commitment implicit in his original project to take the measure of any conflicting purpose that falls across his path. He never lets it come to be that he regards his initial purpose simply as a 'take it or leave it' matter. But that is what happens to the incontinent man.

Such, I am suggesting, is the character of some antecedents to incontinent action. It may still be asked: how can such a transformation in the status of the rationally preferred purpose come to take place? Surely the agent must connive at its losing its claim to adherence? Or surely he must have been rendered incapable of sustaining that? How else can it occur? Either it was permitted, or else it could not be helped – *tertium non datur*, if he realises what is going on. But the incontinent man clearly does not *permit* the outcome to be resolved in this way; that would be to abandon his original deliberative decision. Nor, equally clearly, was he overwhelmed. He retains the power to determine the case on its merits; only he did not. Did he not then know what was going on? But can he not have realised this, only done nothing about it? Is that then 'permission'? Certainly not if that implies he deliberately reconsidered the merit of his original deliberative purpose. His desire brought it about that he did not do what he thought was best. Action upon such desires is voluntary, even if not chosen or permitted, and may be perfectly well recognised at the time. The fault lies in not bringing his will to bear on the desire and taking its measure. And no doubt the desire causes this fault. As such it is a culpable omission, but not a culpable permission. And does this not match the requirements for incontinent action?

There is one other possible origin for incontinent action I want to consider before making some general points about the nature of the case. I have argued previously that excessive passion can seriously imbalance the judgement of practical reason upon what is best to be done, by causing it to give weight beyond due reason to that good that the passion is joined to, because the thought of that good is so insistently present to the agent's mind. What happens when a man comes to act incontinently can, sometimes, have a somewhat similar character to this. His present passional interest suggests to him some purpose is highly desirable, and although with another part of himself he can recognise this suggestion to be spurious, he is too weak and indecisive really to hold firm to this recognition and to determine his conduct accordingly. Taking an analogy with two persons we may represent the case like this. Tempters speak in honeyed tones and flatter and cajole their victims into falling in with their proposals, dismissing reservations, suggesting misplaced inhibitions, until their victim loses his steadiness of judgement and can no longer see clearly what is right and what is wrong. He then is persuaded to say, in effect: 'Well – perhaps you are right. I am not sure anymore, and since you are so confident perhaps I will give it a try.'[4] Something along these lines can occur as a prelude to incontinent action, if not with full explicitness at least implicitly as its originating structure. The practical intellect falters in its conviction for a time under the false glare of some value suggested as desirable by passion.

It would not be true to say that in this case the agent *could* not have seen through the delusive 'patter' he was hearing. He is, indeed, thrown off balance, but not so extremely that he is rendered incapable of recovering the situation. He retains that power, only it is insufficiently employed, because the false alternative is made to seem so plausible. Nor, on the other hand, does the agent change his mind about what he should do. That suggests that, either for this occasion or in general, he makes it his deliberate purpose to do what passion has suggested to him as being what is truly worthwhile. Rather, his consideration is muddled and incomplete; it does not retain its clarity and lead him instead to a different conclusion. It may be true to say that at the time when he acts the agent is no longer convinced of the evil in what he is doing. But that is not because it is his serious judgement that there is a real question

4 See Marlowe, *Doctor Faustus*, Act II, Scene 1, lines 15–29.

about whether it is evil or not; it is because he is quite unsettled in his mind about what is good and what is evil, so that he does not make a serious judgement one way or the other. Thus passion makes and finds its opportunity.

A general doubt about these cases may yet still remain. I have wished to say that the incontinent man *does* not carry through his deliberative intent adequately, not that he *could* not. To say the latter seems to imply that the agent is altogether mastered by his passionally induced impulse and thus that what he then does is involuntary, hence not culpable – unless, indirectly, he is culpable for becoming one who has such overwhelming desires (see Watson 1977; Also Aristotle E.N. 1114a 2ff). Now whilst cases occur (for example, of panic) where we are mastered by certain impulses, these cases are quite inapposite to incontinent action, which is culpable. When he acts incontinently the agent can very well be quite as much 'in control of himself' as one who is doing what he has deliberately elected upon. But still we seek an explanation of how it comes to be that the agent's rationally determined purpose is not enacted by him. And in our allegiance to the principle of sufficient reason we demand from an explanation an account of why things *had to be so* and could not have been otherwise. If the purported 'explanation' leaves open the possibility of there having been an alternative outcome, then the occurrence of the outcome that actually did occur is still left unaccounted for. The mark of a due account appears to be an account which shows it to have been inevitable that things came out as they did and does not leave 'room' for things to have come out any differently. Thus an adequate account of incontinent action will show how it had to be that the agent acted as he did. But if it shows this, it surely follows that the agent had no choice, was mastered by his desire, acted involuntarily, and is more to be pitied than blamed.

The *prima facie* case for this line of argument is strong. But, just as it leads to the conclusion that the incontinent man could not have acted otherwise than he did, it likewise leads to the same conclusion about any action performed by any manner of man in any circumstances. It amounts, that is, to some version of a 'general thesis of determinism'. Now it is not my wish, neither is it within my power, to discuss any such 'general thesis' as this. I shall confine myself to making two points only. First: since this line of argument applies equally to all actions performed by whomever, in whatever circumstances, it provides no *special* difficulty for giving an account of the voluntariness and culpability of incontinent action. Any problem it raises arises quite generally, and it would therefore be wrong to base an argument for the impossibility of incontinence in particular upon it.

Secondly, the argument, if understood as implying that *any* kind of explanation of an action shows it to have been involuntary, is surely mistaken. Only certain histories of the origin of actions show this. Others, where the source of the action lay in an agent's will or desire (within limits), are precisely those explanatory histories of the origin of actions it is necessary to give to show them to be voluntary. This claim needs some qualification, but its essential bent seems correct (cf. Hume, *Treatise*, Book 2, pt 3, sect. 2, esp. 411; Hobart 1934). That an action should necessarily flow from an agent's will or desire so far from rendering it involuntary implies it to be voluntary. If we imagine an action to be cut off from this source, then we have either some reflex, some genuine compulsion, or else an entirely random behavioural display (if this be possible). And this point applies in the case of incontinent action. For in this sort of case, however exactly it works out, the action is certainly basically instigated by the agent's desire and is, thus, voluntary.

As I remarked, the claim that actions originating in desire are *eo ipso* voluntary needs careful working out. Some desires, from which actions come, are uncontrollable (cravings, for example) and the acts they issue in are involuntary (see Frankfurt 1971: 12; Dworkin 1970). The crucial point is whether the agent retains his power to prevent the expression of desire in action. But this the incontinent man, surely, does retain. Though cases where this power is removed do occur, it would be most implausible to say his is such a case. Rather he does not put his power to full or proper use. It is a quite general mistake to suppose that a power does not exist when its exercise is absent.[5]

I have deliberately discussed certain aspects of incontinent action in terms of a dialogue taking place between two persons – personified practical reason and personified desire. This form of description should

---

5 This matter is discussed fully in Ayers 1968. My conclusions concerning the nature of incontinent action are close to those of Rorty 1970, esp. pp. 60–1, though I argue the case very differently.

not be taken too literally. But it is, so far as it goes, an entirely apt form. In temptation it is with us as if we were two persons in one; we are in conflict with ourselves. There are, as I have insisted all along, diverse powers in man, and they can address us in different words, different tones. Or, more correctly, when they actuate us *we* speak in different words, different tones; 'we' are not some third party set apart from both. They are ourselves, showing different aspects of our activity and interest. When we represent the character of inner conflict to ourselves in the form of a dialogue, this is an error, of treating 'ourselves' as a third party to the conflict, we must not slip into.

If anything in the foregoing has been just, then we see that there is no sharp distinction to be made between the deformation of practical judgement by wrong desire and the obstruction of the determination to act upon our practical judgement produced by wrong desire. The idea that wrong desire is a psychic 'force', which knocks us off our intended course and drives us along another, contributes to the idea that he who acts incontinently could do no other, was overwhelmed, compelled by his feelings. But this is grossly to over-simplify what is involved in having and acting from a wrong desire. In wrong desires there are mistaken thoughts about what it would be good to do; and these thoughts can obtrude into the formation and execution of a practically rational intent in much more subtle ways, and more elusively dispossess a man of his rational self-command. Here, as elsewhere, we must recognise the complex inter-relations and interdependencies of thought and desire in the direction of our action.[6]

iii   KINDS AND DEGREES OF FREEDOM

It would clearly be out of the question to discuss here any large range of issues concerning the freedom of man and action. We can, however, look at some aspects of the matter suggested by the discussion of incontinence and of the other states of character.

Consider, first, the condition of one who has habitually to exercise self-restraint over his desires and feelings, if he is to act rightly. The life

---

6 Compare Bambrough 1969: 124: '. . . Socrates held that there are not here two kinds of failure but one; that no man does wrong willingly, wittingly, consciously; that every failure in action is or is a consequence of a failure in understanding . . .'

of such a man will be marked by constant inner struggle and frustration, for if he were ever to 'let himself go' he would, he knows, act badly and that is why he has to keep a tight rein on himself. It seems to me obvious that such a man's life is marked by severe constraints, curbs and limitations. He is divided against himself, and suffers under the hold over him of his wrong feelings. He is constantly prompted to seek things he wishes he did not want to seek, but he cannot rid himself of such desires. There is no unconstrained unfolding of his desires into action, and that is enough to show that he is not wholly free, unimpeded, in his life and activity.

The incontinent man, on the other hand, yields to his desires and thus does not suffer the pain of their frustration. But since he does not abandon his deliberated purposes altogether, he will be, subsequent to his act, apt to feel remorse and self-disgust in that he has betrayed that in which his best intent was lodged. His unfreedom lies in his not making of his life that he would best wish to make of it; he is constantly drawn into paths of feeling and action which deny him that. He fails to realise his conception of how his life should be; this being so, he is not master of himself but is, to a degree, 'in thrall' to his desires.

In both the case of the continent and incontinent man there is a degree of subjection to desire, an element of being possessed and directed by concerns which are not welcomed or endorsed. Such men are not fully in possession of themselves and as such are not fully free in the direction they give to their concern and action. We can see from this how mistaken it would be to say that a free action is the unimpeded expression of desire. For what one desires to do can very well be something one does not think it fit or appropriate for one to do; and then if one acts as one desires one will be acting contrary to one's best intent, one's conception of how one should best act. In the case of animals one might well say that free action is unimpeded action from desire. But in their case there would be no question of such action failing to correspond to their 'best intent', the intent that their lives should take a certain character. They have no such intentions. In the case of (adult) humans, however, this lack of correspondence can often occur. And if it does, the agent has been led away from his deliberated purpose; he is under the domination of a purpose of which he is neither the author nor editor (so to say). And that is not to be a free agent acting freely. Unless and until we come into possession of the direction and effect of our desires, which we can only do by the work of our practical rationality in shaping and moderating them, we shall remain divided in ourselves and the mere subjects of influence upon us, in some respects. One who is 'subject' takes orders from another, and cannot dispose his affairs according to his own chosen election (see Lewis 1967: chap. 5: 'Free'). And such a one is clearly not a free man.

Now, both a virtuous and a vicious man appear to be masters of their lives. For in both cases there exists a unity, a unanimity, between their reasoned purposing and the direction and intensity of their desires. Neither is liable to feel drawn where he would not go; neither is subject to unwelcome pressure from their desirous involvements. So, in the respects in which we have considered the freedom of man so far, their cases would appear to be indistinguishable. However, there are other aspects of the case which enable us to make a distinction between the virtuous and vicious man in respect of their freedom, which may briefly be considered.

The major point of contrast between virtuous and vicious men is in the conceptions each have of what would constitute a satisfactory life. The virtuous man has a sound, appropriate, conception, and the ordering he makes of his desires and actions embodies and enacts that. The vicious man has an unsound, inappropriate conception. The weight he places upon certain goods is excessive or defective and, correspondingly, other matters for concern are given too little or too great an emphasis, are attributed too much or too little importance by him. Now, I have deliberately not considered in this book the question of what might provide a proper criterion of what counts as a sound or appropriate conception of what would constitute a satisfactory life. That would be essential to determining the value of the various virtues; or, rather, to establishing the title of this or that particular state of character to be counted as a virtue – to be counted an *excellent* state of character. However, it is necessary to say a little of a general kind about this matter if any contrast between the freedom enjoyed by the virtuous and by the vicious man is to be uncovered. In particular, a thought along the following lines might be utilised. By giving a wrong weight or importance to some goods, or by taking as good things that are not so at all, a vicious man correspondingly misestimates the significance of other goods or omits them from account altogether. Because he does so, a range of desires, feelings and actions, those which depend upon a due appreciation of these neglected goods, is missing from his life or occupies only a small place in it. But if any of these goods is such as, by its appreciation and pursuit, would give an enlarged and more abundant development and expression to his natural powers and dispositions, then he has blocked or stunted his own self-realisation, his own ability to possess and enjoy the full scope of his personal powers.

This, I suggest, can be understood as a (self-imposed, or self-inflicted) limitation on the vicious man's freedom, for there is an impeded unfolding and expression of his powers and dispositions. Of course, a virtuous man too sets bounds to the development and expression of his powers and dispositions; there is no question but that a satisfactory conception of the ends of desire and action will include a controlled ordering of dispositions. But one may say that this ordering is necessary to facilitate the possibility of each of our powers and dispositions coming to its due and sufficient realisation, and is not an impediment, an obstruction, to this. Locke's famous analogy between the law and that which 'hedges us in only from bogs and precipices' has application here. He goes on: 'the end of law is not to abolish or restrain, but to preserve and enlarge freedom'.[7] As with the civil (or 'natural') law without, so with the moral law within. Or so we may suggest.

It would take a great deal more discussion fully to make clear, let alone make convincing, this line of thought. To attempt this would take me far outside the self-imposed limitations of the present discussion. I therefore leave this here as only a suggestion about a way of approaching this issue.

A point which I have looked at before may, however, be added to this, that the wrong choice of ends can often be the result of the deformation of rational judgement produced by excessive or inappropriate desire (see Plato, *Republic*, 413a ff; 429c ff; Aristotle, E.N. 1140b 17–20; 1144a 34–36). If this is correct then the vicious man is 'in thrall' to his feelings to an even greater extent than either continent or incontinent men are, for at least they preserve their rational understanding intact. In

7 Locke, *Second Treatise*, chap. VI, sect. 57. See also Green 1900; Gibbs 1976: chaps. 1, 9, on 'natural freedom'; Plato, *Republic* 571a–575a, in comparison with 586d–587c. Also, after a somewhat different manner, Herbert, 'The Collar'.

the case of the vicious man it would be that he takes his assessment of the importance of things from the dictation of his desires, and does not dictate to them. And this is to be more extremely governed by them, though perhaps more comfortably so, than is the case where one denies them or, though yielding to them, regrets this. In this case it is not only one's actions which are dominated by desire, it is one's understanding also. And that is to have lost all self-governance, and to be only the tool of one's desires, their apologist not their judge. Hamlet has it thus:

> . . . bless'd are those
> Whose blood and judgement are so well co-mingled
> That they are not a pipe for Fortune's finger
> To sound what stop she please. Give me that man
> That is not passion's slave, and I will wear him
> In my heart's core . . .[8]

iv THE TRUE SELF

Having devoted the previous sections in this chapter to deformations in the relations between practical reason and sense- and passional desire, I want, in conclusion, to return to a consideration of their proper priority and relationship. For I want explicitly to defend the idea, which has been implicit in much of the foregoing, that it is through ordering and shaping his life by his practically rational judgement that someone is his own master, possesses his own self and makes his life the active expression of that self; and the idea that inclincations which someone feels and actions he undertakes which do not express his deliberately purposed conception of how best to live are areas of his life where he is, to a degree, self-estranged or self-alienated, ruled by extraneous influences and not enacting his own being.

We constantly see among the various projects which at different times engage our concern, some as central to what we think of ourselves and our lives, others as peripheral, marginal, insignificant and yet others as alien, hostile, antipathetic intrusions. To do this is essential to having any order and stability in one's engagement in the world. Some-

---

8 Shakespeare, *Hamlet*, Act III, Scene 2. See also Hopkins, 'Thou art indeed just, Lord, if I contend', line 7: 'Oh, the sots and thralls of lust/Do in spare hours . . .'

one who did not, or could not, make any such differentiations would just be a fortuitous agglomeration of impulses thrown together in one place which we could not recognise as making up a unitary person, a single individual at all (Thigpen and Cleckley 1960; Prince 1919); it would be altogether arbitrary what we saw as constituting him as the person with the nature he has.

To be one person requires there to be some kind of stable centre to one's concerns. And as I have said, that emerges out of the sifting and ordering of the multiplicity of interests which beset us. I have tried to explain that it is the work of practical reason to make this sort of ordering, to establish some sense of the enduring significances that things have to us beyond their simply claiming our concern from time to time. So it is through the endeavour of practically rational thought that we fashion ourselves into a single self to which we give an expression in our lives. That self will be truly our own so long as we feel and enact only what we have determined it is important and significant that we should (cf. Dent 1974: 569–70).

It is important to stress here, once again, that through the work of practical reason we do not suppress or put aside our desirous concerns and replace these by objectives we seek upon deliberate judgement alone. That work is very largely concerned to inform and infold those desires into a single unity of self at one with itself, expressing itself completely and undividedly in the general form and particular detail of a life. The picture of the 'rational' man as cold, detached, rigid and machine-like in his attachment to his duty is simply the distorted complement of the distorted picture of passions as blind, a-rational, headlong urges. It is neither alien, nor antipathetic, to the nature of our passions that they should be ordered by true judgement. Nor is it alien or antipathetic to practical reason to have a passional concern bear upon what it judges to be best. For our concern is to act well, and to act well requires the concurrent assent of head and heart, and not just fortunately concurrent but consistently and intentionally concurrent assent. That which is sought in full-hearted and full-minded assent is the unequivocal expression of one's self. Aristotle says that human action comes from 'desiderative reason or ratiocinative desire' (E.N. 1139b 4). Another way of saying the same thing would be to say that a truly human life embodies loving intelligence or intelligent love.

References

Where a reprinting of a book or article is cited, references to it in the text and notes have been to the date of reprinting, which is cited at the end of the entry in the references.

Ackrill, J.L. 1973. Introduction. In *Aristotle's Ethics*, ed. J.L. Ackrill, Faber and Faber

Allan, D.J. 1953. Aristotle's Account of the Origin of Moral Principles, *XIth International Congress of Philosophy* **12**, 120–7

Allan, D.J. 1955. The Practical Syllogism. In *Autour d'Aristote*: Studies for A. Mansion, Louvain, 325–40

Annas, J. 1977. Plato and Aristotle on Friendship and Altruism, *Mind* **86**, 532–54

Anscombe, G.E.M. 1958. Modern Moral Philosophy, *Philosophy* **33**, 1–19. Reprinted in *Ethics*, ed. J.J. Thomson and G. Dworkin, Harper and Row 1968, 186–210

Anscombe, G.E.M. 1963. *Intention* (2nd edition) Blackwell

Anscombe, G.E.M. 1965. Thought and Action in Aristotle. In *New Essays on Plato and Aristotle*, ed. R. Bambrough, Routledge and Kegan Paul

Aquinas, St Thomas. *Summa Theologiae*, First Part of the Second Part (1a 2ae), Questions 1–21. In *Treatise on Happiness*, tr. J.A. Oesterle, Prentice-Hall 1964. Other Questions in *Summa Theologiae*, Blackfriars with Eyre and Spottiswoode from 1963

Aristotle. *De Anima*, Books 2 and 3 tr. and ed. D.W. Hamlyn, Oxford 1968

Aristotle. *Ethica Nicomachea*, tr. W.D. Ross. In *The Works of Aristotle*, ed. W.D. Ross, vol. IX, Oxford 1925

Aristotle. *Ethica Eudemia*, tr. J. Solomon. In *The Works of Aristotle*, ed. W.D. Ross, vol. IX, Oxford 1925

Aristotle. *Politics*. In *Aristotle's Politics and Athenian Constitution*, tr. and ed. J. Warrington, J.M. Dent 1959

Attfield, R. 1971. Talents, Abilities and Virtues, *Philosophy* **46**, 255–8

Ayers, M.R. 1968. *The Refutation of Determinism*, Methuen

Baier, K. 1970. Moral Value and Moral Worth, *The Monist* **54**, 18–30

Bambrough, R. 1969. *Reason, Truth and God*, Methuen

Beehler, R. 1978. *Moral Life*, Blackwell

Bennett, J.F. 1966. *Kant's Analytic*, Cambridge University Press

Benson, J. 1976. Varieties of Desire, *Proceedings of the Aristotelian Society, Supplementary Volume* **50**, 177–92

Bentham, J. 1823. *An Introduction to the Principles of Morals and Legislation*. In *A Fragment on Government with An Introduction to the Principles of Morals and Legislation*, ed. W. Harrison, Blackwell 1967

Blake, W. *Complete Poetry and Prose*, ed. G. Keynes, The Nonesuch Press 1961

Bradley, F.H. 1927. *Ethical Studies* (2nd edition), Oxford University Press

Brandt, R.B. 1970. Traits of Character: A Conceptual Analysis, *American Philosophical Quarterly* **7**, 23–37

Burke, E. 1759. *A Philosophical Enquiry into the Origins of our Ideas of the Sublime and the Beautiful* (2nd edition), R. and J. Dodsley, Scolar Press Facsimile 1970

Butler, J. 1729. *Fifteen Sermons Preached at the Rolls Chapel*. In *Butler's Sermons and Dissertation on Virtue*, ed. W.R. Matthews, G. Bell 1949

Butler, J. 1736. *A Dissertation upon the Nature of Virtue*. In *Butler's Sermons and Dissertation on Virtue*, ed. W.R. Matthews, G. Bell 1949

Davidson, D. 1971. Agency. In *Agent, Action and Reason*, ed. R. Binkley, R. Bronaugh, A. Marras, Blackwell

Davis, L.H. 1979. *Theory of Action*, Prentice-Hall

Dennett, D.C. 1971. Intentional Systems, *Journal of Philosophy* **68**, 87–106. Reprinted in D.C. Dennett, *Brainstorms*, Harvester Press 1979, 3–22

Dent, N.J.H. 1974. Duty and Inclination, *Mind* **83**, 552–70

Dent, N.J.H. 1975. Virtues and Actions, *Philosophical Quarterly* **25**, 318–35

Dent, N.J.H. 1976a. Varieties of Desire, *Proceedings of the Aristotelian Society, Supplementary Volume* **50**, 153–75

Dent, N.J.H. 1976b. Hume on Virtues and Natural Abilities, Paper presented at the Hume Conference, University of Edinburgh (unpublished)

Dent, N.J.H. 1981. The Value of Courage, *Philosophy* **56**, 574–7

Dent, N.J.H. 1983. Common, Civic and Platonic Justice in the *Republic, Polis*, **V** No. 1, 1–33

Dent, N.J.H. n.d. The Importance of Morally Good Action

Dworkin, G. 1970. Acting Freely, Nôus **4**, 367–83

Edgley, R. 1964. The Object of Literary Criticism, *Essays in Criticism* **14**, 221–36

Edwards, R.B. 1967. Is Choice Determined by the 'Strongest Motive'?, *American Philosophical Quarterly* **4**, 72–8

Eliot, G. 1872. *Middlemarch*, Oxford University Press 1947

Eliot, T.S. The Hollow Men; East Coker. In T.S. Eliot, *Collected Poems 1909–1962*, Faber and Faber 1963

Foot, P.R. 1958. Moral Beliefs, *Proceedings of the Aristotelian Society* **59**, 83–104. Reprinted in *Ethics*, ed. J.J. Thompson and G. Dworkin, Harper and Row 1968, 239–60

Foot, P.R. 1972. Morality as a System of Hypothetical Imperatives, *Philosophical*

Review **81**, 305–16

Fortenbaugh, W.W. 1975. *Aristotle on Emotion*, Duckworth

Frankena, W.K. 1970. Pritchard and the Ethics of Virtue, *The Monist* **54**, 1–17

Frankena, W.K. 1973. *Ethics* (2nd edition), Prentice-Hall

Frankfurt, H.G. 1971. Freedom of the Will and the Concept of a Person, *Journal of Philosophy* **68**, 5–20

Frankfurt, H.G. 1976. Identification and Externality. In *The Identities of Persons*, ed. A.O. Rorty, University of California Press

Freud, S. 1917. Mourning and Melancholia. In *The Standard Edition of the Complete Psychological Works of Sigmund Freud*, tr. and ed. J. Strachey, vol. XIV, 1957

Geach, P.T. 1977. *The Virtues*, Cambridge University Press

Gibbs, B. 1976. *Freedom and Liberation*, Sussex University Press

Goldman, A.I. 1970. *A Theory of Human Action*, Prentice-Hall

Green, T.H. 1879. On the Different Senses of 'Freedom' as Applied to Will and to the Moral Progress of Man. In *Works of Thomas Hill Green*, ed. R.L. Nettleship, vol. II, Longmans, Green and Co. 1900

Greenwood, L.H.G. 1909. *Aristotle: Nicomachean Ethics: Book Six*, Cambridge University Press

Hampshire, S.N. 1965. *Freedom of the Individual*, Chatto and Windus

Hampshire, S.N. 1977. *Two Theories of Morality*, Oxford University Press for the British Academy

Harrison, B. 1975. *Henry Fielding's Tom Jones*, Sussex University Press

Herbert, G. The Collar. In *The Penguin Book of English Verse*, ed. J. Hayward, Penguin Books 1956

Hobart, R.E. 1934. Free Will as Involving Determination and Inconceivable Without It, *Mind* **43**, 1–27

Hobbes, T. 1651 *Leviathan*, ed. M. Oakeshott, Blackwell n.d.

Hopkins, G.M. Thou art indeed just, Lord, if I contend. In *Poems of Gerard Manley Hopkins* (3rd edition), Oxford University Press 1956

Hume, D. 1739. *A Treatise of Human Nature*, ed. L.A. Selby-Bigge, Oxford 1888

Hume, D. 1777. *An Enquiry Concerning the Principles of Morals*. In *Hume's Enquiries*, ed. L.A. Selby-Bigge, Oxford 1902

Irwin, T. 1977. *Plato's Moral Theory*, Oxford University Press

Kant, I. 1785. *Groundwork of the Metaphysic of Morals*. In *The Moral Law*, tr. H.J. Paton, Hutchinson 1961. Page references are given as to the Prussian Academy Edition, as cited in this translation

Körner, S. 1973. Rational Choice, *Proceedings of the Aristotelian Society, Supplementary Volume* **47**, 1–17

Laclos, C. de 1782. *Les Liaisons Dangereuses*, tr. P.W.K. Stone, Penguin Books 1961

Laird, J. 1935. *An Enquiry into Moral Notions*, Allen and Unwin

Laird, J. 1946. Act-Ethics and Agent-Ethics, *Mind* **55**, 113–32

Lawrence, D.H. 1928. *Lady Chatterley's Lover*, Penguin Books 1960

Lawrence, D.H. 1929. À Propos of Lady Chatterley's Lover. In *À Propos of Lady Chatterley's Lover and Other Essays*, Penguin Books 1961

Lewis, C.S. 1967. *Studies in Words* (2nd edition), Cambridge University Press

Locke, J. 1690. *An Essay Concerning the True Original, Extent and End of Civil Government* (Second Treatise on Civil Government). In *Social Contract*, ed. E. Barker, Oxford University Press 1947

Lovelace, R. To Lucasta – Going to the Warres. In *The Penguin Book of English Verse*, ed. J. Hayward, Penguin Books 1956

Mabbott, J.D. 1953. Reason and Desire, *Philosophy* **28**, 113–23

McDowell, J. 1979. Virtue and Reason, *The Monist* **62**, 331–50

MacIntyre, A.C. 1971. Some More about 'Ought'. In A.C. MacIntyre, *Against the Self-Images of the Age*, Duckworth

Mackie, J.L. 1977. *Ethics*, Penguin Books

MacLagan, W.G. 1960. Respect for Persons as a Moral Principle, *Philosophy* **35**, I, 193–217; II, 289–305

Marlowe, C. 1616. *Doctor Faustus*. In *The Plays of Christopher Marlowe*, ed. R. Gill, Oxford University Press 1971

Matthews, G. 1966. Weakness of Will, *Mind* **75**, 405–19

Midgley, M. 1978 *Beast and Man*, Cornell University Press

Mill, J.S. 1859. *Essay on Bentham*. In *Mill's Essays on Literature and Society*, ed. J.B. Schneewind, Collier Books 1965

Mill, J.S. 1861. *Utilitarianism*. In *Utilitarianism: John Stuart Mill*, ed. M. Warnock, The Fontana Library 1962

Monro, D.H. 1967. *Empiricism and Ethics*, Cambridge University Press

Nagel, T. 1970. *The Possibility of Altruism*, Oxford University Press

Neely, W. 1974. Freedom and Desire, *Philosophical Review* **83**, 32–54

Neu, J. 1977. *Emotion, Thought and Therapy*, Routledge and Kegan Paul

Pears, D.F. 1978. Aristotle's Analysis of Courage, *Mid-West Studies in Philosophy* **3**, 274–85

Peters, R.S. 1962. Moral Education and the Psychology of Character, *Philosophy* **37**, 37–56

Plato. *The Republic*, tr. D. Lee, Penguin Books 1974

Prince, M. 1919. *The Dissociation of a Personality*, Longmans

Raz, J. 1975. Reasons for Action, Decisions and Norms, *Mind* **84**, 481–99

Rorty, A.O. 1970. Plato and Aristotle on Belief, Habit, and *Akrasia, American Philosophical Quarterly* **7**, 50–61

Ryle, G. 1949. *The Concept of Mind*, Penguin Books 1963

Schopenhauer, A. 1841. *Essay on the Freedom of the Will*, tr. K. Kolenda, Library of Liberal Arts 1960

Schopenhauer, A. 1851. On Ethics. In *Schopenhauer: Essays and Aphorisms*, tr. R.J. Hollingdale, Penguin Books 1970

Scruton, R. 1971. Attitudes, Beliefs and Reasons. In *Morality and Moral Reasoning*, ed. J. Casey, Methuen

Scruton, R. 1975. Reason and Happiness. In *Nature and Conduct*, ed. R.S. Peters, Macmillan Press

Shakespeare, W. *Hamlet; The Tempest*; Sonnet 129. In *The Complete Works of William Shakespeare*, ed. W.J. Craig, Oxford 1954

Solomon, R.C. 1977. *The Passions*, Doubleday Anchor Books

Sorabji, R. 1973. Aristotle on the Rôle of Intellect in Virtue, *Proceedings of the Aristotelian Society* **74**, 107–29

Spinoza, B. de 1677. *Ethics*. In *Spinoza Selections*, tr. W.H. White, ed. J. Wild, Charles Scribners' Sons 1958

Strawson, P.F. 1962. Freedom and Resentment, *Proceedings of the British Academy* **48**, 187–211. Reprinted in *Studies in the Philosophy of Thought and Action*, ed. P.F. Strawson, Oxford University Press 1968, 71–96

Suttie, I. 1935. *The Origins of Love and Hate*, Penguin Books 1963

Taylor, G. and Wolfram, S. 1971. Virtues and Passions, *Analysis* **31**, 76–83

Thigpen, C. and Cleckley, H. 1960. *The Three Faces of Eve*, Pan Books

Tolstoy, L. *Resurrection*, tr. R. Edmonds, Penguin Books 1966

Tolstoy, L. *The Death of Ivan Ilyich*. In L. Tolstoy, *The Cossacks*, tr. R. Edmonds, Penguin Books 1960

Vlastos, G. 1973. The Individual as an Object of Love in Plato. In G. Vlastos, *Platonic Studies*, Princeton University Press

Wallace, J.D. 1978. *Virtues and Vices*, Cornell University Press

Watkins, J. 1975. Three Views Concerning Human Freedom. In *Nature and Conduct*, ed. R.S. Peters, Macmillan Press

Watson, G. 1975. Free Agency, *Journal of Philosophy* **72**, 205–20

Watson, G. 1977. Scepticism about Weakness of Will, *Philosophical Review* **86**, 316–39

Weston, M. 1975. *Morality and the Self*, Blackwell

White, A.R. 1964. *Attention*, Blackwell

Whiteley, C.H. 1952. On Duties, *Proceedings of the Aristotelian Society* **53**, 95–104

Whiteley, C.H. 1979. Love, Hate and Emotion, *Philosophy* **54**, 235

Wiggins, D. 1976a. Deliberation and Practical Reason, *Proceedings of the Aristotelian Society* **76**, 29–51

Wiggins, D. 1976b. Truth, Invention, and the Meaning of Life, *Proceedings of the British Academy* **62**, 331–78

Williams, B.A.O. 1971. Morality and the Emotions. In *Morality and Moral Reasoning*, ed. J. Casey, Methuen

Williams, B.A.O. 1976. Utilitarianism and Moral Self-Indulgence. In *Contemporary British Philosophy*, 4th series, ed. H.D. Lewis, Allen and Unwin

Williams, B.A.O. 1979. Internal and External Reasons. In *Rational Action*, ed. R. Harrison, Cambridge University Press

Wilson, J.R.S. 1972. *Emotion and Object*, Cambridge University Press

Winch, P. 1968. Moral Integrity. In P. Winch, *Ethics and Action*, Routledge and Kegan Paul 1972

Wisdom, A.J.T.D. 1943. A Critical Notice: *Science and Ethics, Mind* **52**, 275–82. Reprinted in A.J.T.D. Wisdom, *Philosophy and Psychoanalysis*, Blackwell 1964a, 102–11

Wisdom, A.J.T.D. 1945. Gods, *Proceedings of the Aristotelian Society* **45**, 185–206. Reprinted in A.J.T.D. Wisdom, *Philosophy and Psychoanalysis*, Blackwell 1964b, 149–68

Wollheim, R. 1975. The Moral Psychology of British Idealism and the English School of Psychoanalysis Compared, *Proceedings of the British Academy* **61**, 373–98

von Wright, G.H. 1963. *Varieties of Goodness*, Routledge and Kegan Paul

Index

221

222

223